The
Welsh Marcher
Lordships

II: SOUTH-WEST

The
Welsh Marcher Lordships

II: SOUTH-WEST

John Fleming

LOGASTON PRESS

First published in March 2023 by Logaston Press
The Holme, Church Road, Eardisley HR3 6NJ
www.logastonpress.co.uk
An imprint of Fircone Books Ltd.

ISBN 978-1-910839-50-8

Designed and typeset by Richard Wheeler in 11 on 14.5 Caslon.
Cover design by Richard Wheeler.

Printed and bound in Poland.
wwwlfbookservices.co.uk

Logaston Press is committed to a sustainable future for our business, our readers and our planet.
The book in your hands is made from paper from sustainable sources.

British Library Catalogue in Publishing Data.
A CIP catalogue record for this book is available from the British Library.

CONTENTS

LIST OF MAPS

LIST OF FAMILY TREES

ACKNOWLEDGEMENTS

I would like first and foremost to express my gratitude to the series editor of *The Welsh Marcher Lordships* volumes, Philip Hume. He has worked tirelessly editing and improving this book. Most importantly, he brought me into this fascinating project. I hope this book is worthy of the faith he has shown in me. I would also like to thank my co-author in this series, Kirsten Lawton-Smith for her guidance in all things historical. Further thanks go to Dr Sara Elin-Roberts and Dr John Kenyon who have kindly contributed guest essays. Paul Davis and Neil Ludlow have spent time helping me with images, illustrations and with some of the trickier aspects of the history of the region. David Stephenson, whose insights into the intricacies of Welsh medieval history on a Monday evening have been something to look forward to during the work on this book. Jason Appleby, for his patience as we worked to construct some of the maps used in this volume. Chris Jones-Jenkins who has kindly offered his interesting reconstruction drawings. I would like especially to thank the team at the National Portrait Gallery for all of their assistance, and Sophie Fuce at the Fylde Borough Council, who went out of her way to provide the wonderful Turner image of Kidwelly Castle from the Lytham St Annes Art Collection.

Su and Richard Wheeler of Logaston Press, whose design and publishing skills have already made the Marcher series a big success. I can only hope that volume two will live up to the standards set by the first volume.

Finally, to the 'proof-reader in chief', my wife Inge, whose support on so many levels has been instrumental in the production of this volume.

John Fleming

The Mortimer History Society

The Mortimer History Society promotes the study and dissemination of information about both the Mortimer family of Wigmore and the medieval Marcher lordships. The Society's conferences and events, journals, annual Essay Prize, newsletters and website are a mine of information: mortimerhistorysociety.org.uk

The fourth in a series of publications for the MHS

Ludlow Castle, which became a main home of the Mortimers at the start of the fourteenth century. Roger Mortimer (d.1330) added new buildings to create a palatial residence (© Philip Hume)

PREFACE TO THE SERIES

It is a great pleasure to welcome the second in this three-volume series of books on the Welsh Marcher Lordships. The first volume, which focussed on the central and northern regions, sold out only five months after its publication in 2021 – a clear demonstration of the great interest in the Marcher Lordships and their lords, who were at the centre of events that affected the history of England and Wales for nearly 500 years. Today, when people envisage the Welsh Marches, it is often the picturesque area that straddles the central part of the English/ Welsh border in Shropshire and north Herefordshire that comes to mind. There are indications that in the eleventh century this was also the perception; however, during the next two centuries, the Welsh Marches greatly expanded to encompass a region that ran from north Wales and the Dee estuary down to the Severn estuary, and across south Wales to the south-west and the coast of Pembrokeshire.

This volume describes the formation of the medieval Marcher lordships of the south-west, a region which many people, indeed, do not realise was part of the medieval March of Wales.

Defined by the 50 or so Marcher lordships that were created, the Welsh Marches became a unique area as a border region that lay between Wales and England, with its own laws and with exceptional powers exercised by their lords. It was referred to as 'Marchia Wallie' to distinguish it from 'Pura Wallia' and was politically separate from both Wales and from England. Many of the areas, having been conquered from the Welsh, were no longer politically part of Wales; other lordships that initially sat in England were effectively withdrawn by their lords from the institutions of English royal governance. The Marcher lords were barons of England and held their lordships from the king, yet they were not subject to many of the institutional and legal structures of the English Crown. They claimed and exercised within their lordships many of the powers which the king exercised in his kingdom. Indeed, the correspondence of kings and royal officials refer to Marcher lords as 'lords royal' who exercise a 'royal lordship'.

There are many examples of the king's writ not running within Marcher lordships. An instance from the south-west was the lordship of Iscennen, that had been created following the Edwardian conquest. When the last Giffard lord of Iscennen was executed for treason in 1322, he was childless and the lordship also became forfeit to the Crown. When the king gave the lordship to his favourite, Hugh Despenser the younger, the grant emphasised that it was not subject to the county court of Carmarthen and all other services; thus, Iscennen functioned as a Marcher lordship independent from the Crown.[1]

The primary aim of this series is to provide the general reader with a broad-ranging synthesis of the fascinating history of the Marcher lordships, and to provide a useful introduction to scholars new to the subject. The books seek to answer questions such as: what were the medieval Welsh Marches? What defined a Marcher lordship and how did they evolve during the two centuries from the first arrival of the Normans on the Welsh border to the Edwardian conquests of Wales in the 1270s and 1280s? What were the distinctive powers of Marcher lords and how did they develop? Why did the Marcher lordships become an anomaly that led to the abolition of their powers in the sixteenth century during the reign of Henry VIII?

To provide a focus on the distinct geographical areas that different readers may be interested in (and to ensure the books are of a manageable size!), the series consists of three volumes – the first covered the Marcher lordships in the northern and central regions; the second, this volume, covers those in the south-west; and the third those in the south-east. Overall, each of the regions has a distinct narrative; however, inevitably there is some overlap as critical events impacted on the whole of Wales and the Marches.

The first half of each book addresses the questions posed above. It starts with a summary of how the Marcher lordships developed together with their distinctive features. This is followed by a narrative history of the significant events in Wales and the Marches, that shaped the development of the Marcher lordships in that region. The narrative starts with explaining the fragmented political situation in Wales in the period before 1066, and the interactions with the Anglo-Saxons as this context shaped the Normans' approach to Wales and the development of the Marcher lordships. It continues with the period of a little over two centuries after the Norman Conquest of England. During this time control of the Marches ebbed and flowed, until the Edwardian conquest and settlement of Wales at the end of the thirteenth century fixed in place the political geography of the Marcher Lordships, and the Principality of Wales that was governed by the Crown. The Marcher lords retained their powers until the reign of Henry VIII, when the Laws in Wales Acts of 1536 and 1542 removed their independence, incorporated the

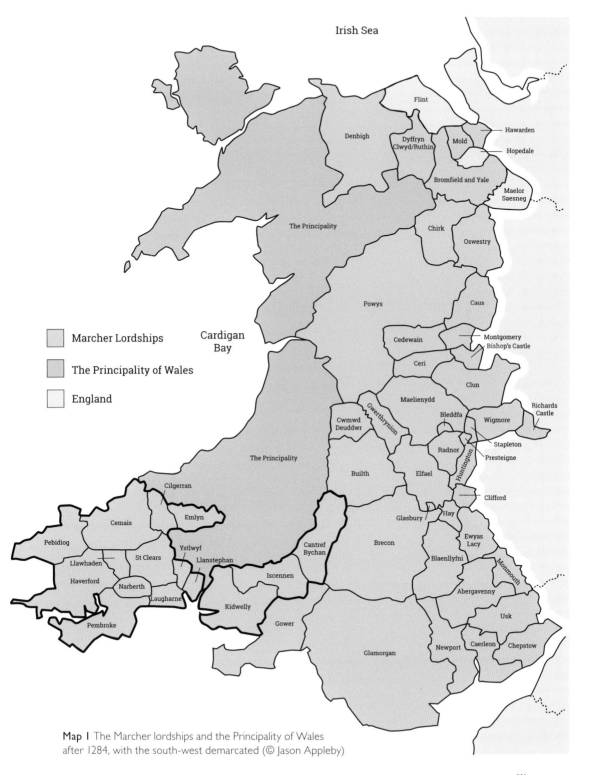

Map 1 The Marcher lordships and the Principality of Wales after 1284, with the south-west demarcated (© Jason Appleby)

lordships into the governance and jurisdiction structures of the new counties of Wales or the border counties of England, and for the first time defined a border between Wales and England.

The second section of each volume provides a brief history of each Marcher lordship in the region, with a list of the lords and ladies who held them.

Series editor: Philip Hume

PREFACE TO VOLUME II: THE SOUTH-WESTERN SECTION OF THE WELSH MARCHES

This volume explores the origins and development of the Marcher lordships in what are now the counties of Carmarthenshire and Pembrokeshire. Additionally, although no Marcher lordships survived there beyond 1284, Cardiganshire will feature prominently in the history of the Marcher lordships of south-west Wales. This is an area that was very different to the regions of the central and northern March that were described in volume one, where some of the lordships were regained fully by the native Welsh rulers for much of the 200 years after the initial conquest; and, a further swathe was withdrawn from England into the March by their powerful lords; or, were lordships newly granted by Edward I after the extinction of native rule in Wales during the period 1277–84.

In contrast, following the major Norman incursion into south-west Wales in the 1090s, nearly all the Marcher lordships comprised lands seized from the native rulers of Wales in the late eleventh and early twelfth centuries. Although the fortunes of the Marcher lords waxed and waned as power was contested for nearly 200 years, their control remained more secure, particularly of the major castles. Unlike the central and northern region, there was only one lordship newly created by Edward I following the end of native rule – the lordship of Iscennen.

One reason why many people are unaware that the Marcher lordships extended to the far west coast of Pembrokeshire is that a March is normally a region that lies between two countries, often in dispute. Yet, the south-west of Wales does not border England nor any other country. It lies firmly within Wales and is bordered to the west and south by the sea. In fact, Devon is closer than Gloucestershire, albeit separated by the Bristol Channel. So, how did these lordships come into existence? what shaped their character? what made them 'Marcher'? and why did the region develop in such a different way to the others? To answer these questions, one must understand the geographical and political nature of the region, and the events that shaped it during the twelfth and thirteenth centuries. Fundamentally, the establishment of the mighty castle of Pembroke, as the bastion of Norman power after the first incursions into south-west Wales in 1093, provided the security and stability to allow for the settlement of the region and the formation of lordships within its sphere. Likewise, the royal castle of Carmarthen, built a little later, performed the same function for the lordships within its control.

NOTES AND EXPLANATIONS
Brut y Tywysogyon (The Chronicle of the Princes)
This is a chronicle that recorded events in Wales and the Marches over several centuries of the medieval period. It survives in three Welsh versions, which are translations of a now lost Latin text. For some time, the scribe who wrote sections of original manuscript, resided in south-west Wales, and, therefore, there are periods when the modern reader gets a rich and detailed description of proceedings in the region. To enhance the narrative, this book incorporates quotations from the *Brut* (shown in a **different typeface**) and, unless otherwise specified, the quotations will be from the version known as *The Red Book of Hergest* (edited by Thomas Jones). The *Brut* is compiled chronologically by date, which makes the entries for each year straightforward to find, thus they are not referenced in the text.

THE GEOGRAPHY OF SOUTH-WEST WALES
This book will refer to several key regions of the medieval south-west that may not be familiar to the modern reader and need to be clarified. The entire region of south and west Wales came to be known as Deheubarth, which had been brought together as a political unit during the tenth century. This encompassed all of modern-day Pembrokeshire, Carmarthenshire, Cardiganshire and, at times, parts of Brecon. Deheubarth consisted of two primary sub-regions: the kingdoms of Dyfed and Seisyllwg. Dyfed was the area west of the Tywi river, whilst Seisyllwg consisted of Ystrad Tywi which lay to the east of the river, with Ceredigion to the north (see Map 5 on p. 27). Within these areas, smaller units of administration had developed – the most local, the *commote*, being a smaller administrative centre within the larger *cantref*. Systematic organisation of territorial divisions is sometimes attributed to Gruffudd ap Llywelyn (d.1063), though these had existed much earlier in some places. By the time the Normans arrived at the border in the years after 1066, the structure of *cantrefi* and *commotes* was common, providing a regional organisation that was often adopted by the Normans to create the boundaries of their own lordships.

There are often many variations of spelling when it comes to names of people and places in medieval history. As in volume one, I have taken a pragmatic approach and will use terms that will be most recognisable to readers, although that will lead

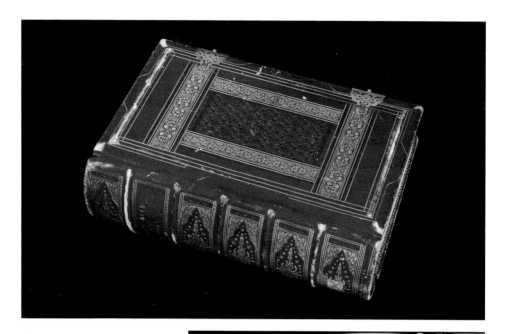

The Red Book of Hergest in its Victorian binding (*52 Jesus College MS 111. Image by kind permission of Jesus College, Oxford*)

A page from *The Red Book of Hergest* (*52 Jesus College MS 111 8v. Image by kind permission of Jesus College, Oxford*)

Edward the Confessor, from the Litlyngton Missal (© *Dean and Chapter of Westminster*)

to some inevitable inconsistencies. Throughout the book, the term 'Anglo-Saxon' has been used to refer to the people of England up to around the mid eleventh century, and as the 'English' thereafter. The 'Norman kings' refers to William the Conqueror and his sons, William (Rufus) II and Henry I. 'Anglo-Norman' refers to Kings Stephen, Henry II and Richard I. Whilst, following the loss of Normandy and the land in France, John, Henry III and Edward I are referred to as 'English' kings. Similarly, with the barons, for families that include several generations with the same name, the date of death of the individual family member is given in brackets. For example, William Marshal (d.1219) has been used to distinguish one from the other, rather than appending Roman numerals.

Any reader of the history of the Welsh marches will be familiar with the phrase, 'The King's writ does not run here'. It symbolises the independence of the Marcher lordships and the judicial power of the individual lord. A writ in its most basic form is a command or mandate from the king, directed at one or more of his subjects to carry out an action. As the use of royal courts grew during the reign of Henry II, a writ became, more commonly, an order purchased from a royal official to initiate a proceeding in a royal court against another subject. Writs were typically used in matters of property or inheritance. In the Welsh March, these royal writs had no force and a person seeking redress from unfair loss of land or inheritance would have had to go to his lord for justice. That contrasts with the rest of England where nobody needed to answer in their lord's court in matters of property without a royal writ. However, it should be noted that those lordships that developed within the sphere of influence of Carmarthen had some obligation to the king's court there. This will be explored more in the Carmarthenshire lordships section. Further, the earls of Pembroke demanded that the lords of the smaller lordships within its orbit hold suit at their court. Whether this happened often depended on that lord's ability to successfully dispute that claim.

TIMELINE OF KEY EVENTS

ENGLAND	DATE	WALES AND THE MARCHES
	1063	Gruffudd ap Llywelyn, ruler of all Wales, killed
Battle of Hastings	1066	
Reign of **William I**, The Conqueror	1067–70s	Earldoms created at Hereford, Shrewsbury, Chester; First raids into Wales; William fitz Osbern builds a line of castles
	1075	Earldom of Hereford forfeit and not continued
	1081	Battle of Mynydd Carn; Rhys ap Tewdwr rules in south Wales; William I progresses to St Davids
Domesday Book	1086	Rhys ap Tewdwr and Robert of Rhuddlan both hold lands from the Crown
Death of William I; accession of **William Rufus (II)**	1087	
	1093	Rhys ap Tewdwr killed; Norman raids increase and overrun south Wales
	1094	Welsh counter-attack; all but two Norman castles in south-west Wales destroyed
	1095–97	Campaigns led by William II and Welsh resistance
Death of William II; accession of **Henry I**	1100	
	1102	Fall of the house of Montgomery
	1116	Uprising of Gruffudd ap Rhys: death of Owain ap Cadwgan
Henry I's son and heir killed in the wreck of the White Ship	1120	
Death of Henry I; accession of **Stephen**	1135	
	1136	General Welsh uprising; comprehensive Norman defeat at the battle of Crug Mawr
Civil War between Stephen and Matilda (and latterly her son, Henry)	1139–54	Welsh resistance reclaims lands from the Anglo-Normans
Death of Stephen; accession of **Henry II**	1154	
	1155	Rhys ap Gruffudd becomes head of the house of Deheubarth
	1157	Henry II leads a campaign against Deheubarth
	1159	Rhys ap Gruffudd leads a revolt in Dyfed
	1165	Henry II leads failed campaign against united army of Wales
Henry II contending with Becket and rebellions of his sons	1166–89	Period of co-existence – Henry II recognises Welsh rulers
	1169–71	Norman invasion of Ireland to support the king of Leinster
Henry II's expeditions to Ireland	1171–72	Henry II agrees truces with Welsh; Lord Rhys is Justiciar
	1175 + 1177	Henry II holds councils with Welsh rulers
Death of Henry II; accession of **Richard I**	1189	Lord Rhys rises in revolt taking several Marcher castles
	mid-1190s	Marcher lords lead expeditions into Wales to claim territories
	1196	Lord Rhys wins battle of Radnor; takes Painscastle but agrees peace
	1197	Lord Rhys dies
Death of Richard I; accession of **John**	1199	Llywelyn ab Iorwerth supreme in Gwynedd
John loses Normandy and most of his other Continental lands	1204–05	
	1208	John starts persecution of de Braose family

	1211 + 1212	John's Welsh campaigns
William Marshal granted Haverford by the king	1213	Llywelyn ab Iorwerth conquers the Perfeddwlad
Magna Carta sealed	1215	Southern Welsh leaders unite behind Llywelyn ab Iorwerth to conquer large swathes of Deheubarth
Death of John; accession of 9-year-old **Henry III**	1216	Llywelyn divides spoils of previous campaign at Aberdyfi
	1218	Treaty of Worcester; Llywelyn confirmed in his conquests
	1223	William Marshal the younger retakes large parts of Dyfed; Llywelyn loses Carmarthen and Cardigan
	1231	Llywelyn retakes Cardigan Castle and several Marcher lordships in the south
	1233-34	Llywelyn joins with Earl Richard Marshal and raids borders
	1234–40	Peace treaties; Llywelyn tries to secure his legacy
	1240	Death of Llywelyn ab Iorwerth; succession disputed
	1241	Dafydd ap Llywelyn forced to submit to Henry III
	1244–45	Death of Gruffudd ap Llywelyn; Welsh revolt
Last male descendant of William Marshal dies without male heir	1245	
	1247	Treaty of Woodstock
	1255	Llywelyn ap Gruffudd secures control of all of Gwynedd
	1257	English army comprehensively defeated near Carmarthen by Llywelyn; several Marcher castles sacked
Period of baronial reform and rebellion	1258–65	Llywelyn sides with the baronial faction to exploit divisions in England
	1265	Government of Simon de Montfort agrees Treaty of Pipton
Royalist victory at Evesham; Simon de Montfort killed	1265	Treaty of Pipton repudiated
	1267	Treaty of Montgomery: Llywelyn recognised as Prince of Wales with many districts ceded to him
	1267–72	Ambiguities in the Treaty cause conflict; Llywelyn late with payments
Death of Henry III; Edward I is absent on Crusade	1272	Further conflicts with regency government
	1273	Llywelyn starts to build Dolforwyn Castle
Coronation of **Edward I** on return from Crusade	1274	Llywelyn doesn't attend the coronation
	1274–76	Tension increases; Dafydd ap Gruffudd and Gruffudd ap Gwenwynwyn in England after failed plot to murder Llywelyn who refuses to meet Edward I to give homage
	1276–77	Edward I's first campaign in Wales; Treaty of Aberconwy humiliates Llywelyn
	1278–82	Welsh tensions increase over English rule
	1282–83	Dafydd's attack on Hawarden sparks rebellion; Llywelyn has no choice but to join; Llywelyn and Dafydd both killed; new Marcher lordships created in north-east Wales
	1284	Edward I's Statute of Wales (Rhuddlan); extinction of native rule; creation of the Principality
	1287–92	Uprising of Rhys ap Maredudd ends in failure; last native prince of Deheubarth to hold a lordship
During the reign of **Henry VIII**	1536 + 1542	The Laws in Wales Acts incorporate Marcher lordships into the new counties of Wales or added to old border counties

Wall painting, possibly Edward I, in Westminster Abbey (© Dean and Chapter of Westminster)

CHAPTER ONE

Defining the Marcher lordships
and their regal powers

A MARCH, when used to describe a geographic area, is defined as the region between two territories, often an area of disputed ownership. There were 'Marches' in many areas in the medieval period, including the Scottish borders and Normandy; however, the Welsh Marches became exceptional through the 50 or so semi-autonomous lordships that developed during the Middle Ages. Unlike a number of those in the central and northern regions of the Welsh Marches that were the subjects of volume one, those in the south-west were mainly created by force, and shaped through conflict for over 200 years. To understand the way of life in the March, a quote from the eminent historian R.R. Davies paints an accurate picture: the people in the March lived in 'a land of war, interrupted on occasion by peace'.[2]

During the period from the 1090s to the end of the thirteenth century, the Marcher lordships became a separate political entity, collectively forming a region which was politically neither part of Wales nor part of England. Until native rule was ended by Edward I, the north and west of Wales became known as *Pura Wallia*, with the east and south known as *Marchia Wallie*, though control of areas moved back and forth during this period. The end of native rule in 1282–84, and the formation of the Principality of Wales as lands administered by the Crown, brought more permanence to the structure of the Marcher lordships (see Map 1 on p. *xiii*) – a structure that endured until the powers of the Marcher lords were abolished during the reign of Henry VIII. The Marcher lords held their lands directly from the English Crown as tenants-in-chief, but their lordships were not part of the English governmental system. It was accepted by both lord and king that 'the king's writ did not run in their lordship'. As an example, in 1241 Henry III confirmed that the bishop of St Davids was to do homage to nobody but the king, which effectively confirmed him in all his rights as a Marcher lord.[3]

A further quick glance at Map 1 shows that the Marcher lordships in the south-west – with the sea to the west and south, and Marcher lordships to the east – did not border England, and therefore did not comprise a 'border region between two countries'. This prompts the question 'in what way was it a March?' The answer lies in the way in which the lordships formed, and the characteristics that came to define a territory as a 'Marcher lordship', particularly the regal-like powers that the lords exercised. This chapter, therefore, will describe the key features of Marcher lordships, with a short summary of the origins of those in the south-west.

The Liberties and Powers of Marcher Lords

During the twelfth and thirteenth centuries, Marcher lordships came to be defined by the powers exercised by their lords. To be a Marcher lord endowed regal-like powers; everyone who lived within the lordship held what they had from the lord and were subject to his courts and will.

There has been a debate amongst historians about whether the powers of the Marcher lords originated from the exceptional rights granted to the first earls established in the border region at Chester, Shrewsbury and Hereford, or were assumed from the native rulers that were displaced in lands conquered in Wales. The answer is probably a combination of the two. The primary driver was force, and the ability of a Marcher lord to exert it. These lords were opportunistic and once they had an area under their control, they exercised power as they saw fit. In other words, Marcher powers were not just granted or assimilated, they were acquired through the exercise of power and the will of the conquering lord. That these powers existed and were recognised by the king is not in dispute. There are many examples in royal correspondence of Marcher lords being referred to as 'lords royal' with 'regal jurisdictions'. An example of an early recognition by the king of Marcher status was the appointment of Bernard, the queen's chaplain, as the bishop of St Davids in 1115 by Henry I. With his appointment the king confirmed that the bishop held his lands directly from the king and exercised full authority within his lands over justice, rents and the right to build castles.[4] Let us now turn to the specific powers that these lords exercised.

One of the most frequently used expressions when referring to the powers of a Marcher lord was that 'the king's writ did not run in a Marcher lordship'. In other words, the king did not have the right to interfere in matters Marcher. It also means that the inhabitants of a Marcher lordship had no recourse to royal justice if they wanted to file a suit or had a grievance. The Marcher lord dispensed justice, patronage and military power in his own name. The lord was responsible for both the promulgation and prosecution of the law. Thus, the lord decreed the law in his lands (see the section on the Laws of Wales/ Law of the March on p. 13), and was responsible for the courts that administered justice

Kidwelly Castle: the right to build a castle without royal licence was one of the many powers of a Marcher lord. (© Philip Hume)

and upheld the law. The lord's court could try every crime except for treason, with the power to pronounce the death sentence and the right to have gallows to execute those so convicted and sentenced. This meant of course that the fines levied by the courts went into the coffers of the Marcher lord, rather than to the Crown through the king's sheriff. This was a key source of revenue for a Marcher lord and, in some cases, it was the chief source of income, accounting for as much as 60% of the lord's revenue.[5]

It is worth noting that, unlike other parts of the March, the position of the south-western lords was compromised at times, as they operated within the scope of the bastion of royal power in Carmarthen. At times, the Marcher lords were expected to hold suit at the county court for certain disputes and crimes. The smaller lords would do that, but when the lordships began to form part of the estates of larger families, this was generally ignored, and justice was dispensed at the lord's court.

The power of a Marcher lord that is most visible to us today was the right to build castles without first requiring a licence from the king. This power, combined with the ongoing military requirements of the protracted disputes with the native rulers, explains the large numbers of ruins and castle sites that survive today. (The development of castles across the south-west is explored in more detail at the end of the chapter.) Further, a Marcher lord had the right to raise his own army, as William Marshal (d.1231) demonstrated with devastating effect in 1223 (he went to Ireland to raise it). They had the right to settle disputes with one another and (when it was still necessary before 1282) with the native Welsh princes, by either making treaties and/ or waging war. With this array of regal powers, being a Marcher lord could be a profitable business, when not fighting your neighbours or the Welsh.

The Marcher lord was effectively the sovereign within the bounds of his lordship. This gave him the same rights as the king enjoyed elsewhere: the right of *primer seisen* (the profits of the lands of a dead tenant until that tenant's heir paid the appropriate relief to enter his or her inheritance); the right of prerogative wardships of the land held of him (when an heir was underage, to have the custody of their lands, and control the heir's wardship and marriage); the right to create boroughs, to establish markets and fairs, and take profits of the toll levied on them; to regulate trade; receive the profit from mills, tolls, wreck of sea, treasure trove and mines; the control of weights and measures; the right to royal fish such as porpoise and sturgeon. As well as the profit from tolls, the lord had the right to exempt his tenants from paying tolls, as William Marshal (d.1219) did in Haverford in the early thirteenth century. All these powers added up to make a Marcher lordship a lucrative enterprise. Marcher lordships were generally exempt from the taxes levied by the king. Although there was an exception in 1292, the Marcher lords were clear that the tax imposed on this occasion should not set a precedent.

THE EMERGENCE AND DEVELOPMENT OF THE MARCHER LORDSHIPS

Map 2 (opposite) illustrates the different ways in which the Marcher lordships developed, and graphically highlights a key difference between the lordships of the south-west and those in the central and northern region detailed in volume one. As explored in that volume, the lordships in that area can be described as:

- disputed areas that were claimed by Norman barons during the incursions at the end of the eleventh century, but in which their hold was so tenuous that control swung from one side to another, with the native rulers in power for long periods (the areas coloured green on the map). Maelienydd, in the central March, is a good example, where the Mortimers of Wigmore ruled for only *c*.80 years out of the 184 years between 1093 and 1277.

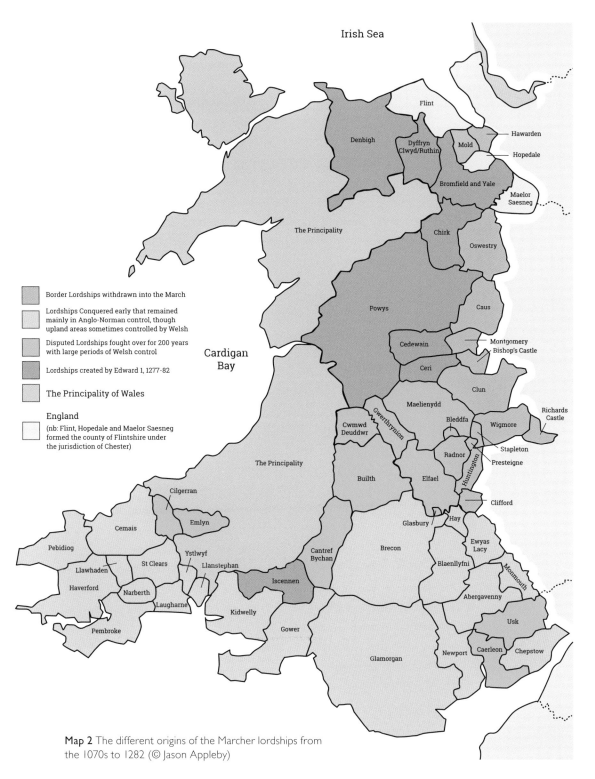

Irish Sea

Flint

Hawarden

Denbigh
Dyffryn Clwyd/Ruthin
Mold

Hopedale

Bromfield and Yale

Maelor Saesneg

The Principality

Chirk

Oswestry

Border Lordships withdrawn into the March

Lordships Conquered early that remained mainly in Anglo-Norman control, though upland areas sometimes controlled by Welsh

Disputed Lordships fought over for 200 years with large periods of Welsh control

Lordships created by Edward 1, 1277-82

The Principality of Wales

England
(nb: Flint, Hopedale and Maelor Saesneg formed the county of Flintshire under the jurisdiction of Chester)

Cardigan Bay

Powys

Caus

Cedewain

Montgomery
Bishop's Castle

Ceri

Clun

Maelienydd

Richards Castle

Gwerthrynion

Bleddfa

Wigmore

Cwmwd Deuddwr

Stapleton

Radnor

Presteigne

The Principality

Builth

Elfael

Huntington

Clifford

Cilgerran

Emlyn

Glasbury

Hay

Ewyas Lacy

Cemais

Ystlwyf

Cantref Bychan

Brecon

Pebidiog

Llanstephan

Blaenllyfni

Monmouth

Llawhaden

St Clears

Haverford

Narberth

Iscennen

Abergavenny

Laugharne

Kidwelly

Usk

Pembroke

Gower

Caerleon

Chepstow

Glamorgan

Newport

Map 2 The different origins of the Marcher lordships from the 1070s to 1282 (© Jason Appleby)

- border lordships that were part of the shire administration of Herefordshire and Shropshire that were granted to Norman barons following the conquest of England. However, during the twelfth and thirteenth centuries, their lords succeeded in withdrawing them from the shire administration and royal judicial structures of the counties of England, taking for themselves the powers of Marcher lords. Thus, the boundaries of the March were pushed eastwards into England through the usurpation of powers, rather than conquest of lands from the Welsh. (Areas coloured orange on the map show the swathe of such lordships from Oswestry down to Clifford.)

- lordships newly created by Edward I following his campaigns into Wales and conquest of the native rulers in 1277, and 1282–3. The lordships coloured pink denote the lands that were taken from the native rulers and given by the king to his closest allies and the senior commanders of his armies in those campaigns. Although Powys also became a Marcher lordship, there was one notable difference – the native ruling family was allowed to hold the lordship in reward for their service to the English Crown, but now as Marcher barons rather than independent native rulers.

In stark contrast (as shown by the swathe of areas coloured grey on the map) nearly all the Marcher lordships of the south-west were lands that were conquered in the early waves of incursions into Wales by the barons. Though contested militarily for nearly 200 years, with some lost for short periods, they mainly remained under Anglo-Norman control. The only exceptions to this are Cantref Bychan and Cilgerran/ Emlyn, which were held for significant periods by the Welsh; in addition, Iscennen, which was formed from the lower half of Cantref Bychan by a grant from Edward I in 1282.

The early formation of the Marcher lordships of south-west Wales
Whilst the circumstances of the early incursions into Wales, and the subsequent events that shaped the Marcher lordships of the south-west, are explored in more detail in chapters three to six, it is useful to provide a summary here.

In the five years after 1066, William the Conqueror established three earldoms at strategic points along the border region with Wales – Chester in the north; Shrewsbury in the centre; and Hereford further south. The king appointed three of his closest allies as earls in each location, granting them exceptional powers to ensure a secure border region. As we will see, royal conquest of Wales was both impracticable and unnecessary. William's objective was stability and a secure border, given the priorities elsewhere across his lands that spanned the English Channel. However, the earls and barons were permitted to push along the strategic access routes into Wales, in order to enhance that secure border. Furthermore, in areas where there was a vacuum in Welsh leadership, those incursions could be extensive – as seen in the north during the 1070s and 1080s. In contrast, in the south, whilst there were incursions by Norman barons into the fringes of the south-east, and also an instance when Normans were hired to support one Welsh faction in their wars with another at the battle on the banks of the river Rhymni in 1072, there were no large-scale expeditions across south Wales.

A good example of William I's approach can be seen in 1081 when the battle at Mynydd Carn between warring factions of Welsh rulers resulted in the victory of Rhys ap Tewdwr of Deheubarth and his ally Gruffudd ap Cynan, a claimant to rule in Gwynedd. The emergence of a new strong ruler in the south caught the attention of the king and he embarked on a 'pilgrimage' to the cathedral of St Davids in the same year. This pilgrimage was in reality a show of strength to demonstrate who held the ultimate power, as he came accompanied by an impressive military force. It is most likely during this 'pilgrimage' that the king received the fealty of Rhys and confirmed him in his lands in Deheubarth for the annual fee of £40 that was recorded in Domesday Book.

St Davids Cathedral: William I made a military expedition here in 1081 to confirm his authority over the native Welsh rulers (© Philip Hume)

After the death of William I in 1087, the new king, William (Rufus) II (d.1100), mostly honoured the arrangements that his father had established with the local Welsh lords. The two catalysts that changed everything, however, were the death of the ruler of Deheubarth, Rhys ap Tewdwr (killed in a battle with the Normans near Brecon in 1093), combined with the need of the king to divert the unrest and rebelliousness of his barons. These two factors opened the way for widespread raids and expeditions into south-west Wales.

From the map, it might be expected that the expeditions would have spilled across the south following the accessible routes from England along the coast; but this wasn't the case. Instead, the power vacuum in Deheubarth in 1093 was filled by the Montgomery family, earls of Shrewsbury, who continued their progress westwards along the River Severn into the uplands, before crossing the hills and descending to the west coast from where they swept down through Ceredigion into Dyfed, building a castle at Pembroke. In that same year, further east, the sheriff of Devon, William fitz Baldwin arrived by sea on a royally-sponsored expedition at the mouth of the Tywi river, building the castle of Rhyd-y-gors, with many of his Devonshire associates establishing smaller lordships within that castle's sphere of control.

The leading Normans and their followers began to build castles throughout the region, to subjugate the local population; however, they soon learned that the conquest of south-west Wales was going to be a difficult proposition. In 1094, according to the *Brut*:

> *... the Britons destroyed all the castles of Ceredigion and Dyfed except two, that is, Pembroke and Rhyd-y-gors; and they took with them the people and all the cattle of Dyfed, and they left Dyfed and Ceredigion in waste.*

This setback may have proved longer lasting, but the two remaining castles were the key to the Normans maintaining a foothold at that time. Pembroke, held by the mighty Montgomery family, was never taken. Rhyd-y-gors was abandoned when its castellan died in 1096, with the Normans losing their hold over the lands at the mouth of the Tywi river for a time. Thus, Pembroke was the only castle still in Norman hands in the south-west, and one of the few in the Marches at the end of the century. Nonetheless, the castles they had built established the foundation for the next wave of settlement.

The balance of power changed dramatically when Henry I became king in 1100, with Pembroke Castle falling into Henry's hands in 1102 following a failed rebellion by the Montgomery family. From that point, the *Brut* records that Henry took a direct interest in matters in the region, appointing his own men to key positions. Two crucial actions by Henry in the first decade of the twelfth century were instrumental in the development of the lordships. Firstly, no later than 1109 and probably earlier, Rhyd-y-gors was replaced by the formidable royal castle of Carmarthen.[6] This centre of royal administration, combined with the royal castle at Pembroke, acted as the anchors for the Marcher lordships to form there. Secondly, his sponsorship of a large influx of Flemish settlers to western Dyfed, established a foreign presence in the region that would replace the Welsh as the local population in one area. The following secular lordships grew within the sphere of influence of the two castles:

- **Pembroke Castle**: Pembroke, Haverford, Narberth, Cilgerran/ Emlyn, Cemais
- **Carmarthen Castle**: Llanstephan, Laugharne, Ystlwyf, St Clears, Kidwelly

As mentioned, there was a non-secular lordship in Pembrokeshire, Pebidiog, which belonged to the bishops of St Davids, and which also had the lands of Llawhaden, the administrative centre of the lordship. This was granted its Marcher status by Henry I in 1115, when the first Norman was selected to be the bishop.

When the Normans seized lands, they often adopted the borders of existing Welsh *commotes* and *cantrefi* as their administrative units. By 1116, most of the Marcher lordships of the south-west had been claimed. We know that the lords felt secure enough to found religious houses, for example at Cemais and Kidwelly. In the easternmost part of Deheubarth, Richard fitz Pons had settled in Cantref Bychan, building his castle at Llandovery, though control there was less secure.

In summary, the Normans were able to establish and colonise reasonably secure lordships in the south-west (in contrast to other parts of Wales, and certainly the central and northern regions) for a number of reasons. The power vacuum resulting from the death of Rhys ap Tewdwr in 1093 created the opportunity for conquest and settlement. Henry I's assumption of Pembroke and, therefore, the subsequent interest and support of the Crown in the area, combined with the favourable geography of a long coastline and a large coastal plain, which enabled the provision of manpower and material for colonisation, meant that the Normans were able to establish themselves in the south in the first quarter of the twelfth century. There was, however, always a northern limit to their expansion based on the geography of the forested uplands, which made long-term settlement problematic. Indeed, there were times when the Welsh were able to push back southwards. For example, the powerful de Clare family were able rapidly to colonise Ceredigion after 1110, but were pushed out 25 years later by a Welsh resurgence. (Chapters Three to Six outline the events during the twelfth and thirteenth centuries that influenced, affected, and shaped the Marcher lordships.)

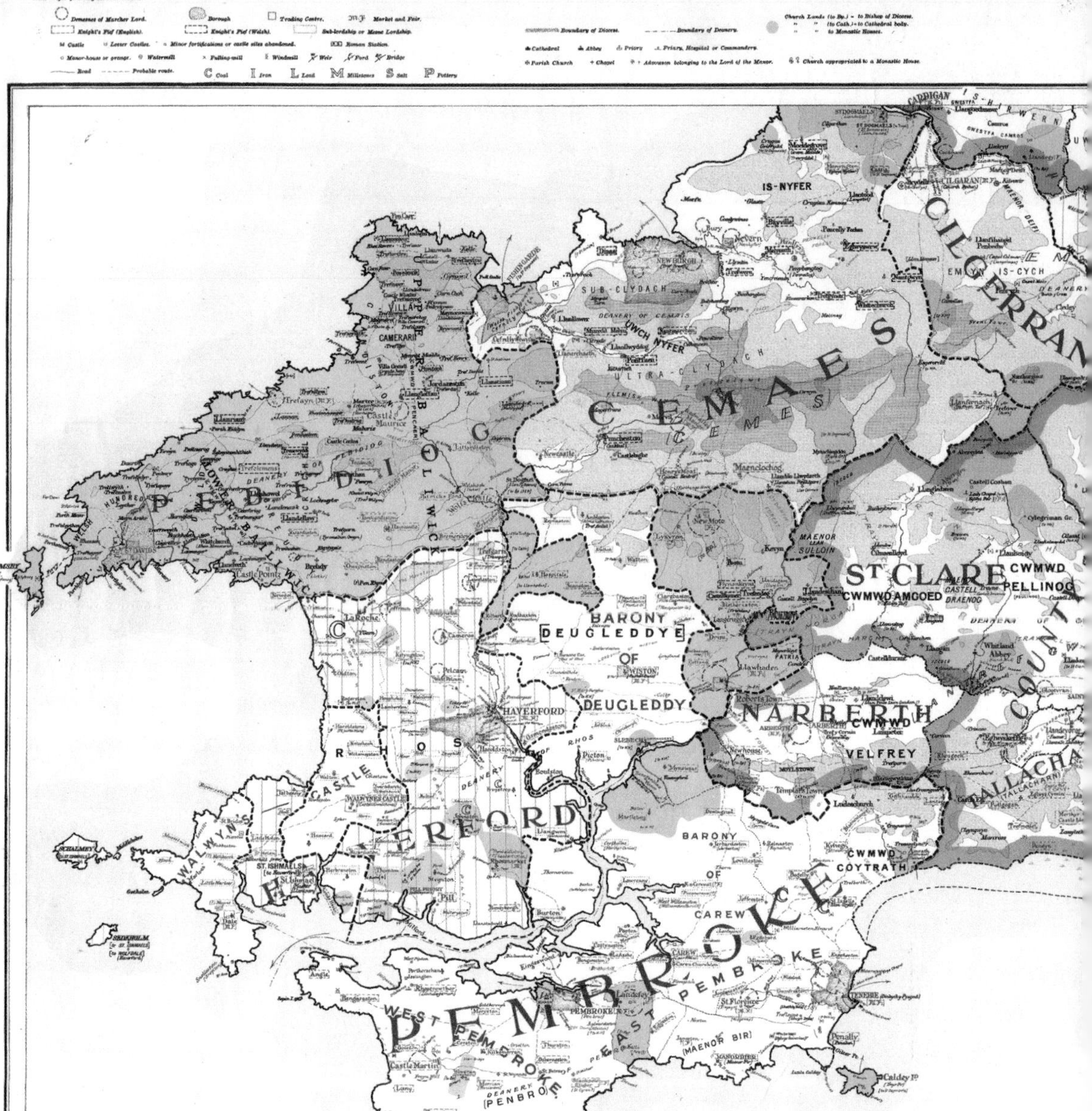

Map 3 The lordships of the south-west March in the fourteenth century
(Produced by William Rees in association with Ordnance Survey)

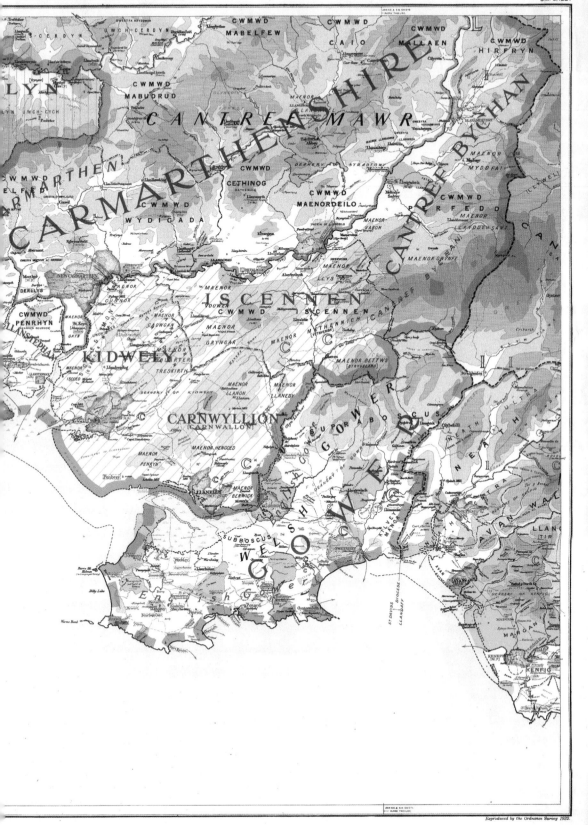

Scale:- half an inch(½") to the mile.

Mile 1 ½ 0 1 2 3 4 5 6 7 8 9 Miles

Pembroke Castle, looking north-west: once built, it was never taken (© Paul Davis)

WELSHRIES, ENGLISHRIES AND THE FLEMINGS

In many of the Marcher lordships, there came to be distinct areas depending on the nationality of the inhabitants. This resulted in the concept of 'Welshries' and 'Englishries', which began to be institutionalised in the thirteenth century, but were beginning to be formed in the twelfth century. This construct of population differentiation repeated itself in various forms throughout the March. Following the annexation or conquest of a region, the new lord would build a castle to maintain control, often forming a borough as well, which encouraged settlers to come and live within the protective sphere of the castle. The Anglo-Normans would naturally choose the most fertile land which was generally in the lower lying areas. The result was that the native Welsh were pushed into the less fertile regions, often the highlands or more forested areas, with the inhabitants of the Welshries living mainly under Welsh law, inheritance-customs, rent and dues. In south-west Wales, there was a large differentiation between the Marcher lordships and their Welshries. The lordships in the far south-west around Pembroke and Haverford had very few Welsh tenants. The lordships that were further inland had very few Anglo-Norman settlers, and these were concentrated around the castle. Cemais,

Cilgerran/ Emlyn, Narberth and Cantref Bychan would have all been predominantly Welsh. Perhaps not surprisingly, the lords of Cemais were noted for their generosity to the native population.[7]

Relationships with the Welsh communities within a lordship were complex. Often native Welshmen were given responsibilities not just within the Welshries, but also in the wider lordship. With many of the Marcher lords of the south-west being absentee lords (managing their estates in England, Ireland and the Continent), it was not out of the ordinary to use a Welsh agent to manage the lordship. An early example was in Cantref Bychan, where the steward of Llandovery, Maredudd ap Rhydderch ap Caradog, a senior Welsh tenant, fought off a Welsh attack in 1116.

Another dynamic that influenced the population settlement in the region was the royally-sponsored immigration of Flemish settlers to the area in the early twelfth century. The Flemish were a hardworking and hard-fighting group of people that originated in the low countries of Europe. Aggressive settlers and capable farmers, they effectively pushed all the Welsh out of the far south-west.

Welsh Law and Marcher Law in south-west Wales
by Dr Sara Elin Roberts

Magna Carta acknowledged three systems of law which could be used to settle disputes: the Common Law of England, the Law of Wales and the Law of the March – a clear acknowledgement that in the March things were done differently.

Cyfraith Hywel, the Law of Hywel, the law which applied to Wales in the Middle Ages, can be said to have been born in Carmarthenshire, and the attribution of *Cyfraith Hywel* to Hywel ap Cadell certainly fixes it firmly in south Wales. However, the origins and the early evidence for the laws are problematic. To start with, the reference to 'Wales' is uncertain. Looking at the evidence of the lawbooks themselves, the books often open with a Prologue, which names King Hywel ap Cadell as the person responsible for the law. Hywel ap Cadell, or Hywel Dda ('the Good', d.949/950) was a tenth-century ruler of the south Wales kingdom of Dyfed and, through conquest and alliance, he managed to extend his dominion to include a large part of Wales – but not 'all of Wales', as is claimed in the lawbooks. His role in lawmaking is less certain. The Prologues to the law manuscripts represent the only evidence, but there is a general lack of evidence for tenth-century Wales. He may indeed have been an active lawmaker; his reign was relatively stable and the conditions for the flourishing of culture,

1215 Magna Carta. Clause 56 acknowledged that the Laws of the March were separate from the Laws of England and the Laws of Wales (Salisbury Cathedral © Ash Mills)

including law, were there for him. He also had contact with Athelstan, the ruler of Mercia from 924, who was known as a lawmaker. Hywel's epithet, 'Good', is interesting and unexplained: it suggests that he may have been a religious ruler (he did go on pilgrimage to Rome), but it may equally apply to his law-making activities, not recorded in any historical evidence.[8]

The Prologues to the lawbooks give the story of how Hywel gathered together learned men, lay and clerical, in Whitland in Carmarthenshire, and there examined the existing laws, maintaining some, rejecting others and adding to them. This meeting is commemorated in the Hywel Dda Centre in Whitland, which has beautiful gardens dedicated to the law, and a heritage centre. The earliest law manuscripts date from the mid thirteenth century, and are not contemporary with Hywel Dda, but there are no earlier manuscripts which do not have the attribution, and this suggests that the tradition may date back to the twelfth century, or even before that. All the Prologues are unanimous in naming Hywel as the lawgiver. The legal scholar and historian, Dafydd Jenkins always took the view that there is 'no smoke without fire' and lack of other evidence for Hywel ap Cadell as a lawmaker does not mean that he was not responsible for any legal activity.

Cyfraith Hywel is very difficult to date, and in any case the laws are unlikely to have been made in one period of activity: the lawbooks contain different sections from different periods. One of the early passages in the lawbooks is the section known as *Saith Esgopty Dyfed* ('The Seven Bishop-Houses of Dyfed'), dated by Thomas Charles-Edwards to the late ninth/ early tenth century.[9] This text borrowed from an Irish collection of canons, showing that early law in Wales was open to external influence. The earliest lawbooks date from the mid thirteenth century, but the texts refer to earlier exemplars. While there is no direct evidence to link the laws to the time of Hywel ap Cadell, there is evidence that there was legal activity taking place in south Wales at an early period. The *Surexit Memorandum* was written on the margins of the Lichfield Gospels, and records the resolution of a legal dispute over a piece of land in the Llandeilo region. This piece was written, in Old Welsh, into the Book of St Chad in the first half of the ninth century, perhaps soon after the case itself had ended. Another piece of Old Welsh, *Breint Teilo* ('the Liberties of [St] Teilo'), included in the twelfth-century Book of Llandaff, has wording reminiscent of the later law texts, and may suggest an early origin for Welsh legal texts in the Carmarthenshire region.[10]

Much attention has been given to the 'golden age' of Welsh law in thirteenth-century Gwynedd, with the manuscripts which were produced there at that time. However, more than half of the law manuscripts originate from south Wales in the fourteenth and fifteenth centuries. The circumstances – political, as well as legal – were different in south Wales in this later period, but Welsh law was still practised there, in a modified form. Several manuscripts were produced in the region, and this attests to an independent written tradition of Welsh law in Deheubarth. The lawbooks from the region show that law was practised in a different way in the south. In north Wales, the justices were professionally trained specialists, but in Deheubarth, landowners could be called upon to sit in justice, which may have been a thirteenth-century development. One reason for this may have been that because of the political situation in south Wales, there were fewer trained justices around: the formal training may have been relaxed out of necessity.

In the southern lawbooks' comments on the role of the justice, which included making judgements, there are hints that taking on this role was difficult. The landowners would not have had the training of the professional justice and may also have been working without the full court personnel, because this was adapted legal procedure in the absence of a royal court. The treatment of the justices in the southern lawbooks also focussed on disputing judgements and wrong judgements. The section is full of practical points, stating what needed to be done when, perhaps as a handbook for untrained jurists. There is no other evidence for the 'landowner justices' in south Wales, but there is evidence from the post-thirteenth-century period of the later situation. Reference is made in the lawbooks, but also in other sources, for men called *dosbarthwyr*, who had some expertise in *Cyfraith Hywel*. *Dosbarthwyr* were legal officials, paid by the Crown; they were usually noblemen, and were often well-known in the cultural and literary life in their communities. They also owned books of law, as reference texts, and this may account for several of the fourteenth-century *Cyfraith Hywel* manuscripts from Deheubarth.

There are references to the Law of the March, and it is clear that this was not a formal written text. However, we know that the Law of the March would vary according to date and according to location.[11] Some of the Welsh law manuscripts from fourteenth-century south Wales were created in what were Marcher lordships. These texts often show a more developed form of the law, and some have English influence; they hint at the different situation in the March, and the more mixed legal traditions. For example, in one manuscript from Cantref Bychan, there is a collection of 'Plaints', outlining how to start the legal process.[12] The form is well-known in medieval England, but the substance of the plaints is rooted in Welsh law. The plaints seem to be models, but the place-names used are all from the area around Llandovery. Peniarth MS 40, in the hand of the poet and scribe Lewys Glyn Cothi, is a law manuscript probably produced for Ieuan ap Phylip, the Constable and Receiver of Cefnllys, and he may have used it in court.[13]

In the March, Welsh law and English laws and practices were combined, and people like Ieuan ap Phylip would need to have had some knowledge of Welsh law, particularly of court procedure. The Cefnllys manuscript certainly focuses on material which would be important and useful to someone who needed to use Welsh law. In addition, while it is not a Welsh law manuscript, there is a highly interesting legal text preserved in a manuscript (primarily containing poetry) by

A page from *Cyfraith Hywel*, Peniarth MS 28, a Latin text of the Laws of Hywel Dda, one of the earliest by a single scribe, dating from the mid thirteenth century (by permission of Llyfrgell Genedlaethol Cymru/ The National Library of Wales)

the poet and scribe Hywel Dafi.[14] Hywel Dafi may also have been a steward in Tretower, and this might explain his interest in the administration of law. In any case, he included in his manuscript a prose text called *dadl croes* ('cross case') from Brecknock, outlining the procedure for claiming land using a cross. In the same manuscript Dafi also included a list, *saith ryw gwyn* ('the seven types of plaints'). This reference to plaints is interesting given that the collection of plaints in another law manuscript seem to originate from the neighbouring lordship to Brycheiniog, Cantref Bychan. The seven plaints are English concepts but written in Welsh. The *dadl croes*, however, is more of a mixture of legal vocabulary and concepts from both regions. These kinds of texts – rare survivals – may reveal a great deal about the mixed legal traditions in the March, and in all the Marcher texts from the region the emphasis is on procedure; the texts may have been committed to writing because there was a need for them.

In south-west Wales and the March, Welsh law was used, and texts were copied and written, but the evidence suggests that there was a developed and modified form of the law. As the law had changed, there was also a need for these texts, and the emphasis on procedure shows the priorities of the scribes and patrons. It may be that there was less segregation of the population in this region (there is evidence elsewhere in the March for 'Welshries' and 'Englishries'), though this would not have been the case in all regions; however, for at least some of the population, *Cyfraith Hywel* continued to be used, in a modified form. The inherent flexibility of the ancient legal system which may have originated in Dyfed made this possible.

Castles of the south-west Marches
by Dr John R. Kenyon

As mentioned earlier, the Marcher lords had the right to build their own castles without requiring permission from the Crown – a power often exercised given the threat posed by native Welsh rulers determined to regain their lands. Thus, it is not surprising that, as shown by Map 4 (opposite) the Welsh Marches had a high density of castles.

The incursion of Roger of Montgomery, earl of Shrewsbury, and the Normans into south-west Wales after 1093, with the death of Rhys ap Tewdwr of Deheubarth in battle near Brecon, resulted in the foundation of several castles. Some were short-lived, whilst others would undergo changes of ownership between Anglo-Norman and Welsh lords as ascendancy swung from one side to another, such as at Llandovery and Newcastle Emlyn. Only Pembroke remained solidly in non-Welsh hands, and even the royal castle and its attendant borough of Carmarthen, founded by King Henry I in the early twelfth century, fell to the Welsh at times, even in the fifteenth century with the Owain Glyn Dŵr uprising in the early 1400s.

Many of the first castles were established close to the coast, such as Llanstephan and Laugharne, or at the highest navigable part of a river, like Kidwelly, and tended to be earth and timber ringworks in origin. There are also good examples of motte and baileys, for example at St Clears and Wiston.

In the south-west, there is evidence for twelfth-century Norman work, of which the outstanding site is Manorbier, with at one end of the castle the ruinous 'old tower', and at the other the fine hall range. Part of the curtain wall at Llanstephan may be late twelfth-century, as might a section of Kidwelly's outer

Map 4 The volume and distribution of castles in Wales and the Marches by 1215 (© Jason Appleby)

curtain. Excavations at Laugharne in the 1980s found the remains of a hall built against the ringwork bank. Carew Castle, like Llanstephan, was founded on an Iron Age site, and another 'old tower' may date to Gerald of Windsor's castle of 1100. This was originally a freestanding tower, later to be incorporated into the inner curtain of the castle constructed later that century.

Recent excavations undertaken at Nevern, the centre of the lordship of Cemais, have uncovered a wealth of information on a castle that underwent Norman and Welsh occupation, the results also causing a rethink about the dating of round keeps in Britain. The summit of the motte is crowned by the remnants of a round tower, interpreted as a keep, as opposed to a shell-keep, this being simply a wall surrounding the perimeter of a motte enclosing one or more buildings within. The dating evidence suggests that this tower was part of the refortification of the castle by William Fitzmartin in the later twelfth century, before the demolition of the castle in 1195.

Shell-keeps are to be found in the south-west. Wiston was founded in the twelfth century by one of the Flemings that accompanied Norman occupation. After various vicissitudes, the castle was refortified with the addition of the shell-keep, possibly soon after c.1220, following Llywelyn ab Iorwerth's destruction of the town. The impressive turreted wall that enclosed the motte of the royal castle of Carmarthen in the early thirteenth century has also been interpreted as a shell-keep.

It is simplistic to view aggression in south-west Wales in the Middle Ages as being Anglo-Norman versus Welsh lords. Welsh disputes between the Lord Rhys of Deheubarth and his sons, for example, even saw the father imprisoned in the castle of Nevern, presumably in the round tower on the motte. One of the sons, Rhys Gryg, was responsible for the core of the stone castles in the Tywi valley east of Carmarthen in the early thirteenth century, namely Dryslwyn and Dinefwr. Perhaps it was Fitzmartin's pre-existing round tower at Nevern that influenced Rhys in his choice of buildings, for Dinefwr is dominated by the great round keep that still stands today, while at Dryslwyn excavations in the 1980s uncovered the remains of a circular keep. Dryslwyn was extended in stone during the thirteenth century by his direct descendants, notably his grandson Rhys.

As elsewhere in the Marches, the thirteenth century witnessed a massive investment in the development of Anglo-Norman castles, especially by the Marshal family, with William Marshal the elder, earl of Pembroke (d.1219), and his sons. The earl built the massive round keep at Pembroke, of four storeys, with an attic under a domed roof. The use of the stone dome in round towers can also be seen at Manorbier, Laugharne and Kidwelly. Marshal's eldest son, another

Dinefwr Castle: family seat of the House of Deheubarth (© Crown copyright 2022 Cadw)

William (d.1231), was finally able to wrest the castle of Cilgerran from the Welsh and began to transform the castle, work that was continued by his brothers (the male line of the Marshals died out by 1245).

What we see today at Cilgerran is basically two great, round towers set close to one another, and while not comparable to their father's keep at Pembroke, those at Cilgerran are of a size equivalent to keeps rather than mural towers. By around the middle of the thirteenth century, Laugharne was in the hands of a Devon family, the de Brians, having been destroyed or badly damaged by Llywelyn ab Iorwerth in 1215. The north-west and north-east corners of the inner ward were dominated by a round tower; and at Manorbier, although the early thirteenth-century curtain walls were largely devoid of towers, the eastern entrance front had rounded towers either side of the rebuilt gateway, one of the towers being circular in the manner of those at Laugharne.

It was a Frenchman and half-brother of King Henry III, William de Valence, becoming earl of Pembroke through marriage, who continued to transform the Marshal castle of Pembroke, by strengthening the outer ward with round towers and a great gatehouse. Before his death in 1296, he may have made domestic improvements to Kidwelly Castle, but it was the previous lords of this castle, the de Chaworths, Payn and Patrick, who strengthened the outer ward with mural towers and gatehouses. They also constructed four great towers at the corners of the inner ward, and these were heightened soon after, leaving the original battlement crenellations 'fossilised' in the new masonry. A similar feature can be seen at Manorbier, where stretches of the curtain walls were heightened (features also to be seen at Caerphilly and Coity in Glamorgan).

A similar layout to Kidwelly's inner ward can be seen at Narberth, a castle largely rebuilt sometime after the original castle had been destroyed by Llywelyn ap Gruffudd in 1257. The rectangular castle has four large, round towers, one of which (the north-eastern) is larger than the others. Another castle that post-dates Llywelyn's successful campaign in 1257 is Newport, with its twin-towered gatehouse and mural towers, although Victorian alterations have obscured parts of the castle of the Marcher lord of Cemais.

One of the most impressive gatehouses in the region is to be seen at Llanstephan. Dating to the later thirteenth century, it was the work of a member of the de Camville family: either William (d.1260) or Geoffrey (d.1308). It has been compared to Gilbert de Clare's inner east gatehouse at Caerphilly, and may have been inspired by Gilbert's work of around 1270, although it might be argued that Llanstephan was the inspiration for Caerphilly.

Llanstephan Castle looking north, with the gatehouse to the left

A feature of some later thirteenth-century developments in castle architecture, and mainly at Marcher castles, is the use of the spurred buttress to strengthen mural towers and gatehouses. Some of the finest examples can be seen at Goodrich in Herefordshire and on Caerphilly's north dam wall. In south-west Wales examples include those on the prominent great west towers at Carew Castle, dating to around 1300, positioned at either end of the magnificent hall. Spurs survive on the outer gatehouse of Laugharne and are a major element in the rebuilding of Carreg Cennen by John Giffard (d.1299) from the 1280s, following the second Welsh war, and also in the Valence chapel tower of Kidwelly and at Newport Castle. Spur buttresses are also a feature of the later medieval gatehouse at the bishop's palace of Llawhaden.

Carreg Cennen is noted for its topographical setting, and much commented upon. Less is said about its design, for Giffard constructed a formidable entrance into the castle, via a number of right-angle turns from the outer gate with its solid turrets through the barbican and the great gatehouse, the approach also overlooked by the intimidating north-east tower.

Royal work was mainly concentrated on repairs and the general upkeep of Carmarthen Castle, the centre of administration (and gaol) of Edward I's new shire. However, at the castle of Haverford (Haverfordwest) new works were undertaken for Queen Eleanor, who was given the castle in 1289 for reasons unknown. Most of what stands today, apart from the Norman keep, dates to this time, although the queen died in 1290. The importance of these two buildings into modern times is reflected by their having, from the later eighteenth century and into the twentieth, places of confinement within their walls.

Churchmen were also lords in the March, and the bishops of St Davids owned estates including in and around Llawhaden. The castle began life as an earth and timber ringwork, probably in the early twelfth century, and suffered along with numerous other castles from Welsh attacks and destruction. Traces of early thirteenth-century masonry survive, and a new hall-block was built by Bishop Thomas Bek, but it was Bishop Adam de Houghton who transformed the site by the 1380s, as well as the adjacent accommodation and chapel ranges. Nevertheless, Llawhaden is arguably more a grand ecclesiastical mansion than a castle.

Administration has always been at the heart of a castle's role, and a particularly good example of this aspect can be seen at Kidwelly, when it became part of the Duchy of Lancaster's estates and later the Crown, from the late fourteenth century. This aspect has recently been studied in depth. The new gatehouse dates to around 1388 to 1401, and references to the work exist, although detailed buildings accounts only survive for 1402. The gatehouse was not completed until 1422 after hiatus and damage during siege by adherents of Owain Glyn Dŵr in 1403. The main purpose of the new gate was not to provide a residence for kings and dukes, but to house officials of the Duchy of Lancaster, and we know that rooms in the chapel tower were kept clean and tidy pending visits by clerks.

Pembrokeshire has several lesser castles-cum-fortified buildings of note. Benton Castle, overlooking the River Cleddau, must be one of the smallest castles in Britain, with its two circular towers and courtyard, much restored in the late nineteenth and twentieth centuries. The Old Rectory, Angle, has all the appearance of an Irish tower-house, while at Picton the original castle of *c.*1300 was a rectangular two-storey block with round towers or turrets at each corner, in the manner of Nunney in Somerset, but more comparable to the Irish castles of Carlow, Ferns and Lea.

Carew Castle, looking south across the Carew river (© Philip Hume)

South-west Wales has two fine examples of castles transformed in the Tudor period, at Carew and Laugharne, with work by Sir Rhys ap Thomas at Carew in the early sixteenth century and by Sir John Perrot at both castles later that century, during the reign of Elizabeth. Both at Carew and Manorbier are outworks added to defend entrances during the civil wars of the 1640s.[15]

CONCLUSIONS

This chapter has described the distinctive features of all Marcher lordships and has begun to show how those in the south-west were shaped by circumstances and forces that were different to elsewhere. As a region bordered on two sides by the sea, lying some distance from the border with England, it was conquest that extended the swathe of Marcher lordships to the sea in the west. Although the grip of the Marcher lords was precarious at times, their presence remained. Chapters three to six explore the events of the twelfth and thirteenth centuries, during which the complex relationships between the kings of England, Welsh rulers and Marcher lords affected the balances of power in the region, shaping the development of the Marcher lordships. Before we embark on that aspect of the narrative, it is necessary first to pose and answer the question: 'Having conquered England, why didn't William I and his successors do the same in Wales in order to exercise direct rule there as well?' The answers to this question, which are rooted in the centuries before 1066, help us to understand the forces and dynamics that led to the formation of the Welsh Marcher lordships, shaping the complex polity that emerged. The next chapter, therefore, briefly outlines some of the key factors in Welsh history before 1066 that shaped the Normans' approach.

CHAPTER TWO

The Formation of Deheubarth and the arrival of the Normans

To understand why the Normans didn't conquer Wales, it is important to consider the underlying topography of Wales, the political fragmentation of the polity of Wales, the growing sense of a Welsh cultural identity, and the relationships that had developed between rulers in Wales and the rulers of Anglo-Saxon England. Awareness of this, together with an outline of the key figures who shaped the formation of the territory that became known as Deheubarth, enables us to understand the interplay of factors that informed the Norman approach to Wales, and thus the development of the Marcher lordships.

The Welsh kingdoms

Wales before 1066 consisted of several kingdoms, jostling and competing for territories. At times, particularly powerful rulers were able to extend their control over other kingdoms, but these often-violent steps towards more consolidation through conquest never survived that person's death. One legacy, however, was the region in the south and west that became known as Deheubarth.

After the Romans withdrew from Britain in the fifth century, there was a mass migration of Angles and Saxons from northern Europe into eastern England. As their settlements expanded, many Britons were pushed westwards, with Cornwall, Wales and areas of the north-west retaining a majority of Britons. Here, they were able to maintain a Celtic identity, but there is very little documentation to show where and how they lived. Another aspect of the general migrations of the fifth and sixth centuries that particularly impacted on south-west Wales was the migration of settlers from Ireland. There is evidence of Irish settlement in areas such as Gwynedd and Brycheiniog, but particularly in the south-west in the kingdom of Dyfed, where the settlers were of high social status, and the first royal line of Dyfed was probably founded by an Irishman.[1] This link between the south of Wales and Ireland continued to be important, with examples of displaced Welsh rulers seeking refuge in Ireland where they could recruit soldiers to reclaim their lands.

Whilst many small kingdoms were initially established, over time they gradually began to merge into larger ones through marriage or annexation by conquest. By the mid eleventh century there were three dominant kingdoms (though their spheres of control constantly changed) with some smaller ones on the fringes:[2]

- In the south, the area that extended from Cardigan Bay down to the Gower peninsula, the kingdom of Seisyllwg, had been joined with Dyfed, which lay to the south-west, to become known as Deheubarth;

- In the north, Gwynedd consisted of the high mountains of Snowdonia and the fertile lowlands of Môn (present-day Anglesey);

- The central area was dominated by Powys, which shared its eastern border with England. Over the preceding centuries the borders of Powys had contracted westwards and northwards, so that by the arrival of the Normans it was the land north of the Severn and west of England. It had also been annexed to the control of Gwynedd since the 850s;

- The south-east was made up of several smaller kingdoms, the two most significant being Morgannwg and Gwent; whilst in central east Wales an independent territory with its own rulers had emerged – Rhwng Gwy a Hafren, which literally translates as 'the lands between the Wye and the Severn'. In the north-east lay an area contested between Gwynedd, Powys and England, which at times maintained independent rule. Confusingly, this area can be referred to as the Perfeddwlad (the middle country), or The Four Cantrefs, or Gwynedd Is Conwy.

Whilst the constant warring between the ruling houses of Wales, ever seeking to expand their territories at the expense of their neighbour, created fragmentation, it also meant that anyone wanting to conquer all the lands of Wales would need to defeat each kingdom. Whereas William the Conqueror, having killed King Harold in a single victorious battle at Hastings, could be crowned King of England, Wales was a much more complicated prospect.

Deheubarth

Deheubarth was the last of the three main kingdoms to be formed, with both Gwynedd and Powys stretching much further back into antiquity. Consequently, although the lands under the control of Gwynedd and Powys had waxed and

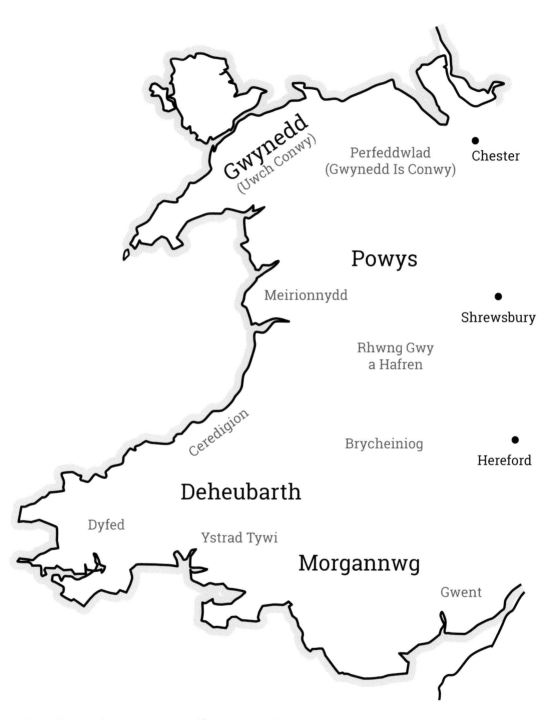

Gwynedd
(Uwch Conwy)

Perfeddwlad
(Gwynedd Is Conwy)

• Chester

Powys

• Shrewsbury

Meirionnydd

Rhwng Gwy
a Hafren

Ceredigion

Brycheiniog

• Hereford

Deheubarth

Dyfed

Ystrad Tywi

Morgannwg

Gwent

Map 5 The pre-1066 Welsh kingdoms (© Jason Appleby)

waned, there was a much stronger identification with a single polity in those areas; an aspect that was less evident in Deheubarth.

By the eleventh century, the region of Deheubarth (which is a geographic descriptor meaning 'the southern part') consisted of several areas that had formerly been kingdoms in their own right, divided by the great rivers of the region. The lands to the north of the River Teifi (medieval Ceredigion, or the traditional county of Cardiganshire), together with the lands of Ystrad Tywi on the eastern side of the Tywi river, formed the earlier kingdom of Seisyllwg. The northern part, Ceredigion, bordering both Powys and Gwynedd, had always been disputed territory. To the south of the River Teifi and the west of the River Tywi was the ancient kingdom of Dyfed. While further east, the kingdom of Brycheiniog had also fallen under the control of Deheubarth.

As described later in this chapter, it was only during the reign of Hywel Dda (d.*c*.950) in the first half of the ninth century that the constituent parts were brought together in a single polity of Deheubarth. Thus, the concept of Deheubarth was only a little over 100 years old by the time the Normans arrived in England.

Hywel's dynasty fortified and built up a new court at Dinefwr, near Llandeilo, on the edge of Cantref Mawr. Dinefwr became their ancestral home and the main court of Deheubarth. Cantref Mawr, lying well inland, many miles from the coastal regions on the eastern edge of Ystrad Tywi, provided a secure refuge. Its dense forests and uplands provided protection for the Welsh when the Normans swarmed across Wales, becoming the area of Deheubarth. This was never conquered or settled by the Normans – though at times, as described later, the native rulers were 'allowed' control of Dinefwr and Cantref Mawr, rather than the Normans attempting to annex it.

TOPOGRAPHY AND ECONOMY OF WALES

One factor that contributed to the fragmentation of the polity of Wales was the divided topography of the lands. The fertile regions of the borders and coastal plains, which enabled arable farming, were separated from each other by the mountains and high uplands that dominated much of the interior and where pastoral farming dominated, and by the valleys that flowed from the mountains. Consequently, transport and communication across Wales, particularly south to north was difficult. For this reason, the landscape lent itself to the formation of smaller kingdoms with strong regional identities. The kingdoms generally developed in areas with fertile plains, mainly along the coast and river valleys, with their hinterlands stretching into the upland interiors. The pastoral economy of the upland areas tended to smaller, more isolated settlements. However, there was no one area that had an abundance of favourable geography, and hence no single kingdom had the concentration of resources needed to dominate the whole of Wales. In the south-west, the fertile coastal plain was a great advantage in feeding the population, but the vulnerable coastline meant that it was often on the defensive against raiders from the sea. The wooded highlands, though, provided a safe refuge for the Welsh to gather their herds, regroup and bide their time to strike back. Allied to the political fragmentation, with its numerous polities and people to overcome, the topography of Wales, with its difficult transport links, meant that full-scale invasion would have been hugely costly of time, men, and resources.

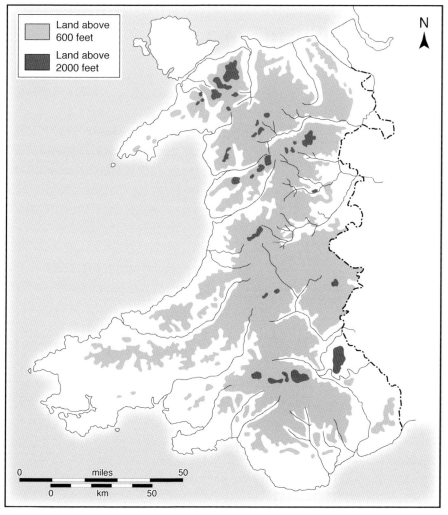

Map 6 The upland interior of Wales with fertile valleys and coastal plains
(© Cath D'Alton and David Stephenson. First published in *Medieval Wales c.1050–1332, Centuries of Ambiguity*, David Stephenson, 2019)

INHERITANCE

Whereas many other medieval societies practiced primogeniture (whereby most of the lands and titles were inherited by the first-born son), Wales practiced partible inheritance. Under this, land and property could be divided between all male heirs related to the second degree – including brothers of the deceased, sons, nephews and cousins. As Welsh law recognised all offspring, whether born in wedlock or not, there could be a large number of heirs, resulting in multiple division of property. This was clearly a factor that mitigated against families building up large concentrations of wealth and property. As it applied to rulership, matters became more complicated still, as there was acceptance that this could not be divided. However, although a ruler sometimes attempted to designate an heir, all male relatives could stake their own claim to rule.[3] Consequently, upon the death of a ruler, there was a large pool of potential replacements, with claimants jostling, feuding and even fighting to exert their own authority in order to take control. It is not surprising, therefore, that the chronicles are full of accounts of killing and maiming to this end.

There were exceptions to this pattern when brothers co-operated together after the death of the ruler. For example, the sons of Rhodri Mawr worked together, with each taking part of the pan-Wales polity that Rhodri had established; though, this also illustrates the forces of fragmentation, as it was accepted that after Rhodri's death the institutions would separate again into the main regions of the north, centre and south. Later in the twelfth century, although the Lord Rhys had established himself as ruler of Deheubarth with influence across all Wales, his death was followed by the bitter and violent feuding between his sons that resulted in the permanent fragmentation of Deheubarth and its ultimate demise as an independent polity.

A DEVELOPING WELSH IDENTITY

A key development in the centuries before the coming of the Normans was the growing sense of a Welsh identity. This is most vividly illustrated through the common Welsh language and the fact that natives of Wales referred to themselves as *Cymry* by the seventh and eighth centuries. *Cymry* translates as 'the compatriots'; whereas 'the Welsh' was a term attached to them by the Anglo-Saxons, and meant 'foreigners'.

A further factor in the emerging Welsh identity was the codification of Welsh law, *Cyfraith Hywel*, and the fact that this was distinct from Anglo-Saxon law. The origins of *Cyfraith Hywel* (as discussed in the previous chapter) were ascribed by tradition to Hywel Dda (d.*c*.950), who was the first ruler of the region that came

Whitland: Hywel Dda Centre and garden. Mosaic commemorating Hywel Dda
and the learned men codifying customs and laws to create a uniform Welsh law

to be known as Deheubarth, and who extended his rule across much of Wales. According to the tradition, Hywel summoned a representative from each of the lands in Wales to a place near present-day Whitland in Carmarthenshire, where he codified the various customs and laws into a uniform law, thus underscoring his supremacy over the other rulers.

Despite this growing sense of a Welsh national identity, the main driver of the polities of Wales was still local. One could just as easily find a Welsh ruler allied with an Anglo-Saxon earl in the frequent internal feuds between rulers within Wales.

OFFA'S DYKE

Another important factor that aided the growing sense of a Welsh identity was the physical barrier of Offa's Dyke. As the strength of the Anglo-Saxon kingdom of Mercia began to grow in the eighth century, the lands of the Welsh kingdom of Powys, which had stretched well into Shropshire, were pushed back eastwards closer to the upland areas. Towards the end of the eighth century, King Offa of Mercia was at the height of his power. It is generally accepted that he ordered the construction of the dyke, although other theories exist as to its origin. It is unclear how long it took to build or when it was finished, but it remains an impressive feat of construction. It runs nearly the full length of the English-Welsh border, and is still conspicuous in many locations, including the most southerly section which runs right up to the Bristol channel near Chepstow. It is still debated what the purpose of the dyke was and whether it was effective. It was most likely a way to regulate and control cross-border movement, including trade, as well as hindering Welsh raiding parties. The fact that the ditch was dug on the Welsh side with

Part of Offa's Dyke near Montgomery, Wales

the raised earth on the Anglo-Saxon side reveals who it was intending to keep out. It did not act as a permanent border as there were examples of Anglo-Saxon and Welsh settlement on either side of the dyke; indeed, the construction of the dyke indicates a lack of intent on behalf of the Anglo-Saxons to conquer lands in Wales. It did, though, act as a powerful symbol that underlined the separation of the two countries, and contributed to the growing sense of a Welsh identity.

Relationships with Anglo-Saxon England

Even though the political landscape in England changed markedly in the ninth and tenth centuries, a lack of intent to conquer Wales remained constant. In contrast to the political fragmentation in Wales, the process towards a unified polity was accelerated in England by the settlements of the Norse invaders in the north and east, which wiped out the indigenous kingdoms of those regions. By the end of the ninth century, when Alfred agreed the formal division with the Norsemen, only Wessex, and a rump of Mercia that was subordinate to Wessex, remained. Thus, when Alfred's successors succeeded in driving the Norse out of England, they were able to become the sole rulers of the English. Their power attracted Welsh rulers seeking their protection (as outlined in the next section), establishing acceptance of the overlordship of the kings of England, and making conquest unnecessary. This was a relationship that the Normans were later able to utilise in order to intervene when necessary to constrain any potential threat to the security of the border region.

Welsh Rulers and the Formation of Deheubarth

RHODRI MAWR

Rhodri ap Merfyn Frych inherited the kingdom of Gwynedd when his father died in *c*.844. Twelve years later, Powys came under his control when the last ruler from the separate royal line of Powys died in 856, creating a unified Welsh presence on the border with Mercia (Powys was to remain under the control of Gwynedd for over two centuries). Then, when the last king of Seisyllwg died in 872, Rhodri claimed and won rule there based on his marriage to the king's sister. Thus, Rhodri controlled lands that ran from Anglesey in the north, through central Wales to the south coast. Only the smaller kingdoms of the south-west and south-east were beyond his rule. It was also during his reign that the Norse invaders began ravaging the coasts of Wales. Rhodri is often best remembered as a Welsh ruler who was able to unite his people to withstand the seaborne assaults, though he was killed in a battle with the Anglo-Saxons in 878. After his death he was often referred to as Rhodri Mawr ('the Great'). It was from his line that the future rulers of Wales descended.

After Rhodri's death, the span of lands under his control fragmented again into their constituent parts. Unusually, it appears that his sons worked together with each accepting rule over one of the distinct regions. Cadell, who had been established earlier to rule on behalf of his parents in Seisyllwg (the kingdom that ran south from the River Dyfi along the lands to the east of Cardigan Bay and on to the Gower on the south coast) continued to rule there, whilst the leadership of Gwynedd was taken by his brother Anarawd.

It was during this period that we begin to see Welsh rulers seeking the protection of the kings of Wessex. First, the lesser kings of Dyfed and Brycheiniog, fearing the dominance of Rhodri's sons, sought the protection of King Alfred. At the same time, rulers in the south-east, fearing the earl of Mercia, also sought the protection of Alfred. This illustrates well the shifting loyalties and alliances, as well as the increasingly dominant role of the kings of Wessex – whereas alliances in earlier generations had been between equals, seeking Alfred's protection also implicitly accepted his overlordship. Indeed, eventually Anarawd himself brokered an agreement with Alfred in 893 and was received at the court of Wessex.

The deaths of Anarawd and Cadell were followed by conflict and rivalry between their descendants, with a clear separation of the dynastic lines. The descendants of Anarawd claimed rule in the north (Gwynedd), whilst the descendants of Cadell ruled in Seisyllwg.

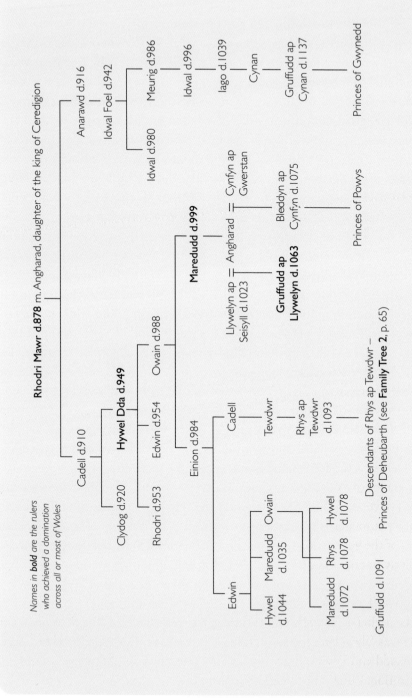

*Names in **bold** are the rulers who achieved a domination across all or most of Wales*

Rhodri Mawr d.878 m. Angharad, daughter of the king of Ceredigion

Cadell d.910

Anarawd d.916

Idwal Foel d.942

Clydog d.920

Hywel Dda d.949

Rhodri d.953

Edwin d.954

Owain d.988

Einion d.984

Idwal d.980

Meurig d.986

Idwal d.996

Iago d.1039

Cynan

Gruffudd ap Cynan d.1137

Princes of Gwynedd

Llywelyn ap Seisyll d.1023 = Angharad = Cynfyn ap Gwerstan

Maredudd d.999

Gruffudd ap Llywelyn d.1063

Bleddyn ap Cynfyn d.1075

Princes of Powys

Cadell

Tewdwr

Rhys ap Tewdwr d.1093

Edwin

Hywel d.1044

Maredudd d.1035

Owain

Maredudd d.1072

Rhys d.1078

Hywel d.1078

Gruffudd d.1091

Descendants of Rhys ap Tewdwr – Princes of Deheubarth (see **Family Tree 2**, p.65)

Family Tree 1 Select descendants of Rhodri Mawr ap Merfyn Frych

Hywel Dda

Hywel, the son of Cadell ap Rhodri Mawr, had probably secured for himself the rule of Dyfed before his father died. Hywel had married the sister of the king of Dyfed, and after the latter's death in 904 no further independent rulers appear in the record. Following his father's death in 910, Hywel inherited Seisyllwg, initially as joint ruler with his brother, Clydog, but as sole ruler after his brother died in 920. It was this combined area of Seisyllwg and Dyfed that became known as the kingdom of Deheubarth. Hywel also appears to have assumed an overlordship of Brycheiniog. He took control of Gwynedd and Powys when, after the death of his cousin Idwal Foel in battle with the Anglo-Saxons, Hywel drove out Idwal's sons in 942, bringing all of Wales under his control, except for the south-east.

Although ruler of most of Wales, Hywel was heavily influenced by the court at Wessex and the reputation of King Alfred. He went on a pilgrimage to Rome, as had Alfred. Upon his return, Hywel was a frequent visitor to the Anglo-Saxon court of Athelstan (d.939), the grandson of Alfred, who drove out the Vikings to claim kingship over all of England. Athelstan received many Welsh rulers at his court, accepting their submissions as honoured subordinates, and receiving annual tributes from them. Although, when witnessing Athelstan's charters, Hywel was always ranked above all the other rulers in Wales, there was a recognition that Athelstan was his overlord. His later reign was generally peaceful by the standards of the time, which may be why the Welsh laws were attributed to him, and why he was termed Hywel Dda (the Good).

When Hywel died in c.950, his sons were not able to maintain their hold over large parts of Wales. Gwynedd and Powys reverted to the line of Anarawd ap Rhodri, but his son Owain ap Hywel Dda, after the deaths of his brothers, did maintain the family's hold of the disparate parts of the west and south as a single polity of Deheubarth, which encompassed Dyfed, Ystrad Tywi, Ceredigion and at times Brycheiniog. When Owain died, his son Maredudd was able to regain some hold over Gwynedd. However, after his death in 999, there commenced a period of instability throughout all of Wales, with a series of interlopers laying claim to leadership of the various kingdoms. This, combined with Viking raiding, made it a particularly fractious period in Welsh history.

Gruffudd ap Llywelyn

During the period of instability and warring, one of the more successful interlopers to emerge was Llywelyn ap Seisyll, who defeated his rivals in battle to hold sway over Gwynedd and Powys. After his death in 1023, the rule of Gwynedd reverted to the traditional line, only to be seized by his son, Gruffudd ap Llywelyn, in

1039. This triggered a protracted and violent feud for control of Deheubarth, which was ruled by Hywel ab Edwin, the great-great grandson of Hywel Dda, who had become the sole ruler of Deheubarth after his brother, Maredudd ab Edwin, was slain in 1035. It would not be until 1055, however, that Gruffudd was able successfully to bring Deheubarth into his realm. Although Gruffudd defeated Hywel in battle in 1041 (allegedly carrying off Hywel's wife as part of the spoils of victory), and again in 1044, when Hywel was slain in battle, Gwynedd's hegemony over Deheubarth did not last long. Gruffudd ap Rhydderch of Gwynllwg, who had his own claim to Deheubarth, defeated Gruffudd ap Llywelyn in 1047, with Gruffudd possibly narrowly escaping with his life. Gruffudd ap Rhydderch remained ruler of Deheubarth until his death in 1055, when Gruffudd ap Llywelyn finally seized control. Even at the time it was noted that this forced consolidation had been achieved through extreme violence. As ruler of all Wales, Gruffudd now set about exerting his influence further afield, with devastating raids into Herefordshire and through alliances with Anglo-Saxon earls.

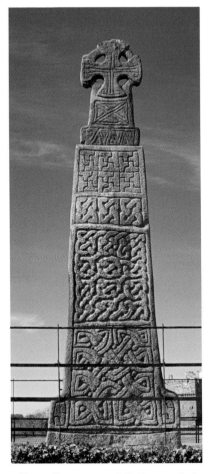

Carew Cross: a carved Celtic cross that is thought to commemorate a ruler of Deheubarth who fell in battle in 1035 (© Crown copyright 2022 Cadw)

Harold Godwinson, the powerful earl of Wessex, was tasked with bringing the borders back under Anglo-Saxon control. In a bold lightning raid across north Wales, he nearly caught Gruffudd at his court of Rhuddlan. Not to be deterred, Harold led an organised campaign deeper into north Wales. The pressure from Harold was enough to force Gruffudd's own men to turn against him in 1063. He was slain, with his head sent to Harold as a prize. It was only three years later that Harold himself, now King of England, died at the battle of Hastings. Shortly thereafter the Normans arrived at the Welsh border. With the memory still fresh of the havoc that Gruffudd wreaked, the threat to the stability of the border region would have been very much in their consciousness.[4]

The arrival of the Normans

The Norman assumption of power in England was rapid, and subsequent conquest of the whole country was brutal. However, when they arrived at the borders with Wales, William I did not continue the forceful subjugation of people to his rule. Instead, he created a strong buffer zone by establishing earldoms at the important points of Chester, Shrewsbury and Hereford, which could control the strategic routes into and out of Wales. The king appointed three of his most trusted companions as earls, giving them a greater level of authority and power than elsewhere, to enable them to create a secure border region.

Whilst the conquest and annexation of the lands of Wales to the direct rule of the Crown would have been too expensive and was unnec-

William I, conqueror of England who established three earldoms on the Welsh border for security rather than attempt a full-scale conquest of Wales (© National Portrait Gallery, London)

essary, it appears that the creation of a secure border region could involve the Norman barons in mounting raids into Wales and annexing lands to their control, particularly in regions where there was a vacuum in native rule. Thus, we see the earl of Hereford, William fitz Osbern, crossing the Wye, building a castle on the western bank at Chepstow, and possibly pushing further west from there. His untimely death in 1071 in battle in Flanders stopped those advances for a time in the south. The first reference to the Normans in the *Brut* shows that they were still active in the south-east soon after, but this time as allies of one Welsh ruler in his conflict with another:

> *One thousand and seventy* [actually 1072] *was the year of Christ when Maredudd ab Owain was slain by Caradog ap Gruffudd ap Rhydderch and the French on the bank of the river Rhymni.*

At the same time, in the central region, Roger of Montgomery, earl of Shropshire, having established a castle (Hen Domen) overlooking a crossing of the River

Severn, pushed further up the valley, building several castles to secure Norman control of that strategic route from central Wales into England. From there he launched raiding parties into Ceredigion and Dyfed in 1073 and 1074.

In the north, where there was a vacuum in Welsh leadership, earl Hugh of Chester and his cousin, Robert, campaigned across north-east Wales, annexing land first to the control of Chester. As Robert pushed further westwards, he was permitted to take the lands into his personal control, building a castle at Rhuddlan in 1073, from which he became known as Robert of Rhuddlan. With considerable violence, Robert moved further along the coast, establishing a castle as far west as the Conwy at Deganwy. From there, he secured his control over the *cantrefi* of Rhos and Rhufoniog.

William fitz Osbern and Roger of Montgomery both established a string of lordships in the border region between the lands of the Welsh and the caputs of their earldoms at Hereford and Shrewsbury respectively. When both earldoms were forfeited to the Crown and discontinued (after the failed rebellion in 1075 of Earl William's son, Roger of Breteuil, and the failed rebellion led by two of the sons of Earl Roger in 1102), those lords in the central Marches became tenants-in-chief of the Crown. It was these lordships that, over the course of the next two centuries, were withdrawn out of the shire administration and into the March.

Rhys ap Tewdwr and the House of Deheubarth

This chaotic picture of Normans allying with one Welsh ruler in his battle with a rival, securing strategic routes, raiding deeper into Wales when they could, and in the north annexing territory to their control, is bound up in the 18 years of chaotic and bloody feuding that erupted after the death of Gruffudd ap Llywelyn in 1063. Following Gruffudd's death, Edward the Confessor asserted the overlordship of the English Crown in order to recognise Gruffudd's maternal half-brothers, Bleddyn ap Cynfyn and Rhiwallon ap Cynfyn, as the rulers of Gwynedd/ Powys. In Deheubarth, Maredudd ab Owain had restored the power of the traditional dynasty of the house of Merfyn Frych. Inevitably, this settlement was challenged by Gruffudd's own sons, Maredudd and Idwal, sparking a series of feuds between warring families. Although Maredudd, Idwal and Rhiwallon were killed at the battle of Mechain in 1069, other claimants joined the fray. As noted above, in 1072 Caradog ap Gruffudd of Gwynllwg, with the assistance of the French, defeated and killed Maredudd ab Owain of Deheubarth. Six years later, Caradog, having in the meantime seized Morgannwg, defeated and killed another claimant to Deheubarth, Rhys ab Owain ab Edwin, who had killed the remaining half-brother of Gruffudd ap Llywelyn, Bleddyn ap Cynfyn. After the death of Rhys ab Owain, another relative, Rhys ap Tewdwr (d.1093), staked his claim to Deheubarth, which provoked Caradog to invade in 1081, driving Rhys to seek sanctuary at St Davids.

This period of destructive warfare across all of Wales was brought to a sudden end by the battle of Mynydd Carn in 1081, which resulted in the death of Caradog alongside most of the other contenders for power. Two men emerged still standing and victorious from the battle – Rhys ap Tewdwr (d.1093) and Gruffudd ap Cynan (d.1137), both from the traditional branches of the ruling families of the north and the south. Returning north, however, Gruffudd was captured by the Normans and forced to languish in captivity in Chester for some ten years. The vacuum caused by his absence enabled Robert of Rhuddlan to dominate north Wales. In contrast, Rhys ap Tewdwr was able to secure his domination over the lands of Deheubarth.

Rhys's control, though, did not go unchallenged. In 1088, according to the *Brut*:

> *And then Rhys ap Tewdwr was expelled from his kingdom by the sons of Bleddyn ap Cynfyn, that is Madog, Cadwygan and Rhiddid. And he fled to Ireland. And forthwith after that he assembled a fleet and came back again. And then the battle of 'Llychcrei' took place, and the sons of Bleddyn were slain; and Rhys ap Tewdwr gave immense treasure to the seamen, Scots and Irish, who had come to his aid.*

In 1091, Rhys was faced with yet another challenge to his rule when he had to defeat descendants of the original kings of Dyfed.

Establishing the overlordship of the English Crown

Having laid the basis for a secure border region, with the understanding that his barons could raid into Wales, William I, with greater priorities elsewhere, was content to let the chaos play out. However, soon after the decisive battle of Mynydd Carn in 1081, which enabled Rhys ap Tewdwr to establish his rule over the large territory of Deheubarth, the king took action to assert his authority. Although the *Brut* records that it was a royal pilgrimage:

> *1081:* [at the end of a long list of the princes slain at Mynydd Carn] *And then William the Bastard, king of the Saxons and the French and the Britons, came on a pilgrimage to Menevia* [St Davids] *to offer prayers*

St Davids Cathedral: the destination of William I's 'pilgrimage' in 1081 (© Philip Hume)

The Anglo-Saxon Chronicle is clear that, with a large armed retinue, this was more accurately a show of military strength – of the authority of the English Crown, and the overlordship in Wales of the King of England. Compiled five years later in 1086, Domesday Book records that Rhys ap Tewdwr held south Wales from the king for an annual fee of 40 pounds. Almost certainly, therefore, Rhys would have met with William I during his progress across south Wales in 1081, with the two men coming to an agreement that Rhys would give fealty and tribute to the king, who in turn recognised Rhys's right to rule. Both men gained from the agreement. For the king, this acknowledged his superior position as overlord, and gave the prospect of greater stability. For Rhys, it extended him the benefit of the protection of the powerful king of England, and thus protection from the Norman barons who would not dare to threaten him or his lands in Deheubarth.

Further detail in Domesday Book provides an interesting contrast and further insight into William's approach in Wales. In the north it records that the *cantref* of Tegeingl in north-east Wales was part of the lands of the earldom of Chester, whilst the lands to the west of the River Clwyd were held directly from the king by Robert of Rhuddlan for the sum of 40 pounds, which suggests that the Norman's status was like that of Rhys ap Tewdwr in the south. Whilst, at first glance, this might appear inconsistent, this is not the case, as the key point is that both men held their land from the king of England. In the south, William was happy to accept the rule of a dominant native ruler, provided that he was subject to the king; in the north, where there was a vacuum in Welsh leadership, William recognised Robert's right to have lands annexed to his control, but with recognition that they were held from the Crown. This is a factor in the emergence of the Marcher lordships – that lands annexed in Wales would become discreet lordships, held from the king, rather than being merged into their other holdings in England.

Although the barons were allowed to grab what they could around the edges, and plunder further into Wales, William's campaign across south Wales in 1081 – and his agreements with Rhys in the south and Robert in the north – were a clear indication that he had no intention or need to conquer and annex Wales to his direct rule.

The death of William I in 1087, however, shifted the dynamics. William left Normandy to his eldest son, Robert Curthose; England to his middle son, William (Rufus) II; and a sum of money to his third son, Henry. This division, which effectively gave the barons, who held lands in both territories, two masters, was to influence Norman politics for the next 20 years and have significant consequences for the March. In 1088, William (Rufus) II withstood a rebellion by dissatisfied and unsettled barons, many of whom were from the border region with Wales.

Although the king quickly quelled the revolt, he was remarkably generous towards the defeated rebels, possibly because he could not afford to alienate so many of the barons from the Welsh March. Instead, he may have encouraged them to look westwards into Wales as a safer outlet (for him) for their aggression and desire for more lands. One of those barons, Bernard de Neufmarché, began to penetrate into Wales, moving along the valleys of the Usk and Wye, and building a castle at present-day Brecon. With Brycheiniog forming a buffer between the Normans and the heartlands of Deheubarth, Rhys ap Tewdwr was forced to respond. In 1093, Rhys marched on Brecon, ready for battle, and was killed in the resulting skirmish.

KING WILLIAM the SECOND
Surnamed Rufus 3ʳᵈ Son of William the Conqueror was Crowned Octo. 5ᵗʰ 1087 Built the great Hall at Westminster was Slain by accident as he was hunting in New Forrest He was Buried at Winchester he Reigned about 13 Yˢ

King William Rufus: encouraged Norman expansion into Wales as a means of rewarding his barons
(© National Portrait Gallery, London)

Up to this point, the *Brut* contains very few references to the Normans. However, the chroniclers were aware that the death of Rhys was a momentous event – '*And then fell the kingdom of the Britons*'. Certainly, Rhys's death opened the floodgates, according to the *Brut*:

> *and then, two months after that, about the Calends of July, the French came to Dyfed and Ceredigion which they have held to this day, and they fortified them with castles; and they seized all the lands of the Britons.*

Indeed, from 1093 onwards the interactions with the Normans become central to the narrative; however, (as explored in the following chapters) this contact, which forged the Marcher lordships, was complex and nuanced. As power swung back and forth, it depended not only on the attention and abilities of the kings of England, but also the powers and abilities of the native rulers of Wales.

This chapter has sought to sketch out the forces that shaped the Normans' approach to Wales, which provided the context for the complex events that were to follow in the twelfth and thirteenth centuries – events that led to the emergence of the Marcher lordships. In summary, the key elements were:

- The lands of Wales were fragmented geographically and politically, consequently any attempts at conquest would require the simultaneous defeat of several rulers. Allied to the mountainous topography, conquest would be hugely expensive, requiring considerable resources of money, men and time. The richer fertile lands of the south and the east, on the other hand, were readily open to encroachment from England;

- The kingdom of Deheubarth that spanned the west and south of Wales, giving it the resources of the large coastal areas, had been the last of the main regions of power to be formed in Wales. Having been brought together by marriage and conquest only a century or so before the arrival of the Normans, there was less identification with a united polity of Deheubarth;

- The Normans were aware of the potential threat posed by a powerful ruler in Wales, such as Gruffudd ap Llywelyn, thus recognised the importance of a secure border region and the necessity to constrain the ambitions of successful Welsh rulers;

Part of Offa's Dyke, Llanfair Hill, north of Knighton (© CPAT image 4236-3414, photograph by Julian Ravest)

- The Norman kings were able to draw on the precedent of Welsh rulers seeking the protection and overlordship of their Anglo-Saxon predecessors. Consequently, while there was conflict and raiding in the border regions, there was no desire or need to annex the lands of Wales to the direct rule of the Crown;

- Although Offa's Dyke had significance as a boundary of culture and identity, it was a fluid border with Welsh settlement to the east of it, and Anglo-Saxon settlement to the west;

- The lands of the south-west, of course, were far removed from Offa's Dyke; however, the long coastline made it vulnerable to raiders from the sea. Also, the proximity to Ireland had led to generations of intermingling;

- Following his victory in battle in 1081, Rhys ap Tewdwr emerged as the ruler of Deheubarth and the dominant ruler in the south. Because of this, William I moved quickly to establish his authority as Rhys's overlord;

- The death of Rhys ap Tewdwr in 1093 presented an opportunity for Norman barons to raid into Deheubarth to annex territory to create their own territory, thus forming the early Marcher lordships.

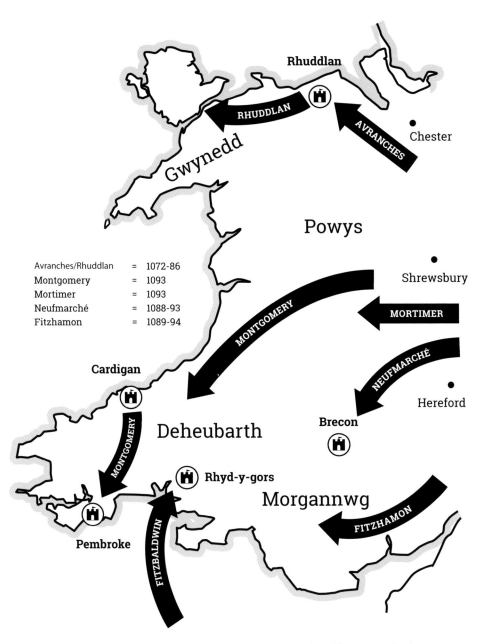

Map 7 Norman invasion routes in the late eleventh century (© Jason Appleby)

CHAPTER THREE

Norman Conquest and consolidation
1093–1135

Ask 'in what year was the Norman Conquest?' and the inevitable reply is '1066'; however, for south-west Wales the answer would be the year 1093. It was in this year that the Normans staged a two-pronged invasion of the region, establishing their control via that most Norman of structures, the castle. The invasion was, for the most part, a private enterprise by Norman barons, though it also had elements of royal sponsorship. As outlined in the previous chapter, the strategies of the Norman kings of England did not include conquest and direct rule of Wales; it was to be another two centuries before circumstances changed.

The Norman incursions of 1093 created what became the Marcher lordships of south-west Wales. Their hold was initially tenuous, as they were expelled from nearly all areas before the end of the eleventh century. The ebb and flow of power between Marcher lord and native Welsh ruler was influenced by several factors, with the two most significant being the competing strength of the local Welsh rulers, and the corresponding influence of the king. The political landscape in Wales changed depending on whether the king was willing and able to exert royal influence in the region or whether he was preoccupied elsewhere. This chapter will focus on the reigns of the two brothers, William (Rufus) II and Henry I, whose actions defined the Marcher lordships of the south-west in the eleventh and twelfth centuries.

INITIAL CONQUEST AND WELSH RESURGENCE 1093–1100

As discussed in the last chapter, William (Rufus) II came to view Wales as a place where he could direct the military and acquisitive instincts of the barons. It may be that both the king and Rhys ap Tewdwr did not feel as bound by the agreement that William the Conqueror had made with Rhys in 1081. The Norman advances up the Wye and Usk valleys forced Rhys to respond militarily, resulting in his death in 1093 at the hands of the encroaching Normans. This death created a power vacuum that could not be filled by his very young heir, Gruffudd, who was sent to Ireland where he could grow up in safety. Into this void first stepped

Cadwgan ap Bleddyn from Powys, who ransacked the area before returning home with his plunder. A few months later Roger of Montgomery, earl of Shrewsbury, who had been steadily driving further up the Severn valley to secure the strategic route into the heartlands of central Wales, crossed the watershed to sweep through Ceredigion, building a castle at, or near, what is now Cardigan. He and his followers then moved to the south coast, building the castle of Pembroke, which he granted to his youngest son Arnulf.

In addition to the overland invasion by the Montgomery family, there was a royally sanctioned seaborne invasion from England. Led by the sheriff of Devon, William fitz Baldwin, this was calculated by William (Rufus) II to make sure that the conquest of south-west Wales had a royal element attached to it. William fitz Baldwin built a castle at Rhyd-y-gors, near present-day Carmarthen, whilst the group of Devonshire magnates who came up with him set up satellite lordships within the orbit of Rhyd-y-gors. The striking feature of the Normans' incursion was that, unlike the prince of Powys, they had not come for plunder, they had come to stay.

Although the *Brut* records that the death of Rhys ap Tewdwr was disastrous for the Welsh in 1093, the Norman hold was tenuous. In 1094, *'the Britons threw off the rule of the French, being unable to suffer their tyranny'*. Towards the end of that year the Welsh ravaged all of Dyfed and Ceredigion, destroying all the castles that had been built there, except for Pembroke and Rhyd-y-gors. According to the *Brut,* open warfare raged, with much of the land left as waste. When William fitz Baldwin died in 1096, the castle of Rhyd-y-gors was abandoned, leaving only Pembroke Castle in Norman hands. This was now held by Gerald of Windsor, the steward of Arnulf of Montgomery (with the lord holding many lands across two countries, it was common practice to leave a lordship in the hands of a trusted steward). Gerald was a prime example of a senior Norman of non-aristocratic background who could make his livelihood in the newly-conquered lands. When the Welsh moved against Pembroke with a large warband later that year, the story of Gerald's defence of Pembroke castle was afterwards told in detail by another Gerald – Gerald of Wales. Having been abandoned by all the senior knights, Gerald of Windsor fooled the Welsh attackers into believing that the defenders were in a much stronger position than they were, causing the Welsh to take their spoils and return home without seizing the castle. Indeed, the Norman castle of Pembroke was never sacked, becoming the anchor of the Norman occupation. When William (Rufus) II was killed in a hunting accident in the New Forest in 1100, his younger brother, Henry, became king. Henry I was a formidable ruler with a forceful personality. He rarely had to resort to direct military intervention in Wales, only twice making military invasions to achieve his goals. With great skill, he used diplomacy and coercion to become a ruler to be respected and feared.[1]

THE RISE OF HENRY I

Henry I effectively seized the throne in 1100 by swiftly securing the royal treasury at Westminster. His elder brother, Robert Curthose, ruler of Normandy, was away on Crusade, which made Henry's path easier. When Robert returned, he also claimed the throne of England. Gathering an army, he set sail for England to enforce his claim in 1101; however, the two sides came to an agreement before there was any fighting. Robert Curthose returned to Normandy, whilst Henry I was affirmed as king. With the matter of the English throne now settled, several barons in England found themselves exposed. The Montgomery family held extensive lands in Normandy as well as England, and they had supported Robert against Henry.

THE FALL OF THE HOUSE OF MONTGOMERY

When the first earl, Roger of Montgomery, died in 1094, the eldest son, Robert de Bellême, inherited the family lands in Normandy, while the second son, Hugh, became the second earl of Shrewsbury. However, when Hugh was killed in 1098 on the coast of Anglesey in a skirmish with the boats of the king of Norway, Robert de Bellême became the 3rd earl of Shrewsbury. The youngest son, Arnulf of Montgomery, was still at Pembroke, styling himself as the earl of Pembroke (although it is debatable whether he officially held the title of earl). When the brothers rebelled against Henry I, Robert de Bellême recruited two brothers from the royal dynasty of Powys (Iorwerth and Cadwgan ap Bleddyn) to support them, while Arnulf turned to Ireland for assistance. According to the *Brut*,

> *And whilst those things were being done, Arnulf thought to make peace with the Irish and to obtain help from them. And he sent messengers to Ireland, that is Gerald the steward and many others, to ask for the daughter of king Muircertach for his wife. And that he easily obtained.*

By the time the Irish support arrived, the rebellion was over. Henry had managed to coax one of Robert's Welsh supporters, Iorwerth ap Bleddyn, to turn against them. With his Welsh support now in tatters, Robert submitted to the king; Arnulf was left with the option of subjecting himself to Henry or leaving his lordships and going into exile abroad. When Arnulf chose the latter, playing no further role in the Marches, Henry took Pembroke into royal hands, giving himself a direct interest in the newly-conquered territory.

A depiction of Pembroke Castle c.1130 (© Neil Ludlow)

THE DOMINATION OF HENRY I

The promise that Henry I had made to Iorwerth and Cadwgan, in exchange for their help in defeating the Montgomery family in 1102, was that they would be given Ceredigion, Dyfed and Ystrad Tywi. Despite this, Henry immediately went back on his word, giving them only Ceredigion but not the lands in the south. It was likely that he felt that the family would become too powerful if allowed to control such a large part of Wales. He therefore appointed two others as stewards, splitting the control of the two regions. He appointed a knight, Saer, to be steward of Dyfed. Arnulf's castellan, Gerald of Windsor, was probably seen as too close to Montgomery, as he appears to have been removed from office. The stewardship of the other half of the south of Deheubarth, Ystrad Tywi, was granted to a Welsh prince, Hywel ap Goronwy, a descendant of the ruling dynasty of Rhwng Gwy a Hafren, who had been the leader of the war band that attacked Pembroke Castle in 1096. Henry was consummate at balancing power, having no scruples about ruthlessly going back on a promise if it worked to his advantage. In fact, when Iorwerth went to Henry's court to complain, he was brought up on charges and thrown in the king's prison for seven years! This completely removed a potentially strong Welsh ruler from the nascent Norman March.

By 1105, the Normans were back in Rhyd-y-gors and its surrounds. Richard fitz Baldwin, the brother of William, and now sheriff of Devon, seized, restocked and outfitted the castle to make it defensible again, expelling Hywel ap Goronwy from his lands. Although Hywel ravaged the surrounding countryside, he could make no impact on the castle, and the following year was slain by treachery. A man who had been a close comrade, Gwgan ap Meurig, invited Hywel to stay a night at his house, but informed the Normans where he could be found:

> And they [the Normans] *came about cock-crow and surrounded the hamlet and the house where Hywel was. And they raised a shout, and with the shout Hywel vigorously awoke and sought his arms and awoke his comrades and called upon them. And the sword which he had placed at the head of his bed, and the spear at his feet, Gwgan had removed whilst he was sleeping.*

Hywel was brutally murdered thus precipitating Norman control in the region.

Gerald of Windsor was also now back in favour, having been installed again as the castellan of Pembroke Castle in *c.*1105. Furthermore, he had married the daughter of the slain Rhys ap Tewdwr, the princess Nest. She had been the mistress of Prince Henry (as he then was) after she was brought back to the royal court following the death of her father in 1093. It is unclear how Gerald came to get back into good favour, but the marriage to Nest was a powerful move for him, as she lent the fledgling Norman outpost local credibility. From Pembroke, Gerald was able to expand Norman control over other parts of Dyfed. He built a castle at Cenarth Bychan, which was most likely at Cilgerran, and also at Carew to the east of Pembroke. The Normans continued to augment their control by expanding their settlements and religious houses. However, the peace was shattered by an infamous event in 1109, that is described in detail in the *Brut.* Gerald was at his castle at Cenarth Bychan with Nest, when her cousin Owain ap Cadwgan of Powys attacked, gaining entry to the castle through a hole that had been dug under the gate:

> And then he came to the chamber in which Gerald and Nest, his wife, were sleeping. And they raised a shout around and about the chamber in which Gerald was, and kindled tapers and set fire to the buildings to burn them. And when he heard the shout, Gerald awoke, not knowing what to do. And then Nest said to him, 'Go not out to the door, for there thine enemies await thee, but follow me.' And that he did. And she led him to the privy which adjoined the chamber. And there, as is said, he escaped by way of the privy hole. And when

Nest knew that he had escaped, she cried out from within and said to the men who were outside, 'Why do you cry out in vain? He whom you seek is not here. He has escaped.' And after they had entered, they searched for him everywhere. And when they did not find him, they seized Nest and her two sons and her daughter and another son of his by a concubine, and they sacked and plundered the castle. And after burning the castle and collecting spoil, and have intercourse with her, he returned to his land.

As will be seen, this outrage to one of the king's servants would have serious repercussions.

Henry I had also become much more directly involved in south-west Wales after 1106, having consolidated his hold over both England and Normandy by defeating Robert Curthose at the battle of Tinchebray. As undisputed ruler of both England and Normandy, there was a noticeable acceleration of the conquest and settlement of Deheubarth. Firstly, there was a massive influx of Flemish settlers into the region, starting in or around 1107 (though the precise origins of this are somewhat obscure). There can be little doubt that the settlement was sanctioned by Henry.[2] With population growth in their own lands fuelling emigration, it appears that the king agreed to their settlement in south-west Wales. The main area of immigration was around Haverford where the Fleming, Tancred, built a castle. Other castles were built by the Flemish settlers. For example, Wiston Castle (see opposite) was built by Wizo the Fleming, to consolidate their position, with the result that the Welsh (and the Welsh language) were almost completely removed from the two western-most *cantrefi* of Dyfed. Over time, this area became known as 'Little England beyond Wales'.

Further east, the castle of Rhyd-y-gors disappeared from the records, when a new royal castle was built at Carmarthen sometime before 1109, which became the royal hub of Ystrad Tywi and eastern Dyfed. The castle provided both security and an administrative centre for the Marcher lordships that had established themselves nearby. There were other new men brought in by Henry. Bishop Roger of Salisbury, who was a royal favourite, a high-ranking official and a great builder of castles, was granted the lordship of Kidwelly. He set about constructing a new castle on the high ground above the tidal river. As well as building the castle, he established Kidwelly Priory as a daughter house of the abbey at his main residence at Sherbourne in Dorset. Where the Normans went, there were first the castles followed quickly by their religious institutions. The other Marcher lordships in the region, such as St Clears, Llanstephan, Ystlwyf and Laugharne, would all have been re-established by their lords within the security of Carmarthen castle.

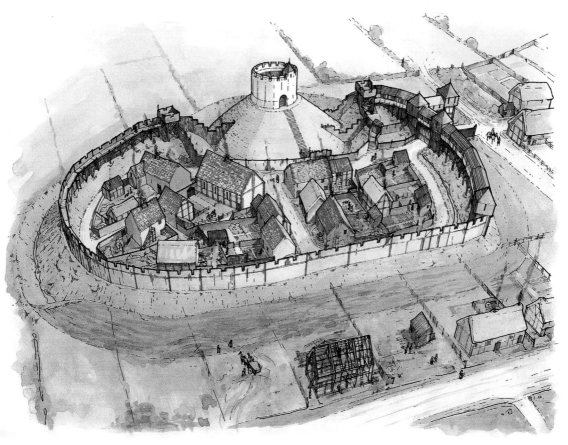

Reconstruction of Wiston Castle: built by Wizo the Fleming in the early years
of the Flemish settlement of western Dyfed (© Chris Jones-Jenkins)

Another Devonshire magnate, Robert fitz Martin, built a castle at Nevern in
Cemais. Furthermore, we know that by 1116 Richard fitz Pons had established
himself in eastern Ystrad Tywi in Cantref Bychan, with his main castle at Llandovery, which he had conquered from his lands in Brycheiniog. This was the time
of the great Norman settlement in the south-west. Such was Henry's mastery that
the Welsh dared not strike back against the invaders.[3]

AN ECCLESIASTICAL MARCHER LORD: THE NORMAN BISHOP OF ST DAVIDS

When Henry I came to the throne in 1100, the See of St Davids had a Welsh bishop,
Wilfred, who had been consecrated in 1085. St Davids was the prime ecclesiastical
centre of the Welsh Church, but Wilfred learned to accept the Norman occupation, working with the Norman Church, and even submitting to the primacy of
the Archbishop of Canterbury (though this was probably a matter of self-preservation). He would have been thankful to Archbishop Anselm for sending a letter
in c.1100 to the Norman invaders, imploring them to stop plundering the lands
of St Davids and ordering them to return any property they had stolen.[4] When
Wilfred died in 1115, the clergy of St Davids were expected to choose his successor

(or so they thought). They may have been somewhat surprised, therefore, when Henry summoned them to London and 'advised' them to choose the Queen's chamberlain, Bernard, as their next bishop. They had no choice but to comply. Very little is known about Bernard, but he appears to have been a capable and energetic man. Henry granted charters to Bernard, that effectively made the lands of St Davids – known as Pebidiog and Llawhaden – a Marcher lordship, with the bishop holding it directly from the king. Norman control of south-west Wales was now effectively complete. The Norman Marcher lordships of the south-west were firmly established. Furthermore, the most senior church in Wales had a Norman bishop who was a Marcher lord.

Powys and Gwynedd

Before turning back to Deheubarth, it is important to take a brief glance at events in the rest of Wales, where the involvement of the Normans developed very differently. In the north, during the 1090s Gruffudd ap Cynan, having escaped from his long captivity in Chester, led the resistance to the Norman incursions in alliance with Cadwgan ap Bleddyn of Powys. In 1093, Robert of Rhuddlan was killed in a Welsh raid, possibly led by Gruffudd, with the following year seeing the destruction of the Norman castles in Gwynedd, and also the defeat of a Norman force by Cadwgan. William (Rufus) II had twice led armies into north Wales (in 1095 and 1097), but on both occasions the Welsh avoided open conflict, allowing the natural terrain to thwart him, and forcing the king to return home empty-handed. Although an expedition in 1098, led by the earls of Chester and Shrewsbury, resulted in Gruffudd and Cadwgan taking refuge in Ireland, they soon returned to make an agreement with the Normans – a strong indication that the Norman barons had accepted, for the time being, that they did not have the resources to hold onto lands deep into central and northern Wales.

Henry I. His direct involvement in Wales created the environment for Marcher expansion and settlement (© National Portrait Gallery, London)

Henry I confirmed Gruffudd's rule over the lands to the west of the Conwy but retained the lands to the east, the Perfeddwlad, as part of the earldom of Chester. The agreement heralded a period of relative peace in Gwynedd, which enabled Gruffudd ap Cynan to establish there his own undisputed authority, which lasted until his death in 1137. In the early years, Gruffudd took a non-confrontational approach to Henry I, avoiding direct conflict where possible. When, in 1114, Gruffudd did raid into Tegeingl, the *cantref* closest to Chester, the king mounted a military campaign as a sharp reminder of who wielded the supreme power, with Gruffudd quickly making his peace, and swearing oaths of allegiance. Despite this, during a series of battles from 1118 to 1124 amongst the native rulers of the district, Gruffudd extended his control of the other three *cantrefi* of north-east Wales – a hold which he and his successors maintained and expanded for the next 150 years.

During the years of Gruffudd's imprisonment after the battle of Mynydd Carn in 1081, the sons of Bleddyn ap Cynfyn (the half-brother of Gruffudd ap Llywelyn who had been recognised, along with his brother, by Edward the Confessor as the rulers of Gwynedd and Powys), were able to retain hold of Powys, thus establishing a separate polity for the first time in two centuries.

After the imprisonment of Iorwerth ap Bleddyn at the start of the twelfth century, his brother, Cadwgan ap Bleddyn held Ceredigion, while Owain, Cadwgan's son, ruled Powys. Their tenure faltered when Owain committed his famous crime of passion in 1109, with this act against an agent of Henry I resulting in severe consequences for them. Cadwgan, understanding the gravity of the situation correctly, made a dash to Henry begging his forgiveness. Henry was inclined to help, but he wanted Owain apprehended, ordering the Welsh to bring him in to face justice. This made Owain a fugitive, which set him on the course of an outlaw. For a time, he went on a rampage, causing great difficulty for the settlers, raiding deep into Dyfed and killing a prominent Flemish leader who was travelling there.

Realising that Cadwgan could not control his son, Henry pensioned him off on the condition that he not set foot in his own lands. In 1110, he summoned Gilbert fitz Richard de Clare (d.1117), the powerful lord of Clare, to whom, according to the *Brut*, he said, '*thou wert always seeking of me a portion of the Britons. I will now give thee Cadwgan's territory. Go and take possession of it.*'

Gilbert de Clare was ruthless in his execution. He established himself at the castle of Cardigan, with his followers setting up castles throughout the entirety of Ceredigion.[5] Owain's return from exile in Ireland resulted in further skirmishes between him and the Marcher lords. When de Clare complained to the king, Henry mounted an invasion in 1114 to settle the matter, though his three-pronged assault never led to a battle. Suitably awed by the display of power, the Welsh rulers received the king's peace after paying a large tribute in cattle. Indeed, Owain was knighted and accompanied the king on campaign in Normandy.

Owain might have managed to get back on good terms with the king, but others still harboured resentment, and he was killed by archers friendly to Gerald of Windsor when he was on the king's business near Carmarthen in 1116. Throughout this period, Powys had been characterised by relentless internal feuding between the descendants of Bleddyn, but following the death of Owain ap Cadwgan, Maredudd ap Bleddyn emerged from the violence to rule Powys until his death in 1132.

Gruffudd ap Rhys

When Rhys ap Tewdwr was killed in 1093, his son, Gruffudd ap Rhys, who was too young to inherit, fled to Ireland for safety. By 1115, Gruffudd had returned to Dyfed. Here, in another example of the complex ties between Anglo-Norman and Welsh, Gruffudd sometimes stayed with Gerald of Windsor (his brother-in-law); even though he was a fugitive, he clearly felt safe there. Aware of the potential threat posed by Gruffudd, Henry I was determined to have him captured. When Gruffudd ap Rhys turned to the ruler of Gwynedd seeking protection, he found no friend in Gruffudd ap Cynan. Indeed, he was betrayed and barely escaped with his life as he fled. Gruffudd was determined to regain Deheubarth, which led him to stage an uprising in 1116. He first burned Narberth Castle, whose lord at that time is unknown, before attacking and burning the castle of Richard fitz Pons at Llandovery, then turning his attention to Carmarthen Castle. Once again, Gruffudd burned the town and took the spoils, but was not able to take the castle. His lack of siege equipment meant that he did not have the necessary firepower to completely dislodge the inhabitants. Nevertheless, these were seen as victories for the son of Rhys ap Tewdwr and *'Thereupon, hot-headed youths of the land gathered to him from all sides, thinking because of that incident that he had overcome everything.'*

Gruffudd's force successfully rampaged through Gower before setting their sights on Ceredigion. However, the rebellion fizzled out before the walls of Aberystwyth Castle, as the lack of discipline amongst the Welsh finally showed the weakness of the movement. They were routed by an organised Norman army, led by a steward of the de Clare family. Following the defeat, Gruffudd ap Rhys went into hiding in the woods of Ystrad Tywi. Despite this, he did manage to get back into the king's good graces a few years later. At the time of Henry's death, Gruffudd had been granted one single *commote* in Cantref Mawr as his own – a far cry from the extensive lands his father had held.

Old Aberystwyth Castle: the uprising of Gruffudd ap Rhys faltered before the walls of this castle in 1116
(© Crown copyright: Royal Commission on the Ancient and Historical Monuments of Wales)

Following the failed uprising of Gruffudd, the Marcher lordships would have been able to expand their settlements and administrative structures. The two royal castles at Pembroke and Carmarthen provided the anchor by which the lordships could survive. The fitz Martins, fitz Geralds and fitz Pons/ Cliffords all had castles in the more exposed north and east of the region. The Flemish were firmly established around Haverford, with several smaller castles such as Roch and Wiston built there. The illegitimate son of Henry I by Princess Nest was now lord of Narberth. The Marcher castles along the south coast, such as Llanstephan, Laugharne, St Clears and Kidwelly, which were all built on rivers that would have enabled them to be supplied by sea, were inhabited by families from the West Country, which established a lasting bond between the two regions. (See Map 8 overleaf for an illustration of the Marcher holdings at the end of the reign of Henry I.)

By the time of Henry I's death in 1135, the structure and form of the Marcher lordships in the south-west had been established. Although these lordships would be fought over until the matter was finally settled by Edward I at the end of the thirteenth century, the fact that the lordships existed at all was no longer a matter of debate.

In conclusion, it is necessary to reflect on why the involvement of the Normans in south-west Wales developed from the outset in such a different way to that witnessed in other regions – particularly in Powys and Gwynedd where Henry acknowledged the role of the native rulers (with the proviso that they accepted his pre-eminance and did not threaten regional stability):

- a key factor was that the vacuum in Welsh leadership in Deheubarth after the death of Rhys ap Tewdwr in 1093 created the opportunity for the Normans to fill the void. In this they were aided by the easy access to the region both from the sea and via the low-lying inland routes along the coast. The low coastal plains also provided fewer areas in which the Welsh could seek refuge and regroup to bide their time before striking back;

- a further significant contribution was the failed rebellion of the Montgomery family in 1102, which brought the king's direct involvement into Deheubarth, with Pembroke Castle taken into royal control. The addition of the royal castle at Carmarthen by 1109 meant that there were two powerful royal centres in the region, giving the Crown a stake that it did not have elsewhere in the Welsh Marches. The stability provided by the castles encouraged an influx of settlers to populate the new lordships that had developed around them, particularly the Flemings in the region around Haverford. In many places the local Welsh were completely displaced by the newcomers. Combined with the strong Norman hold in Ceredigion established by the de Clare family (Richard fitz Gilbert, d.1136, having inherited when his father died in 1117), it effectively meant that the entire south-west of Wales, apart from Cantref Mawr in Ystrad Tywi, was firmly in Norman hands;

- a testament to that is one key surviving document from the reign of Henry I, the Pipe Roll of 1130.[6] A Pipe Roll is a record of the accounts owed and paid, compiled by the Chancery of the Exchequer. This extremely instructive document is the only surviving Pipe Roll from Henry's reign. Pembroke was rendered as if it were an English county. We can see that it was lucrative, owing a rent of £60 a year, which was a significant amount. We can also see that many of the names in the list are Flemish;

- another intriguing aspect of this period is that the marriage of Nest ferch Rhys ap Tewdwr to the steward of Pembroke, Gerald of Windsor, resulted in individuals and families that were related to and descended from both Rhys ap Tewdwr and the Normans. Their descendants would dominate local politics for much of the twelfth century.

When Henry died in 1135, the hold on the region established by the Crown and the barons looked ominous for the Welsh. However, the events of the next two decades demonstrated that it was more precarious and subject to the personal abilities of the monarch and distractions elsewhere. Whereas Henry 1 combined the personal authority and military strength to stamp his will on others, his successor, King Stephen was a weaker monarch whose reign was beset by civil war. This was to change the dynamics of the balance of power in Deheubarth for the next 60 years.

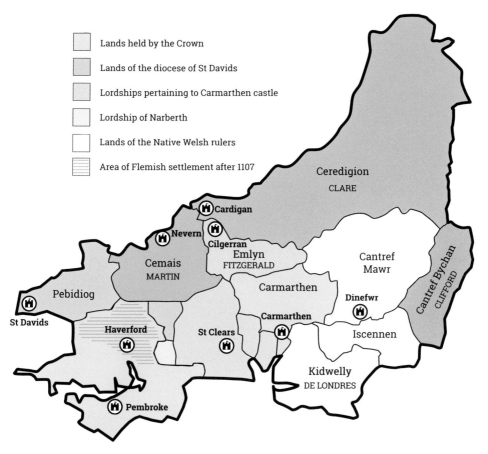

Map 8 The Marcher lordships of south-west Wales in 1135 (© Jason Appleby)

Fontevrault Abbey near Chinon in France: the final resting place of Henry II and Richard I

CHAPTER FOUR

The rise of the Lord Rhys and the dominance of Henry II

THE previous chapter described how, during the reign of Henry I, the balance of power in south-west Wales tilted decisively towards the Normans, with new lordships established and the Welsh only holding on to a few *commotes* in Ystrad Tywi and the uplands of Pembrokeshire. This chapter will describe how the dynamics swung back in favour of the Welsh during the civil wars in England, only for the pendulum to swing again when Henry II re-established the authority of the English Crown. When confronted, however, with a combination of myriad problems elsewhere in his sprawling empire, together with the rise of a commanding ruler in Deheubarth, the powerful monarch settled for a period of stability when he appointed Rhys ap Gruffudd his Justiciar of south Wales, with the latter becoming known as the Lord Rhys.

When Henry's son and heir had died in 1120 in the infamous 'wreck of the White Ship', Henry made his barons swear an oath to support the succession, upon his death, of his only legitimate child, his daughter Matilda. When Henry died in 1135, however, it was her cousin Stephen of Blois who acted decisively. Having gained, with the support of his brother, the bishop of Winchester, control of the royal treasury, Stephen was able to arrange, within a few days, a quick coronation ceremony at Westminster. In a period when there had been no ruling queens, as a nephew of Henry I and grandson of William I, Stephen had a legitimate claim to the throne, which gained him support amongst many leading barons. His early reign passed without any major disturbances from Matilda's supporters; however, it was the personality of the king that set the tone for his rule. Stephen was personable, but also indecisive. His first real test came in Wales.

THE WELSH FIGHT BACK

The Welsh historian J.E. Lloyd characterised the events in Wales of 1135, 'The National Revival ... Everywhere the foreign yoke was cast off, the power of the new settler was dauntlessly challenged, and a new spirit of daring and independence seemed to have seized the whole Welsh race'.[1] It is less well-accepted now that this was a co-ordinated national revival, but there is no debate that the uprisings were widespread and significant. The result left the Marcher lords in precarious positions across all regions of the March, or indeed completely pushed out in some. It would be easy to assume that the uprisings were a direct consequence of the death of Henry I; however, there were already signs of discontent before Henry's death. Indeed, there had been some minor uprisings whilst he was still alive.

When the uprising came, it was the response of King Stephen (or lack of one) that made the early Welsh victories so meaningful and long-lasting. The first recorded act was an attack by a Welsh war band in Gower on 1 January 1136. During these raids, 500 Anglo-Norman fighters and settlers were killed, a shocking setback and the first since the accession of Henry I. Gruffudd ap Rhys, who still held only one *commote* from the Crown, at once sensed that there might be the opportunity for a major uprising. Harbouring ambitions to regain the familial seat at the head of the house of Deheubarth, he set off for Gwynedd to seek an alliance with Gruffudd ap Cynan. Although the leader of Gwynedd was now too old to engage in military campaigning himself, he had two sons, Owain and Cadwaladr, who were in their prime and were readily convinced to act.

Following the Welsh victory in Gower, the Normans went on the offensive to re-establish local supremacy. Maurice de Londres, who had his main seat at Ogmore Castle in Glamorgan, began to mount a counterstrike against the Welsh in the region around Kidwelly (at around this time, and certainly by 1139, control of Kidwelly had passed from Bishop Roger to Maurice). With Gruffudd absent in north Wales, his wife, Gwenllian, the daughter of Gruffudd ap Cynan, decided to move against de Londres. She took to the field with two of her sons. It was a bold action, but she was soundly defeated, resulting in her death and the loss of her sons. Although the attack may have been futile, the bravery and the sentiment of her action further fuelled the flames of rebellion.

Memorial to Gwenllian: her bold counter-attack against the Normans helped fuel the Welsh uprising

Revenge Stone: erected at or near where Richard de Clare was killed in an ambush in 1136 in revenge for Norman atrocities (© Paul Davis)

The uprising quickly gained further momentum in April 1136. The powerful lord of Clare and Ceredigion, Richard fitz Gilbert de Clare, was returning to Cardigan Castle from the court of King Stephen by way of Abergavenny. Although he had apparently received warnings that the route was dangerous, he set off with only a small party (Gerald of Wales even stated that Richard had minstrels playing as they progressed). A young Welsh ruler and his war band ambushed him, with the result that Richard and his entire retinue were slain. When news of the death of the lord of Ceredigion reached Gwynedd, the fighting men swept south, led by Owain and Cadwaladr, sons of Gruffudd ap Cynan, sacking Aberystwyth Castle and several others. It was becoming clear that the Norman hold in the region was precarious.

In early autumn of that year, Owain and Cadwaladr, now joined by Gruffudd ap Rhys and several Welsh princes from Brycheiniog and Rhwng Gwy a Hafren, staged another invasion of Ceredigion. The *Brut* records that the Welsh marched not only with large numbers of foot soldiers, but also armoured knights: the Welsh had learned how to fight the Anglo-Normans on their own terms. The target was Cardigan Castle, with the plan to sack it and remove the Normans from Ceredigion completely. The Marcher defence was organised from inhabitants drawn from the whole of south-west Wales. The lord of Cemais, the sons of Gerald of Windsor, the constable of Cardigan Castle together with a host of Normans and Flemish combatants were assembled to fight off the Welsh attack. They met a few miles north of Cardigan at the battle of Crug Mawr which resulted in a decisive Welsh victory. The *Brut* described the carnage,

*The Flemings and Normans took to flight ... and after some of them had been
slain and others burnt, and the horses of others ham-strung and others carried
off into captivity, and the greater part had been drowned like madmen in the
river, and after losing about three thousand of their men, sadly despondent they
returned to their land.*

Despite this crushing defeat, the Welsh attackers were only able to burn the town,
while Cardigan Castle survived, to remain a thorn in the side of the Welsh for
many years. As a result of the battle, the Anglo-Normans and Flemish of the
south-west, lost the ability to dictate the proceedings, fighting from then on to
maintain what they had gained, with the prospect of further conquest now gone.
It is of note that it was the local Anglo-Norman and Flemish settlers who rose
to meet the Welsh threat, not a royal army. These were frontiersmen who fought
together when the need arose; however, against an organised Welsh army, they
were no match in a pitched battle.

Royal response

Following such a devastating defeat, the settlers would have been expecting or
hoping for royal intervention to tilt the balance back in their favour. Despite this,
King Stephen made only half-hearted attempts to intervene. Firstly, he sent a rescue
party to Cardigan Castle to bring the widow of Richard fitz Gilbert de Clare back
to England. In a bold strike across what was now Welsh-controlled territory, Miles
of Gloucester and a small group of knights managed to reach the castle before
returning her safely to England. Secondly, King Stephen organised for Baldwin,
a younger brother of the murdered Richard, to lead a force into Ceredigion with
the goal of bringing it back under Norman (and de Clare) control. Upon reaching
Brecon, however, it became clear that the Welsh were going to present a much
more formidable opponent than Baldwin was prepared to take on. Thus, rather
than conquering Ceredigion, he stayed in the environs of Brecon until his money
ran out, returning to England without striking a blow. Another expedition by
Robert fitz Harold of Ewyas had more success, as he managed to get through to
Carmarthen, where he shored up the defences of several Marcher lordships before
he too returned to the safety of England.[2] Stephen then made no further attempts
to relieve the Anglo-Norman settlers. It would have been clear to the Marcher
lords by now that their fate lay in their own hands, which probably explains to some
extent why most of the Marcher barons sided with Matilda when civil war came.

In 1137, Gruffudd ap Rhys, shortly before his death, turned his attention to
Dyfed, overrunning the Flemish territory of Rhos. When he died soon after, he

left four sons to carry on the fight. Unusually for a Welsh ruling family at that time, they worked together to achieve their goal of re-establishing the house of Deheubarth. This cooperation was strongly influenced by two factors: firstly, their father had not left them with a large, landed inheritance over which to fight; and secondly, there was no need to fight amongst themselves as they had plenty of settler targets to plunder.

In the same year, the princes of Gwynedd swept through Ceredigion again, burning several castles as they made their way to Carmarthen, where they destroyed the castle before returning north. In 1138, the two eldest sons of Gruffudd, Anarawd and Cadell, joined the forces of Owain Gwynedd (now the ruler in the north after the death of his father, Gruffudd ap Cynan) and his brother, Cadwaladr, to try once again to take Cardigan Castle – this with a hired Viking/ Danish fleet to help them besiege it. However, they were unsuccessful, and the main result was that the hired troops sacked St Dogmael's Abbey for its treasures before departing. One can only speculate as to whether King Stephen might eventually have sought to regain Anglo-Norman control. However, in 1139 Matilda landed with an army in England to contest her claim to the Crown, which forced Stephen to devote all his attention to political matters in England.

The Earl of Pembroke

Although King Stephen had assumed the throne with no resistance, things began to change soon into his reign, with the king having to put down several small rebellions amongst his barons in the summer of 1137. In 1138 he decided that one method to secure baronial support was to double the number of earldoms that had existed in the time of Henry I, expecting the loyalty of the newly-created earls. As part of this, he made Gilbert fitz Gilbert de Clare (d.c.1149, the brother of the murdered lord of Ceredigion) earl of Pembroke, no doubt in the hope that de Clare would help stabilise a situation that was becoming precariously unstable in south-west

King Stephen: his lack of royal response to the Welsh uprising set back Marcher ambitions and gave the Welsh the upper hand
(© National Portrait Gallery, London)

Wales (see Family Tree 3 on p. 69). In doing this, Stephen gave away one of the Crown's key assets in Wales and paved the way for the development of an influential earldom in the hands of a powerful family – Gilbert now held the new earldom of Pembroke, plus the lordship of Striguil (Chepstow) that he had inherited from his childless uncle, Walter; while the earldom of Hertford descended to the sons of Richard who had been killed in the ambush in 1136. Gilbert didn't go to Pembroke immediately, perhaps because he considered the Welsh to be too dangerous to permit safe passage. When the Empress Matilda landed with a force in England to claim the throne in 1139, the new earl of Pembroke, like all the magnates in England and Normandy, became fully committed to the ensuing civil war.

Although they had suffered a catastrophic defeat at the battle of Crug Mawr, the Marcher lords and settlers were still able to hold onto much of their territory. The Welsh did not press their advantage; rather, they returned to their homes loaded with plunder. There was, though, at least one lordship that was taken by the Welsh during the early uprisings – Cantref Bychan fell in 1141. Its proximity to the east, with no access to the sea, made it untenable in the face of the scale of the rebellion.

By 1145, Gilbert fitz Gilbert, now supporting the Empress Matilda, had decided that it was time to pay his first visit to west Wales. It is unclear whether he travelled all the way to Pembroke, but he is on record as having rebuilt the defences of the ruined Carmarthen Castle as well as building a new castle at Pencader on the border of Ceredigion. Thus, we get a glimpse of what an organised Anglo-Norman army was able to achieve with the right resources – something that King Stephen never attempted. Gilbert, though, was soon back in England, where he switched back to the side of the king, as his strong presence and military backing were missed. His departure immediately put the Marcher lords of the south-west on the defensive again.

CONTINUING FEUDS BETWEEN WELSH RULERS

Although the Welsh were in the ascendancy during this period, bitter rivalries were still to be witnessed between the competing kingdoms. The head of the house of Deheubarth, Anarawd, had been killed by the warband of Cadwaladr of Gwynedd in 1143. Given that Anarawd was an ally of Cadwaladr's brother, Owain Gwynedd, and betrothed to Owain's daughter, this caused a split in that family, with Owain dispossessing Cadwaladr of his portion of Ceredigion to give to his own son, Hywel. The next eldest son of Gruffudd ap Rhys, Cadell, assumed the leadership of Deheubarth. After de Clare returned to England, Cadell took action to undo his achievements. In 1146, he allied with Hywel ab Owain to sack

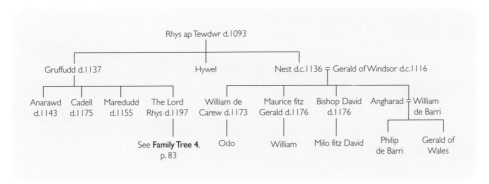

Family Tree 2 Select descendants of Rhys ap Tewdwr

and hold the newly-repaired Carmarthen Castle, before they proceeded to capture Llanstephan Castle, which lies directly south of Carmarthen, with a view to holding this too. They placed the safekeeping of that castle into the hands of Cadell's younger brother, Maredudd.

As a response to the sacking of Llanstephan, we find the Marcher families on a war footing once again. A group of local Anglo-Norman and Flemish fighters, led by the sons of Gerald of Windsor, came to retake the castle. They were repulsed by Maredudd in a battle (which the *Brut* described in detail, see p. 209).

There was a further interesting development in 1147, where the *Brut* notes that the sons of Gruffudd worked together, not just with Hywel ab Owain, but also with William fitz Gerald, to settle a dispute with the Fleming, Wizo of Wiston Castle. Together they sacked the castle, with the Welsh attackers able to carry off many spoils. Life in the March was clearly complicated: the rivals could fight to the death at Llanstephan in 1146, and then work together to settle a dispute in 1147. It must be remembered, however, that they were cousins, both sides sharing Rhys ap Tewdwr as their grandfather. As a further sign of the brothers' growing strength and confidence, in 1150, Cadell ap Gruffudd '*repaired the castle of Carmarthen, for the splendour and strength of the kingdom; and ravaged Cydweli* [Kidwelly]'.

They were in full control of the area in and around Carmarthen in 1150, with the result that Marcher lords continued to suffer further attacks.

CEREDIGION REGAINED BY DEHEUBARTH

The three remaining brothers now turned their attention to reclaiming Ceredigion for Deheubarth. In 1150, they overran the lands of Hywel ab Owain Gwynedd (their ally of just three years earlier) up to the Aeron river, completing the conquest of Ceredigion the following year. Cadell was not to enjoy the victory for long, though. In 1151, when he was spotted in the woods by the men of Tenby, he was beaten

Tenby: aerial view of the castle and town (© Gareth Davies Photography, Tenby)

brutally and left for dead. Although he recovered, he had lost his will to fight, taking no further part in the struggle to re-establish the authority of Deheubarth. The two remaining brothers, Maredudd and Rhys, although young, were able to maintain their hold on Ceredigion, despite the best efforts of Owain Gwynedd. They also gained some revenge on the men of Tenby by sacking the town in 1153. As another example of the complicated relationship between Marcher lords and the Welsh, Tenby was handed over to their cousin, William fitz Gerald, after they had taken it. By 1154 Maredudd and Rhys were in a very strong position in the south-west. They had solidified their hold over Ceredigion, refortified Carmarthen Castle and built a new castle at Dinefwr, thus fortifying the principal seat of the family's power.

In this way, the Welsh of the south-west held the upper hand while the Anglo-Normans were hanging on where they could. The area around Pembroke Castle and Haverford remained firmly in Marcher control, as it seems did Kidwelly. It is difficult to tell how much control the fitz Martin lord had in Cemais, because he was certainly in England mainly during the civil war, although there is no specific reference to Cemais falling. There are also no records that specify whether the other Marcher lordships near Carmarthen were held by their Marcher lords or not; however, if they were it seems likely that the hold would have been tenuous.

The Welsh resurgence after the death of Henry I found expression across all of Wales. In Gwynedd, although Gruffudd ap Cynan, who had built up a prosperous kingdom during his long years, was becoming increasingly infirm, his sons were more than ready to act in his stead in his final years. When he died in 1137, the rule of Gwynedd passed to Owain (unusually, he became known as Owain Gwynedd to distinguish him from another Owain, who was the son of Gruffudd ap Maredudd of Powys, who became known as Owain Cyfeiliog). Owain was supported by his brother, Cadwaladr, who held the lands in northern Ceredigion. This chapter has already described the activities of the brothers in Ceredigion and further south; in the north-east, Owain succeeded in taking Rhuddlan Castle, making himself the master of Tegeingl and pushing his boundaries almost within sight of Chester.

In Powys, Maredudd ap Bleddyn had been able to secure his rule after he emerged from the bloody family feuds in Powys during the first part of the twelfth century. After his death in 1132, he was succeeded by his son Madog, who ruled until 1160. Although Madog lost territory to Gwynedd in the north-east, he was able to exploit the divisions in England to push eastwards, where he occupied Oswestry and built or rebuilt the castle.

In the central regions of Rhwng Gwy a Hafren, the native rulers had also expelled the Normans in the 1130s. Although Hugh Mortimer (d.1181–85), loyal to King Stephen, retook Maelienydd in 1144, with the de Braose family taking Elfael at the same time, both were lost within a decade.

By the first half of the 1150s, the political landscape across Wales looked very different to that during the domination of the Crown and Marcher lords that had been secured during the reign of Henry I. Although it would be an exaggeration to refer to the uprising as a 'national revival', the Welsh resurgence following the death of Henry I was momentous. While the involvement and support of Henry I, particularly in the south-west, had demonstrated the importance to the Marcher lords of the Crown's support, the reign of Stephen demonstrated the same point from the opposite perspective. Following the battle of Crug Mawr in 1136, there was no effective royal response, which left the Marcher lords to fend for themselves. On their own they lacked the resources to mount an effective fight-back, with the result that the Anglo-Normans and Flemish lost the upper hand and were left scrabbling to defend what territories they had established in the first third of the twelfth century.

The period had also seen the growing complexity of interrelationships within Wales and the March. As shown earlier, the descendants of Gerald of Windsor and Nest ferch Rhys ap Tewdwr could cooperate with their cousins, the sons of Gruffudd ap Rhys, when they had a common cause; yet at other times, they were locked in deadly battles of conquest and re-conquest. This affords an interesting insight into a kind of *mode de vie* for life in the March.

SIGNS OF CHANGE

Although the civil war, which had raged in England throughout the 1140s, reached a stalemate by 1150, significant changes were beginning to happen. In 1148–49, Gilbert de Clare died, leaving his son Richard fitz Gilbert de Clare (d.1176) as the earl of Pembroke and lord of Striguil. Unlike his father, Richard would become a key player in the south-west Marcher lordships. With the Empress Matilda back in Normandy, her son, Henry, started to press his rights to the throne. The succession became clearer when the son of King Stephen, Eustace, died in 1153, and the king was pressed to make peace with Henry. They agreed to the Treaty of Winchester, which made Henry the king's adopted son and heir. It didn't take long for the succession to take place, for in 1154 Stephen died, to be replaced by a far more forceful monarch. A year later, in 1155, Maredudd ap Gruffudd died at the young age of 25, with the *Brut* recording,

> ***Maredudd ap Gruffudd ap Rhys, king of Ceredigion and Ystrad Tywi and Dyfed, died in the twenty-fifth year of his age, a man who was of great mercy towards the poor and of eminent prowess against his enemies and strong in righteousness.***

This left his younger brother, Rhys, as the last remaining son of Gruffudd ap Rhys ap Tewdwr, to rule Deheubarth. The sons of Gruffudd had shown that they were capable warriors and a powerful force, having re-established the house of Deheubarth in Ystrad Tywi, and removed the princes of Gwynedd from Ceredigion, which brought back to Deheubarth some of its historical boundary. Most of the lands of Dyfed, dominated by the castle at Pembroke, however, remained in the hands of the Marcher lords. Over the next 40 years, Rhys ap Gruffudd matured into a man able to dominate the affairs of south Wales.

MARCHER LORD AND ROYAL DOMINATION RESTORED BY HENRY II

When Henry II came to the throne, the Welsh princes were in a dominant position, with the Marcher lords holding on in those regions where they could, with Llanstephan, Carmarthen and most of Ceredigion in the hands of the sons of Gruffudd ap Rhys. Henry II, though, was a powerful ruler with a dominant and

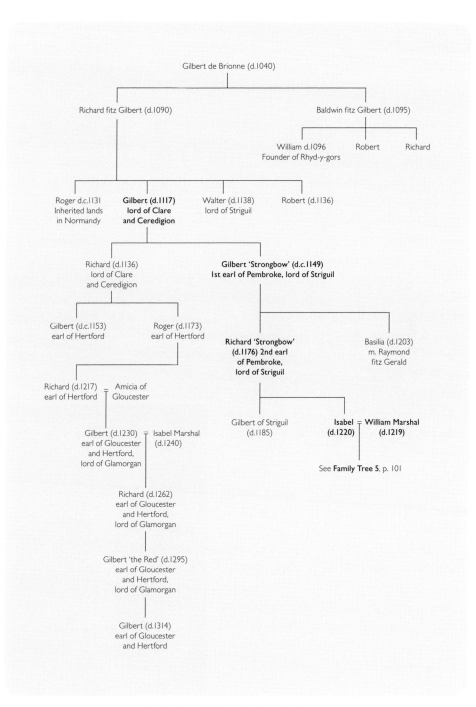

Family Tree 3 Select de Clare family tree

forceful personality. Although young, he was determined to reassert the rights of the Crown after the chaos of Stephen's reign, and to stamp his own authority across all his lands, bringing to heel barons and Welsh rulers alike. Viewing the preceding years as an aberration, he moved to set the clock back to the reign of his grandfather.

In Wales, Henry's reign can be seen in two contrasting parts – the period from 1154 to 1165 was dominated by military interventions, which were designed to show that the days of unchecked baronial and Welsh progress were at an end, and to assert his own overlordship of Anglo-Norman barons and Welsh rulers alike. During the second part of his reign from the 1170s, which saw growing disputes across his vast empire, including rebellions by his sons, he maintained stability through diplomacy, which involved recognition of the Welsh rulers and protecting them from further incursions from the Marcher lords.

Across England, Henry II moved quickly to restore order and the rule of law, which was welcomed by many barons. The few, such as Hugh Mortimer (d.1181–85) of Wigmore, who misjudged the intent and ability of the young king, were taught a swift lesson. Hugh Mortimer, though, despite submitting only after the king had besieged three of his castles (and taking one), escaped punishment, probably because Henry recognised that he couldn't afford to alienate an experienced warrior in the central Marches.

As Henry began to turn his attention towards Wales and the Marcher lordships, the political dynamic, as noted earlier, changed in Deheubarth when Maredudd died in 1155, leaving Rhys ap Gruffudd as sole ruler at the age of around 23 years old. With Rhys so young, Owain Gwynedd promptly challenged his authority by preparing for an invasion of Ceredigion, with the hope of recovering it for himself. However, Rhys acted swiftly by building a castle at a strategic crossing on the River Dyfi on the border between Ceredigion and Gwynedd, which forced Owain to abandon his plans.

When Henry II decided to move against the Welsh in order to restore his authority, he chose to move against Gwynedd first.

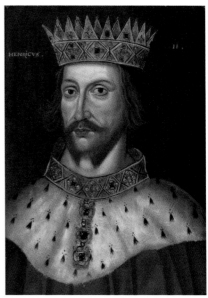

King Henry II: established royal authority in Wales following the reign of King Stephen (© National Portrait Gallery, London)

As described earlier, Owain Gwynedd had extended his lands across all north-east Wales to almost within sight of Chester, and also taken territory in the region from Powys. Following the murder of Anarawd ap Gruffudd by Cadwaladr, Owain had expelled his brother from his land in Ceredigion and Gwynedd. Henry used the restoration of the rights of Cadwaladr as pretence to launch a military campaign in 1157, with the goal of bringing the region back into balance. The plan was to move along the north coast with a great host to meet a fleet of Anglo-Norman and Flemish fighters from the south-west, that were sailing to join the king. The campaign almost ended in an early disaster when Henry was nearly killed in an ambush by Welsh skirmishers. He regrouped and the campaign proceeded as planned, though Owain, recognising that the assembled force was too great to withstand, withdrew towards his mountain stronghold. Henry looked to press his advantage but was unable to penetrate the mountains.

The fleet that had been sailing to support Henry had made a stop at Anglesey looking for plunder. They sacked several churches and villages before heading back to their ships. However, they were overwhelmed by the locals, suffering many casualties, with the dead including the bastard son of Henry I, Henry fitz Henry, the lord of Narberth. Despite this setback, the superior strength of Henry's force brought a submission from Owain, who handed over hostages and surrendered Tegeingl.

While Henry was campaigning in north Wales, Rhys ap Gruffudd was in open rebellion in the south-west. Following Owain's submission, Henry turned his attention to Rhys's uprising; however, as Henry was organising an army in 1158, Rhys became convinced that submission was a wiser option than battle. He was escorted to the king where he submitted and received peace terms. Henry promised Cantref Mawr and one other *cantref* to Rhys, which would have given him a solid group of lands around his chief castle at Dinefwr. Although this was a larger holding than his father had at the end of the reign of Henry I, it also meant that he was forced to make significant sacrifices in territory that he and his brothers had gained as he had to cede Ceredigion, which reverted to the de Clares. Furthermore, Cantref Bychan was granted to Walter fitz Richard (later known as Walter Clifford), the heir to Richard fitz Pons, and Carmarthen Castle was recovered for the Crown. Rhys soon found that Henry was less than generous with his grants of land. Apart from Cantref Mawr, his other *cantrefi* were a group of smaller *commotes* within territories claimed by Marcher lords which were thus of little value. When the men of Cantref Bychan plundered Rhys's lands later the same year, he took to arms again. This time Henry did come south with an army. The force on display was enough to convince Rhys to submit, though we don't know what terms Henry would have exacted from Rhys, as the king departed for the Continent to deal with the complex political situation in France following the death of his younger brother, Geoffrey. He did not return for four years, which left the March exposed once again.

With the king on the Continent, Rhys felt secure enough in 1159 to launch another full-scale uprising. The *Brut* records that he had '*conquered the castles which the French had set up all over Dyfed and he burned them all*'. He then besieged Carmarthen which brought a response from the officials of the Crown, with five earls being sent to subdue the rebellion. They were joined by several princes of Gwynedd, who were now aiding the king. Wisely, Rhys withdrew from the siege, taking to the safety of the forests and highlands of Cantref Mawr, in the region of his castle at Dinefwr. The relieving army dared not pursue him, agreeing a truce

Dinefwr Castle: the chief seat of the Lord Rhys before 1172 (© Philip Hume)

which brought peace for a time. Rhys, though, was back at war in 1162, when he moved against the castle of Llandovery in Cantref Bychan, which the Pipe Rolls show was receiving funds to shore up its defences. This time he captured the castle, thus bringing it into Welsh hands, (where it remained for over a century), as a consequence of which it disappeared from royal records.[3]

When Henry II returned to England in 1163, he embarked on a military expedition to south-west Wales, penetrating deep into Rhys's territory and forcing him to submit. Rhys then accompanied the king back to Woodstock in England where he, Owain Gwynedd, Malcolm of Scotland and several lesser Welsh princes all gave homage to him. The oath that Henry received diminished the relationship between the king and the Welsh rulers from that of client ruler to the more demeaning one of dependent vassalage.

HENRY II DEFEATED BY THE TERRAIN

Whilst Rhys was in the king's custody, his nephew was murdered. The culprit was most likely working on the instructions of the de Clares. When Rhys returned to Deheubarth, he took his revenge by attacking the de Clare lands in Ceredigion, destroying all the castles apart from Cardigan itself. In the north, Owain Gwynedd, unwilling to accept the new subordinate client status that Henry had extracted from the rulers, sent his son to raid deep into Tegeingl.

Angered, Henry was determined now to deal with the Welsh problem decisively. In 1165, he gathered an army from across the Angevin empire, the *Brut* stating that he came as far as Oswestry, *'purposing to carry into bondage and to destroy all the Britons'*. Owain and Rhys now joined forces with several other Welsh rulers, to form a combined army to meet the threat. They made their encampment at Corwen in the Dee valley. Henry unwisely chose to lead his army by the direct route over the Berwyn range, which turned into a disaster. Despite it being August, the chronicle described a hurricane of wind and rain as they made the crossing. With the harsh conditions and slow going they were soon low on provisions and had to turn back. A hired fleet from Ireland arrived but were too few to allow Henry to continue the campaign. It was clear Henry had lost without even fighting a battle. He vented his fury on 22 Welsh hostages, having them blinded, including a son of Rhys and two of Owain. Following the defeat, Henry spent the next four years on the Continent, dealing with matters in that part of his massive empire.

With the king back across the Channel, the two Welsh rulers each regained lost territory. In the north, Owain again brought Tegeingl back under his control, pushing his kingdom close to the bounds of Chester once more; while Rhys returned to the south-west where he besieged and finally sacked the castle of Cardigan, removing the de Clares from there once and for all. He then moved south-east to sack Cilgerran Castle in Emlyn. In 1165–66, the Anglo-Normans and Flemish made two attempts to recapture Cilgerran, but both failed. The house of Deheubarth once again had the upper hand in the south-west, with the Anglo-Normans and Flemish unable to resist.

Cilgerran Castle: its northern location made it vulnerable to attack

ANGLO-NORMAN CONQUEST OF IRELAND

In 1166, Diarmait Mac Murchada, the king of Leinster, was expelled from Ireland by a force led by the high king of Ireland. Diarmait had connections with the Normans, including a personal contact with Henry II, having supplied the fleet for the failed campaign of 1165. He travelled all the way to Aquitaine in southern France to track Henry down, where he pleaded for assistance in the re-conquest of Leinster. Henry was lukewarm to the idea but did grant Diarmait permission to recruit help from within the Angevin empire. When he returned to south Wales, he found several willing candidates that would assist him in his re-conquest of Leinster. The highest-ranking supporter was the lord of Striguil and former earl of Pembroke, Richard fitz Gilbert de Clare (d.1176), later referred to as 'Strongbow'. Richard had lost the title of earl of Pembroke when Henry II came to the throne. As part of his strategy to turn the clock back, Henry had reduced the number of earls and taken away many of the titles newly granted by Stephen. Richard's prospects were therefore limited in England and Wales. He offered tacit support in return for the hand of Diarmait's daughter and the succession to the lordship of Leinster. Diarmait also found several willing Anglo-Normans amongst the descendants of Gerald of Windsor and Nest who, now dispossessed of their lands in Cilgerran and Emlyn, were also frustrated by their lack of opportunity in Wales. Robert fitz Stephen (d.b.1192), another son of Nest by the former castellan of Cardigan Castle, who was being held in Rhys's prison after his capture at Cardigan, was released by Rhys on condition he join the invasion to Ireland.

The conquest took place in three waves, with the first expedition securing Leinster. In August 1170, when Strongbow himself joined the third invasion, they soon controlled Leinster, Wexford, Dublin and Waterford, a stunning achievement given their resources and fighting numbers. In May 1171, when Diarmait Mac Murchada died, Richard fitz Gilbert de Clare claimed the kingship in the right of his wife, though he wisely sought the approval of the king. Concerned at the growing power of Richard, Henry travelled to Ireland directly to assert the authority of the Crown. Henry's terms to Richard were that he would have to return his lands in France, England and Wales in order to consolidate their gains. Faced with this choice, Richard relinquished his claim to Dublin and all his other Irish conquests except for Leinster, which he now held from Henry. In the time that Henry was in Ireland he received the homage of the native Irish and the Norman lords, dividing the Irish kingdoms between them.[4]

Throughout the 1160s, Henry had become entangled in the bitter dispute with Thomas Becket, Archbishop of Canterbury, which eventually embroiled him in one of the biggest scandals of the Middle Ages, when several of his household knights murdered Becket in his own cathedral in December 1170. His expedition to Ireland not only allowed him to assert his authority and limit the scope for independent action by his barons, but also provided him with an opportunity to let things cool down while he worked on a rapprochement with the papacy. The latter was greatly aided when Henry brought the Irish Church into the Roman fold. When Henry received word that the Pope was ready to discuss his forgiveness for the murder of Becket, he departed for England, leaving the south and east of Ireland under the sovereignty of the English king. The political landscape in Wales was also dramatically altered, as many of the barons now had Irish estates added to their Marcher lordships – henceforth, Ireland would remain a major focus and source of revenue for many of them.

The Lord Rhys

It is not possible for us to discern whether Henry II intended to use his overwhelming force in 1165 to coerce once and forever the Welsh rulers into submission to his authority, or to move to outright conquest. What is clear is that having been thwarted in that campaign by the terrain and the weather, and in the subsequent years confronted with the mounting problems across his vast swathe of lands, Henry pursued a very different policy in Wales and the Marches when he returned from his four-year absence on the Continent. The political and military challenges that he faced abroad were compounded by the fallout from the death of Becket and, in subsequent years, were deepened by the rebellions of his fractious

Laugharne Castle: Henry II made Rhys ap Gruffudd Justiciar of south Wales
at a meeting here in 1172, thus becoming the Lord Rhys (© Philip Hume)

sons. Not only did Henry not have the time and resources for further military interventions in Wales, but he needed stability and allies, turning to unexpected quarters to find them. Rather than punishing the Welsh rulers for regaining the territory that they had previously ceded to him, they had now become potential allies to secure a stable region.

On his way to Ireland in 1171, Henry had met Rhys ap Gruffudd, with Rhys offering hostages and many horses and cattle to gain the king's peace, which Henry accepted. On Henry's return journey from Ireland, he met Rhys, first at Pembroke and then at Laugharne. Even though Rhys still controlled all the lands he had conquered since Henry's failed campaign of 1165 (including Ceredigion, Cantref Bychan, Ystlwyf, Cilgerran and Emlyn), in a dramatic turn of events Henry appointed Rhys as the Justiciar of south Wales.

As another sign of royal favour, Henry only accepted a portion of the tribute that Rhys had previously offered and released the hostages. Furthermore, he confirmed Rhys in his lands, including the conquests, to be held from the king directly, with the Marcher lords who had lost land being compensated with territories elsewhere. Rhys was now responsible for keeping the peace in the south, with the other local Welsh rulers subordinate to him. Henry's policy towards Wales had changed from one of confrontation to one of cooperation. For the rest of his reign,

Rhys and the other Welsh rulers were protected from further incursions by the Marcher lords. Henry expected the Marcher lords to keep the peace, and the Lord Rhys (as he was now referred to) to keep the Welsh rulers in check.

For a time, this worked. When Henry II faced the first challenge to his authority by his own sons, a full-scale rebellion in 1173, the Lord Rhys sent a contingent of Welsh troops, led by one of his own sons, to support the king to quell the rebellion. The Lord Rhys set about building a new castle at Cardigan on the ruins of the old Norman castle, which became his main seat and where he held the first Eisteddfod in 1176 shortly after the death of Cadell (his elder brother, who had been left for dead at Tenby all those years ago).

As ruler of Deheubarth and the king's Justiciar of south Wales, the Lord Rhys became the pre-eminent figure across all of Wales. In part this was due to the instability in other regions when the deaths of Madog ap Maredudd (d.1160) and Owain Gwynedd (d.1170) eventually ended their long reigns. The death of Madog resulted in the division of Powys into two separate regions, whilst the death of Owain resulted in over two decades of warfare between his sons and grandsons. The Lord Rhys was at the head of a group of southern and central Welsh rulers who met Henry at Gloucester in 1175, all swearing their fealty to the king. Two years later in 1177 at the Council of Oxford, although attended by many Welsh rulers, only the Lord Rhys, and Dafydd ab Owain Gruffudd, did homage to King Henry, reflecting the dominant positions of Deheubarth and Gwynedd. As a sign of his stature within Wales, Rhys founded Talley Abbey to the north of Dinefwr in around 1185.

The Lord Rhys and Henry II kept this mutually supportive agreement in place for many years. Rhys was also connected to a vast array of southern and central Welsh rulers through marriage, which gave him a direct connection to many of the lesser rulers in the region. Although he was able to maintain the peace in the south-west, he was powerless to stop the hostilities that broke out elsewhere. Years of infighting and treachery meant that outbreaks of violence could occur at any time. The most infamous example of this was the 'Massacre of Abergavenny', during which a group of noble Welshmen was lured to Abergavenny Castle by William de Braose and murdered on Christmas

Talley Abbey, founded by the Lord Rhys in around 1185

Day 1175 without warning. The killers then mounted horses before word could spread, hunting down the leader's seven-year-old son, to kill him in his mother's arms. The resentment and hatred this engendered led to years of retribution and violence in the region.

Another factor was the death of the second earl of Gloucester, and lord of Glamorgan, in 1183. His heir was a young daughter, Isabella, who had been betrothed in 1176 to Henry II's youngest son, the future King John (at the time of the betrothal, the king had disinherited Isabella's sisters to make her the sole heir). Although they weren't officially married until 1189, royal officials were put in place to manage the lordship of Glamorgan. This royal intrusion caused turmoil and resentment, which resulted in major Welsh uprisings in 1184–85.

Towards the end of Henry's reign, as well as the Lord Rhys's long life, the sons of Rhys were becoming increasingly impatient for their own power, and beginning to spread their wings militarily. Despite all of this, Henry and Rhys maintained a friendly relationship, often meeting when Henry was in England. With both Gwynedd and Powys experiencing succession struggles, the Lord Rhys remained the most senior Welsh ruler. Although there had been intermittent uprisings of varying significance, the peace that they agreed in 1172 had endured for the most part.

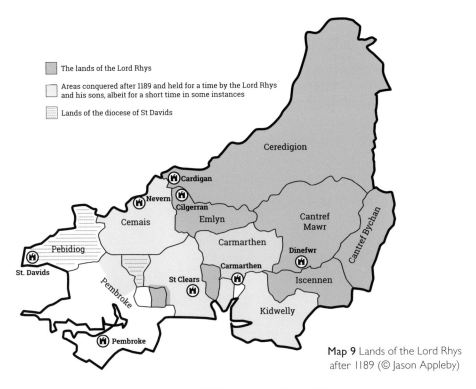

The lands of the Lord Rhys

Areas conquered after 1189 and held for a time by the Lord Rhys and his sons, albeit for a short time in some instances

Lands of the diocese of St Davids

Ceredigion

Cardigan

Nevern

Cilgerran

Emlyn

Cemais

Carmarthen

Cantref Mawr

Cantref Bychan

Pebidiog

Carmarthen

Dinefwr

St. Davids

Pembroke

St Clears

Iscennen

Kidwelly

Pembroke

Map 9 Lands of the Lord Rhys after 1189 (© Jason Appleby)

CONCLUSIONS

Although much of the period that has been the subject of this chapter witnessed volatile fluctuations, with the balance of power moving one way then the other, an equilibrium emerged in the last two decades of the reign of Henry II. During the reign of King Stephen – one that was beset by civil war in England – the native rulers had been able to regain much of their lands. The accession of a young, powerful monarch in 1154 altered the balance again, with Henry II determined to reassert royal authority across his lands. Initially, his approach was like that of his grandfather, Henry I – to assert his authority over Welsh rulers and Marcher lords, backed by demonstrations of the military power of the Crown when the expansionist ambitions of Welsh rulers pushed the boundaries too far. Consequently, in Deheubarth, the sons of Gruffudd ap Rhys were pushed back into the heartlands, with the Marcher lords regaining territory. Ceredigion was returned to the de Clares, Cantref Bychan was restored to Walter fitz Richard Pons, and the Crown regained Carmarthen.

It is impossible to say whether Henry's intention in 1165 was to end native rule in Wales, as feared by the chronicler of the *Brut*; or whether it was an attempt to force the Welsh rulers once and for all into submission to him. However, after being defeated by the terrain and the weather, and with problems mounting across his vast empire, including the controversy that resulted from the murder of Becket, and the shock of the rebellion by his sons, Henry II adopted a new approach of cooperation with the Welsh rulers. Particularly with the appointment of the Lord Rhys as his representative in south Wales, Henry was able to assert the royal authority of the Crown through his overlordship of the Welsh rulers, who, in turn, were protected from encroachment by the Marcher lords. Indeed, during the latter part of Henry II's reign, the Marcher lords had been pushed back again. The Marcher lordships of Cantref Bychan, Cilgerran/ Emlyn and Ceredigion were lost. However, the conquest of Ireland opened new opportunities for expansion, and many of the Marcher lords of the south-west had also become lords in Ireland, with the descendants of Gerald of Windsor and Nest, who had played such a key role in the early settlement of south-west Wales, focusing their attention there. The lordships that had access to the sea or were in the environs of Pembroke Castle, were still in the hands of the Anglo-Norman and Flemish settlers, albeit there are few records to show how much control they were able to exert. Indeed, William fitz Martin (d.1209) in Cemais married a daughter of the Lord Rhys to seal a pact of mutual security. However, that was all soon to change following the death of Henry II in 1189.

Although Henry II's policy from the 1170s onward ensured a degree of stability and recognition of his authority, it was based on his personal power and

Chinon Castle: Henry II died here 1189

relationships, with no formal structure to sustain it. Consequently, his death at Chinon Castle in France in 1189, and burial at Fontevrault Abbey, followed by the accession of Richard I, opened the way for a further period of volatile and violent change.

Indeed, it was not just the accession of Richard I that changed the dynamics. The Lord Rhys was moving into the last phase of his life, and his numerous sons were already impatient for their own power, jostling and feuding to be the one who would succeed their father. The bitter rivalry and infighting between his sons would begin to erupt in the years before his death, adding a further element of destabilisation, that would eventually fragment control in Deheubarth forever. As the next chapter will explore, this happened at the same time as the emergence of a new and powerful Marcher lord in Pembroke, and the rise of a remarkable ruler in Gwynedd.

CHAPTER FIVE

The Decline of Deheubarth and the rise of Gwynedd

T HE death of Henry II in 1189 heralded an abrupt change across all of Wales and the Marcher lordships. A new reign saw the period of relative peace and stability that had prevailed since 1172 suddenly shattered. This chapter will explore how, in the south-west, the significance was magnified in the subsequent decades by the decline and death of the Lord Rhys, the bitter feuds between his sons that destroyed his legacy, the rise to power of William Marshal, earl of Pembroke, and the domination of all Wales that was secured by Llywelyn ab Iorwerth.

INITIAL WELSH UPRISING

When Henry II died in July 1189, it appears that the Lord Rhys considered their agreement to be no longer valid. Certainly, before Richard I had even been crowned, Rhys captured the castles of St Clears, Llanstephan, Kidwelly and Laugharne, having raided through the lordships of Haverfordwest and Pembroke (and Swansea in the south-east). He also attacked Carmarthen Castle but was unable to take it. Following these raids, Richard I sent his brother, John (d.1216), at the head of an army to break the siege. It was arranged that Rhys would accompany John back to Oxford to swear his loyalty to Richard, potentially renewing the agreement that had been made with

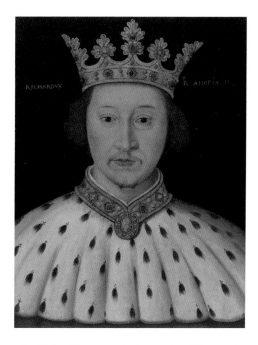

King Richard I: spent only six months of his reign in England (© National Portrait Gallery, London)

Henry II.[1] Richard, however, didn't arrive in Oxford, leaving Rhys to return home feeling slighted. It is a matter of some debate why Richard failed to meet with the Lord Rhys, though it may have been because he thought the terms offered by John were too generous. Certainly, throughout the period from 1189 to his death in 1197, the Lord Rhys and his sons led numerous raids against the Marcher lords.

The sons of the Lord Rhys

The final chapter in Rhys's illustrious career was dominated not only by conflict with the Marcher lords, but also strife within his own family. This, following Rhys's death, led to the break-up of the polity of Deheubarth and contributed to their dynasty losing a senior role on the political stage of Wales. In addition to the many sons that Rhys had with his wife, Gwenllian, there were other sons who were the children of his numerous mistresses. With so many sons vying for prominence, the question of succession was always going to be problematic. In practice, Rhys effectively compounded the problem by maintaining the Welsh custom of sending his children to be fostered in other households, thus breaking (or at least weakening) sibling bonds and loyalty to family that might otherwise have developed. There are suggestions that Rhys regarded his eldest son, Gruffudd, as his heir who would inherit the ancestral core, whilst other sons would be given conquered territories on the periphery. If so, his strategy was a failure, as their lack of unity meant that the kingdom of Deheubarth would be left fragmented by the infighting that erupted. There were four main antagonists amongst Rhys's sons:

- Gruffudd (d.1201), the eldest son from his marriage, who was probably regarded by his father as the presumptive heir to the head of the house of Deheubarth, and who had been married to Maud de Braose, a daughter of arguably the most powerful Marcher lord at the time. His power-base was in Ystrad Tywi, with the family seat at Dinefwr, though his descendants would become based in parts of Ceredigion.

- Maelgwn (d.1231), Gruffudd's main rival, was an older son, but a child of one of Rhys's mistresses. He was clearly a multifaceted character, for he is described in the *Brut* as:

  ... the man who was a shield and a bulwark for all the south: for his fame was of the brightest, and he was comely and beloved by all ... and all the leaders whose lands bordered upon him dreaded him ... the man who slew many of the Flemings and drove them to flight.

His affinity was in Ceredigion, from where he drew his support.

- Rhys Gryg (d.1234) ('the hoarse') was another key rival. He was willing to cooperate with either brother, depending on where he perceived the greatest advantage. His importance grew gradually until he eventually held the seat of Dinefwr for himself.

- Hywel Sais (d.1204), who was given lands in the far south-west. He was also willing to work with either brother.

It would be no exaggeration to say that Gruffudd and Maelgwn hated each other. Indeed, Gruffudd had Maelgwn imprisoned in his father-in-law's castle at Brecon in 1189 in order to keep him under control, after Maelgwn had destroyed the town of Tenby two years earlier.

Following the failed meeting at Oxford, Richard departed to lead the Third Crusade. The Crusade itself, followed by his period in captivity and his campaigning on the Continent against the king of France, all meant that Richard I spent only six months in England throughout his reign. Without a strong royal presence, it was again left to the Marcher lords to fend for themselves for the most part. Prince John, as lord of Glamorgan, may have been expected to bring order

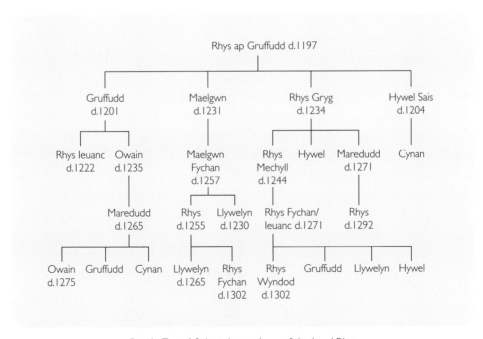

Family Tree 4 Select descendants of the Lord Rhys

to the region, but he wanted to be near the centre of power while the king was away – indeed becoming involved in treacherous activity. Thus, the next few years saw both attacks on Marcher lordships, and battles within the family of the Lord Rhys, as the situation in the region descended into near chaos for a time.

In 1191, the Lord Rhys attacked the lordship of Cemais, even though it was held by his son-in-law, William fitz Martin. Following his capture of the castle at Nevern, he handed it over to his son, Gruffudd. Despite this, when Maelgwn escaped from his imprisonment the following year, Gruffudd was made to cede Cemais to him. Perhaps to unite his feuding sons, Rhys brought together Gruffudd, Maelgwn, Rhys Gryg and Hywel Sais in 1192 to attack the lordship of Gower, besieging the castle at Swansea. If creating unity was Rhys's objective, it proved a dismal failure when, with the brothers preferring to pursue their sibling feuds, the siege failed. On his own, the Lord Rhys struck west, taking the castle of Llawhaden from the bishop of St Davids and handing it over to Hywel Sais, who went on to capture Wiston.

Indeed, Hywel's capture of Wiston was their last successful raid as the family became more and more embroiled in battles between themselves. In 1194, Maelgwn and Hywel, having taken up arms against their father, defeated him, imprisoning the Lord Rhys in the castle at Nevern, now held by Maelgwn. The captivity didn't last long though, as Hywel had a change of heart and freed his father from the castle in the same year. The chaotic political infighting continued when Rhys Gryg and his brother, Maredudd (d.1201), took Dinefwr and Llandovery castles from their father. However, although he was now quite aged, Rhys raised support, retaking both castles and imprisoning the two recalcitrant sons in a remote castle in Ceredigion.

While this was happening, the Marcher lords were assembling resources to strike back. Firstly, there were Marcher counter-attacks on the south coast, with both Llanstephan and Kidwelly regained for the de Camvilles and the de Londres respectively. Pipe Roll evidence shows that they were both receiving money for the upkeep of their castles by 1194.[2] Furthermore, although the king was in England for only a few months in 1194, it appears that a decision was made that the Crown would provide financial support for a new campaign. However, when it came in 1195, the main focal point of the aggression was a drive into the central Marches against the rising threat posed by Gwenwynwyn, the ruler of southern Powys. In the south-west, the powerful William de Braose, the pre-eminent lord of the central Marches, raised a large force to stage a campaign through the region, taking St Clears for himself before moving on to Ceredigion.

In 1196, the Lord Rhys decided that the best way to counter the attacks of William de Braose was to go on the offensive himself, with an attack on Carmarthen.

Yet again he was only able to burn the town while the castle survived. He then turned north to the lands of William de Braose, capturing and burning the castles of Colwyn and Radnor before turning his attention to the stronghold of Painscastle, newly captured by de Braose's wife. Although he captured Painscastle, the Lord Rhys and de Braose came to an agreement by which de Braose ceased his operations in Ceredigion in exchange for the return to him of Painscastle.

The following year Rhys died from a great pestilence that swept through the kingdom. The *Brut* laments:

> *... grief and misery came to the whole race of the Britons when Death, in that accursed year, broke the wheel of Fate to snatch the Lord Rhys ap Gruffudd on its wings under the subduing power of Death; the man who was the head and the shield and the strength of the South and all of Wales and the hope and the defence of all the race of the Britons.*

Although he had been excommunicated for the attack against the castle of the bishop of St Davids at Llawhaden, Rhys was buried at St Davids Cathedral. This was allowed because he was posthumously reinstated to the Church through having his corpse do 'penitence' for the offences he had committed, by being scourged before burial by the bishop, Peter de Leia. His desire to be buried at the holiest place in Wales demonstrated his own awareness of his place in history. This would

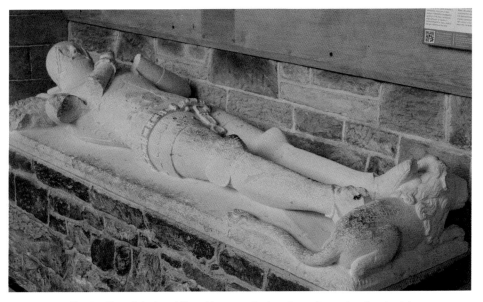

Tomb effigy of the Lord Rhys: his corpse had to do penitence to allow burial in the cathedral at St Davids (© Philip Hume)

not have been allowed except that his sons arranged to have him posthumously reinstated.[3] Rhys would be the last sole ruler of Deheubarth. His success on the battlefield and his ability to negotiate peace had put him and Deheubarth in a pre-eminent position during his lifetime. Not surprisingly, given the bitter and violent feuds within his family, the dominant role of Deheubarth within Wales did not survive his death, particularly as it coincided with the advent of a new and powerful Marcher lord in the south-west, and the emergence of a strong prince in Gwynedd, who would change the political dynamic of the Welsh polity.

THE DECLINE OF DEHEUBARTH

Following the death of the Lord Rhys, the sibling disputes escalated as each brother fought to enhance their own position. The ever-aggressive Maelgwn looked to increase his power by attaching himself to the rising strength of Gwenwynwyn (d.1216), the ruler of southern Powys, joining forces with him to capture Aberystwyth Castle. In the following year, the pair took Cardigan Castle, which put Maelgwn in control of most of Ceredigion. When Gruffudd ap Rhys moved to check their gains, he was captured and sent to the English, who imprisoned him in Corfe Castle.

Gwenwynwyn, continuing to press for a superior position in mid Wales, gathered an army to lay siege to Painscastle in 1198. This move provoked the English government to release Gruffudd from custody, in the hope that he would restore the balance of power in the region. When he attempted to broker a truce with the besieging Welsh, Gwenwynwyn felt no need for negotiation and refused the offer. However, his judgement was flawed, and his army was routed in the ensuing battle, which left him in a much-weakened position. Gruffudd now moved against the lands of Maelgwn in order to assert his authority as the ruler of Deheubarth, taking most of Ceredigion into his control, and capturing Cilgerran Castle and Emlyn.

After the death of Richard I in 1199, while on campaign in France, King John took a much more active role in Welsh affairs than his brother had. As elsewhere, John's strategy from the outset was to play the Welsh rulers against one another, thereby balancing power such that no one ruler could grow to dominate the region and pose a threat to the king's interests. With Gruffudd having now reversed nearly all Maelgwn's earlier conquests, apart from two castles in Ceredigion, Maelgwn turned to King John for support, offering to relinquish Cardigan Castle to the king in return for affirmation of his hold over northern Ceredigion and Emlyn including the castle of Cilgerran. The writer of the *Brut* laments that Maelgwn,

Tomb effigy
of Richard I
at Fontevrault
Abbey in France

Sold Cardigan, the key to all Wales, for a small price to the Saxons for fear and hatred of Gruffudd, his brother.

Cardigan Castle would remain in royal hands, a key development in the future power struggles in the March.

Gruffudd ap Rhys died suddenly in 1201 and was buried at Strata Florida Abbey. His death, though, only escalated the contest to become the sole legitimate ruler of the house of Deheubarth. Gruffudd's two sons, Rhys Ieuanc and Owain, ably replaced their father in the struggle for the head of the Deheubarth dynasty; however, Maelgwn and Rhys Gryg worked against the two sons of Gruffudd and their claims. The following years witnessed a series of conquests and re-conquests of the key castles and *cantrefi* of Deheubarth. For example, one of the most heavily contested regions was the ex-Marcher lordship of Cantref Bychan, with its castle of Llandovery changing hands every year from 1201 to 1204.

WILLIAM MARSHAL (d.1219)

It was not only the lack of one strong ruler in Deheubarth that coloured the political landscape in the early thirteenth century, but also the arrival of a new powerful Marcher lord. For his services to the royal family over many years, William Marshal had been granted marriage to the de Clare heiress of Striguil (Chepstow) and Leinster by Richard I in 1189. King John then bestowed the re-creation of the earldom of Pembroke on William Marshal in 1199 as a reward for his support when John claimed the throne after Richard's death.[4] Although Isabel de Clare was the grand-daughter of the 1st earl of Pembroke, the de Clare earldom of Pembroke had lapsed, thus William Marshal was created the 1st earl of Pembroke of the second creation of the title (nearly 50 years later there would be a third creation). At a stroke William Marshal became a dominant force in south-west Wales. It is likely that William visited Pembroke Castle as early as 1200, as he was recorded travelling to Ireland.

The entry in the *Brut* for the year 1204 illustrates the growing complexity, in the region, of relations between the sons and grandsons of the Lord Rhys on the one hand and William Marshal on the other:

> *1204: ... Hywel Sais, son of the Lord Rhys, was wounded in Cemais through treachery by the men of Maelgwn, his brother; and of that wound he died ... that year Maelgwn ap Rhys lost the keys to all his territory, to wit, Llandovery and Dinefwr, for the sons of Gruffudd, his brother, manfully won them from him. That year William Marshall, and a mighty host along with him, came to lay siege to Cilgerran, and he gained possession of it.*

The other momentous event that happened in 1204 was that King John lost virtually all the Angevin lands on the Continent. One long-term impact was to turn the attention of the Crown firmly onto its lands in Britain. The short-term impact was that many of the leading barons, who held land in both France and England, were forced to make a choice as to where their future loyalty would lie. Those who abandoned their Continental holdings were usually compensated with the confiscated English lands from the barons that chose to hold their Norman lordships from the French king. Even though it required him to swear allegiance to both kings, it is testament to William Marshal that he managed to use his influence and prestige to hold on to his estates on both sides of the Channel. However, when William Marshal refused to take part in an invasion of Poitou in 1205, because it conflicted with his loyalty, King John was enraged. The notoriously insecure king became distrustful of William, who

King John (© National Portrait Gallery, London)

remained out of favour for some time. Marshal spent the next years in Ireland consolidating his lordship in a country that was still dominated by the families of the original invaders and settlers, most of whom were not supportive of the new lord of Leinster. Matters came to a head when King John brought about the downfall of the powerful Marcher baron William de Braose in 1208. De Braose fled to Ireland for safety and Marshal took him in, before de Braose moved on to the de Lacy's lordship of Meath. This was treasonous in John's eyes, and brought about a royal Irish campaign, securing John's authority in Ireland. William Marshal was forced to give a son as a hostage as a sign of his loyalty. William survived this brief storm, making sure that he never again antagonised the king to such an extent that he fell completely out of favour.

LLYWELYN AB IORWERTH

During the early years of his reign, King John gave his support to both Gwenwynwyn of Powys and to Llywelyn ab Iorwerth, who had become the sole ruler of Gwynedd after years of familial infighting following the death of his grandfather, Owain Gwynedd, in 1170. Undoubtedly, John, as ever, was manipulating people to create a balance of power, including agreeing a peace treaty with Llywelyn, which was sealed by Llywelyn's marriage to John's illegitimate daughter Joan in 1205. However, when Llywelyn began to move into lands beyond Gwynedd and exert influence more broadly in Wales, King John decided it was time to clip Llywelyn's wings. When the King launched a campaign in 1211 against Gwynedd, it is interesting to note that the descendants of the Lord Rhys marched with the king, no doubt out of alarm at the increasing power and ambition of Llywelyn.

Outmatched, Llywelyn withdrew to the mountains of Snowdonia, and the starving royal army was forced to return to Chester. However, the king regrouped to lead a second expedition across north Wales, bringing Llywelyn to the point of surrender. With his wife, Joan, acting as intermediary with her father, Llywelyn and King John agreed terms by which Llywelyn ceded the lands in north-east Wales, paid a heavy tribute and handed over hostages. Within a year, though, Llywelyn had rallied his forces to strike back, regaining by force in 1212 the lands in north-west Wales that he had ceded to the king the year before. This time, most of the Welsh rulers, including Maelgwn and Rhys Gryg, marched with Llywelyn. Whereas the previous year they had seen King John as the defender of their independence from Gwynedd, they now saw John as the greater threat. When John's plans for a massive campaign of retaliation were abandoned due to the mounting problems elsewhere in his kingdom, Llywelyn and his allies struck further south. They first sacked the new Aberystwyth Castle, which John had recently built, and then moved against Swansea, burning it to the ground.

Despite this show of Welsh unity, there was further infighting amongst the heirs of the Lord Rhys. In 1213 Rhys Ieuanc, with no lands of his own, appealed to King John for support. The *Brut* recounts his response:

> And then the king sent to the seneschal of Hereford and to Falkes, seneschal of Cardiff, and commanded them to cause Rhys Gryg to give up the castle of Llandovery and the land, or else to flee from the whole kingdom. And after Rhys Gryg had been summoned to answer the king's command, he said in answer that he would not share a single acre with Rhys Ieuanc.

Following Rhys Gryg's refusal to comply, Rhys Ieuanc raised an army of Welsh and English, taking both Dinefwr Castle and Llandovery into his hands.

MAGNA CARTA

In England, King John's relationship with his barons was rapidly deteriorating. However, while the earl of Pembroke may have been out of favour after 1205, he had never completely fallen out with the king. In 1213, when John was looking for allies, he found one in William Marshal, granting him further lands including the lordship of Haverford, and also Carmarthen and Cardigan castles in order to solidify their pact. Despite the support of William, when John's attempt in 1214 to regain Normandy ended in a humiliating retreat to England, the baronial revolt was gaining momentum. The civil war that ensued resulted in John being forced to put his seal to Magna Carta in 1215; however, when John successfully appealed to the Pope that he had been forced to sign under duress, the barons were excommunicated. In response, the barons invited the son of the king of France to take over the English throne.

Taking advantage of the chaos in England, Rhys Ieuanc, the son of Gruffudd ap Rhys, allied with his uncle, Maelgwn, to seize all of Dyfed, except Cemais. Whilst Maelgwn and Rhys's brother, Owain ap Gruffudd, travelled north to join forces with Llywelyn, Rhys Ieuanc marched east to gain possession of Kidwelly and all the castles of the Gower. Llywelyn, also taking advantage of the turmoil in England (and with the support of most of the Welsh rulers), led an army through central Wales, annexing lands there to his control. With the king powerless to intervene, Llywelyn swept into south-west Wales where his forces succeeded in capturing Cardigan Castle, and taking all of Ceredigion and Emlyn from the Marshals, before moving on to sack Carmarthen, St Clears, Laugharne, Cemais,

Llanstephan, and Kidwelly. However, they did not press their campaign into the far south-west around Pembroke and Haverford, and this therefore remained the only region with an English presence in south-west Wales.[5]

The dominant position that Llywelyn had achieved in Wales was demonstrated in 1216 when he used his authority to summon a formal assembly to meet at Aberdyfi in Ceredigion. Llywelyn used the meeting to divide the inheritance of the Lord Rhys, and the lands of the previous year's conquests, between Maelgwn, Rhys Gryg and the two sons of Gruffudd, Rhys Ieuanc and Owain, signifying both his own ascendancy over all the other rulers in Wales, and the permanent fragmentation of Deheubarth. The division orchestrated by Llywelyn is shown on Map 10, below. The sons of Gruffudd ap Rhys, Rhys Ieuanc and Owain, were granted most of Ceredigion with the castle of Cardigan. Rhys Gryg received a cohesive unit of land within Ystrad Tywi, which included the castle of Dinefwr and the Marcher lordship of Kidwelly. Maelgwn received more scattered territory which included parts of Cantref Bychan, with the castle of Llandovery, two *commotes* in southern Ceredigion and the Marcher lordships of Cemais, Emlyn/ Cilgerran, St Clears, Ystlywf, Laugharne and Llanstephan. This put Maelgwn in a more tenuous position, as his lands were more dispersed and many of his holdings were lands previously held by Marcher lords, who would demand their return one day.

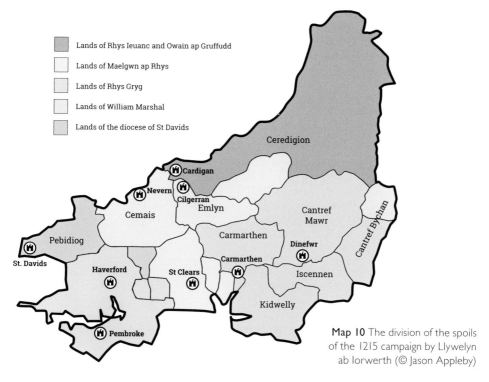

Map 10 The division of the spoils of the 1215 campaign by Llywelyn ab Iorwerth (© Jason Appleby)

John, meanwhile, attempted to fight back, but he was still not in control of large parts of the country when he died of a gastric infection on a stormy night at Newark Castle, Nottinghamshire. His young son Henry (d.1272) was heir to the throne. As Professor David Carpenter stated, 'No king of England came to the throne in a more desperate situation than Henry III'.[6]

THE YOUNG KING HENRY III

John's nine-year-old son Henry was in a precarious position when his father died. The civil war was still raging, with the rival claimant to the throne, Prince Louis of France, in control of large parts of the country; however, two of the leading English magnates, William Marshal and the earl of Chester, remained loyal to Henry. William Marshal took the young prince into his possession at King John's funeral in Worcester, before swiftly moving him to Gloucester to have him crowned. William Marshal was chosen to be the regent of the royal government, effectively granting him control of the country. His biography states that he exclaimed that his loyalty to the boy king was so deep that, 'I'd carry him astride my neck and bear him unfailingly from isle to isle, from land to land, even if I had to beg for my bread'.[7] One of the first acts of the new regency government was to reissue Magna Carta to re-establish authority. With the unpopular John now dead and a legitimate heir on the throne, who had the backing of the Church, the rebel barons began to come back into the king's allegiance. When the remaining baronial opposition was decisively defeated at the Battle of Lincoln in 1217 by an army led by the 69-year-old William Marshal (himself in the thick of the action), a negotiated agreement was reached. This led to the departure of the French prince from England, thus effectively ending the civil war.

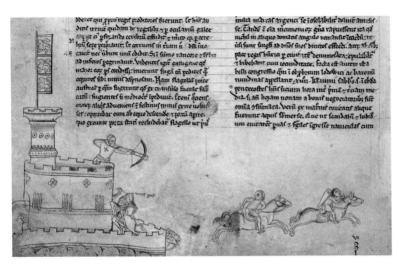

Matthew Paris' *Chronica Maiora II* (MS 016ii): a depiction of the decisive Battle of Lincoln which ended the baronial revolt in 1217 (© Parker Library, Corpus Christi College, Cambridge)

In Wales, Llywelyn continued to take advantage of the weakness of the royal government in England. When King John had persecuted the de Braose family, they had allied with Llywelyn; with the change of regime, they now submitted to the new regency government in 1217, abandoning their alliance with Llywelyn. In retaliation, Llywelyn subdued the de Braose lordships of Brecon and Gower, following up with another campaign deep into south-west Wales, this time penetrating as far into Dyfed as Haverford. It was only on payment of 1,000 marks, in a deal brokered by the bishop of St Davids, that Llywelyn refrained from sacking the castle and town. The Marcher lords were completely powerless to stop his advances, nor were they able to recover what they had lost.

Establishing peace in Wales was becoming a priority for the new regency government led by William Marshal. In a meeting arranged by the archbishop of Canterbury, Llywelyn met with the child-king and his advisors at Worcester in 1218, to agree a peace. Llywelyn emerged triumphant when the Treaty of Worcester acknowledged his domination of Wales, confirming him in all the territory he had won. Although Llywelyn agreed to return the royal castles of Cardigan and Carmarthen, they were immediately granted back to his custody until the king came of age, which might be as late as 1228. Llywelyn also agreed to do his best to have the Marcher castles returned to the owners recognised as rightful before the war. There was no urgency on Llywelyn's part to enforce this, however, and none were returned. One of the biggest losers from the treaty was William Marshal, as Llywelyn retained much of what he had taken from the earl of Pembroke. Presumably, however, as leader of the regency council, Marshal put peace and the interests of the country above his personal interests (a situation that, after his death, was much resented by his successors).

Although the treaty endorsed Llywelyn's domination of Wales, he was frustrated in two respects – whilst it confirmed him in all his possessions, it was by right of conquest and not by hereditary right, thus leaving the door open to the Marcher lords (and others) should Llywelyn die; secondly, the treaty withheld formal recognition that Wales was a single polity ruled over by Llywelyn. Llywelyn gave his homage to the child-king, but so did the other rulers and lords in Wales. Although it was Llywelyn's responsibility to see that the native rulers gave their homage to the king, which underlined his superior position among the native rulers, this was very different from those rulers giving homage to him. The desire to secure this recognition would affect much of his actions during the years of his long ascendancy.

William Marshal died in 1219 at the age of 72 at Caversham on the River Thames. His son, William Marshal (d.1231), was confirmed as earl of Pembroke and Lord Marshal of England, though was not given a similar role to that of his father in the governance of England. The younger Marshal also strongly resented the concessions given to Llywelyn, and the loss of Marshal lands that his father, as leader of the regency council, had agreed to but was powerless to reverse.

In the Treaty of Worcester, Llywelyn had committed to compel those Welsh rulers who had gained lands and castles from Marcher lords to return them. As of 1220, none had been returned and the government urged him to comply with the treaty. Llywelyn agreed, marching south at the head of a large army with the stated intent of bringing to heal Rhys Gryg, who still held the de Londres fortress of Kidwelly and Gower, which had been taken from the de Braoses. Llywelyn and Rhys Gryg met at Carmarthen, with the result that Llywelyn forced him to surrender Kidwelly, the Gower and other lands to their Marcher lords. He then moved against the holdings of William Marshal, who he accused of consistently violating an agreement struck at Shrewsbury in May of 1220. Somewhat surprisingly, Llywelyn was joined in this campaign by none other than Rhys Gryg, the humbled Welsh ruler quickly recovering from his previous censure. The castles of Wiston and Narberth were soon destroyed, and the town of Haverford burned up to the castle gates. Llywelyn was still in complete control of the political landscape;

Kidwelly Castle: once lost in 1215, it was not recovered by the de Londres heir until 1241

indeed, Kidwelly Castle was returned to Rhys Gryg. The new earl of Pembroke remained powerless to oppose him. With the regency government still trying to mend the damage of the civil war and refill royal coffers, there was no support offered. In fact, the government worked hard to stay on good terms with Llywelyn.

Welsh setback

Once again, the baron who had lost the most from Llywelyn's incursions was the earl of Pembroke. Although deeply dissatisfied that the Welsh were not keeping their part of the bargain, the agreement that had been reached in 1220 was renewed annually until 1223 and peace prevailed. However, on the day that it expired in 1223, the *Brut* relates that

> *William Marshal came from Ireland, and with him a multitude of knights and foot-soldiers, in a mighty fleet landing at Menevia* [St Davids] *about Palm Sunday. And on Easter Monday he attacked Cardigan. And that day the castle was surrendered to him. And the following Wednesday he drew towards Carmarthen, and he took that castle also.*

He also took Cemais and Cilgerran before moving against Kidwelly, where he was fought to a standstill by Llywelyn's son, Gruffudd, who had been sent south with an army to resist the advance. The royal authorities at first reacted with shock at the turn of events; however, they soon recognised the opportunity this presented to regain lost footing in the region. With royal support in the form of William Longespée, earl of Salisbury, another campaign was launched which succeeded in retaking the remaining Marcher castles of St Clears, Llanstephan, Ystlwyf, Laugharne and Kidwelly, with the Welsh pushed back into their traditional strongholds in Ystrad Tywi and northern Ceredigion. The Marcher lords now had the upper hand with the strong presence of the earl of Pembroke leading the way.[8] Despite this, the simmering feuds between the descendants of the Lord Rhys resurfaced when a grandson, Cynan ap Hywel, was in the Marshal's army that retook Cilgerran. Cynan was rewarded with a grant of the eastern half of Emlyn as well as Ystlwyf, to be held directly from the Marshals – a definite sign of the Marshals' growing power in the region. It was after this that construction work on the stone castle at Cilgerran we see today, would have been started by the Marshals. As a further reward for his service, William Marshal was granted Kidwelly, to hold while the heiress was a minor. He also held Cemais, whose lord, Nicholas fitz Martin (d.1282), was a ward in the custody of one of the Marshal's enemies.

Reconstruction of Cilgerran: the stone castle was begun by the Marshal family (© Chris Jones-Jenkins)

Following the campaign, Llywelyn came to terms, relinquishing the royal castles of Cardigan and Carmarthen, which were granted to William Marshal while the king remained a minor, a bitter blow to Llywelyn and his allies. The strength of the earl of Pembroke was now far greater than that of the fragmented princes of Deheubarth, whilst Llywelyn did not have the power to reverse these losses either.

THE KING COMES OF AGE

Henry III declared himself of age in 1227. Until then, he could only make grants and gifts with the consent of his council. Almost immediately, he began to exert his authority. In south-west Wales, Henry took Cardigan and Carmarthen castles back from William Marshal the younger, putting his own castellan in charge. He also reissued Magna Carta again, which put him on a more solid footing with his barons. However, he was still young and reliant on his senior advisers, one of whom, the Justiciar, Hubert de Burgh used his position to amass enormous land holdings in the Marcher lordships, including the custody of Carmarthen and Cardigan – acquisitions that would lead to further unrest. Although most of de Burgh's lands were in the southern Marcher lordships, when a clash erupted it was in the central region, where, in April 1228, he had been given the new royal castle at Montgomery together with the lordship. When a further quarrel resulted in a Welsh siege of Montgomery, a royal army marched into the neighbouring district of Ceri where de Burgh started to build a castle. However, Llywelyn, recognising the threat that this castle posed to his own security, now became personally involved. Llywelyn's army slaughtered the English invaders, forcing them to withdraw from the area with the castle only partially constructed. When Henry III undertook to demolish the unfinished castle, it was dubbed 'Hubert's Folly'.

Another significant result of the failed Ceri campaign was the capture of William de Braose (d.1230). As part of the ransom for his release, de Braose agreed to the marriage of his daughter Isabella to Llywelyn's son and heir, Dafydd, along with the castle of Builth, a strategic castle in the central March, as her wedding dower. However, when William returned to Llywelyn's court at Easter 1230, to finalise the arrangements for the wedding, he was found in the bedchamber of Joan, Llywelyn's wife. Convicted of treason, William was hanged publicly from a tree in front of many witnesses. Despite this, the wedding of Dafydd and Isabella went ahead and the castle of Builth came into Llywelyn's possession, with the result that a key piece in the line of defence at the top of the Wye Valley was established. William had no male heirs and the de Braose inheritance was divided between his daughters, to be split between Dafydd, the Mortimers, the Bohuns and the Cantilupes, with the lordship of St Clears divided between the three Marcher families.

Llywelyn ab Iorwerth – the final chapter

The sudden death of William Marshal the younger in 1231, following his return from a campaign in France, changed once again the dynamics in the region. Dying childless, he was succeeded by his younger brother, Richard (d.1234). Despite this, it was events elsewhere that provoked the conflict that developed during 1231. When Hubert de Burgh executed some Welsh prisoners at Montgomery, Llywelyn was pushed into action. He campaigned vigorously in the central Marches, burning the town at Montgomery before moving on to capture Radnor, Hay and Brecon castles. No doubt seeing an opportunity to strike at the power of de Burgh in the Marcher lordships, Llywelyn continued his campaign into the south-east and the south-west,

Cardigan Castle: a flashpoint of Anglo-Norman conflict in Ceredigion (© Paul Davis)

taking Caerleon, Neath and Kidwelly, which was still held by the Marshals. The son of Maelgwn ap Rhys (d.1231), Maelgwn Fychan (d.1257) with the help of Owain ap Gruffudd, took Cardigan back into Welsh hands. The *Brut* records that,

> *... he and Owain ap Gruffudd and the men of Llywelyn ab Iorwerth came to lay siege to the castle. And before the end of a few days they breached the castle with engines. And the garrison was forced to leave the walls and to surrender the castle.*

Seized from the custody of de Burgh, Cardigan remained in Welsh hands for the rest of Llywelyn's life. Once again, there was a royal campaign to attempt to counter the Welsh advance, but it achieved nothing more than the building of a new stone castle at Painscastle in the central March.

Richard Marshal held considerable lands in Normandy and Brittany, occasioning a short delay while the matter of Richard renouncing his allegiance to the king of France was completed. Having lost their French estates, the Marshals were granted Carmarthen and Cardigan to hold in their stead; however, Richard was in no position himself to wrest Cardigan from Welsh control. Although earl of Pembroke for less than three years, Richard's tenure was dominated by the open rebellion that he led in the final months of his life, often referred to as the 'Marshal War'.

Hubert de Burgh was eventually forced out of office by Henry III in 1232, to be replaced by the energetic bishop, Peter des Roches, who took possession of the lands of de Burgh after his fall, dispensing them to his favourites. Then in 1233, when Peter des Roches, looking to further his gains, took an estate from one of the Marshal's close allies, Richard Marshal was compelled to act. He demanded it be returned on the grounds that it had been taken without a fair judgement, something that Magna Carta specifically forbade. He received no joy. In September 1233, Richard rose in rebellion, allying himself with none other than Llywelyn ab Iorwerth, his family's long-time foe. The seasoned Welsh ruler was not going to let an opportunity like this pass without taking advantage of it. The key battleground was in the south-east, where Marshal took the castles of Cardiff, Newport, Abergavenny and Usk; however, when his forces failed to take Monmouth, a stalemate ensued. The rebellion became a series of skirmishes, some of which were embarrassing to the king, especially when one of Richard Marshal's key supporters sacked the baggage train of Bishop Peter and took it for himself.

In the south-west, meanwhile, Richard Marshal and the southern Welsh rulers, led by Rhys Gryg, joined forces to besiege Carmarthen, as described in the *Brut*:

> *That year* [1233] *Maelgwn Fychan ap Maelgwn ap Rhys and Owain ap Gruffudd and Rhys Gryg and their sons and the host of Llywelyn ab Iorwerth and the host of the earl of Pembroke gathered together at Carmarthen. And they laid siege to it for three months, and they made a bridge upon the Tywi. And then the sailors came armed, with the tide, to break down the bridge. And when the Welsh saw that their expedition would be fruitless, they returned to their lands.*

As a consequence, Rhys Gryg was severely wounded, dying a short time later, and was buried at St Davids with his father. His sons and grandsons would carry on as rulers of their dominion in the Tywi valley, often as rivals, from their castles at Dinefwr and Dryslwyn. The rebellion was now in a state of impasse and, receiving very little support from other barons, Richard took refuge in his lands in Ireland where he needed to resolve several political problems. However, he was wounded in battle and died in captivity a short time later in April 1234. Although the rebellion had not become widespread, it cost the bishop his position as Justiciar, while the original disseisin of land was reversed and the Marshal's man was restored to his lands.

Like his older brothers, Richard died childless, with the next brother, Gilbert (who had been Richard's lieutenant in Ireland), now becoming heir to the earldom of Pembroke. However, the family was at war with the king whose cooperation was necessary to succeed to the title, and Gilbert, as a younger son, had been trained as a cleric. Gilbert travelled to Wales and, through intermediaries, was reconciled with the king. On 11 June he was knighted at Worcester, thus cancelling his status as a cleric, being created earl of Pembroke and Marshal of England immediately afterwards. Gilbert was granted Carmarthen and Cardigan, but, like his brother, he was unable to make good his claim to Cardigan.

The last years of the Marshals

With the end of the Marshal rebellion, Henry and Llywelyn concluded a peace treaty later in June 1234. The truce was brokered by the Archbishop of Canterbury and several other powerful ecclesiastics at Middle near Shrewsbury. The Truce of Middle was formally to last for two years, and it only put the clock back to the situation at the outbreak of the recent conflict, thus confirming again Llywelyn in the lands that he held by conquest whilst avoiding the issue of who held them by right. However, it was in both parties' interest to maintain peace, thus the truce was renewed annually resulting in no further conflict between Llywelyn and the Crown.

Throughout the period from the Treaty of Worcester in 1218 until his death in 1240, a priority for Llywelyn was to secure his legacy. As mentioned earlier, he failed to secure formal recognition from the Crown to a title such as 'Prince of Wales'. Also, to help ensure his legacy, Llywelyn had controversially designated the son from his marriage to Joan, Dafydd, to be his successor at the expense of an elder son, Gruffudd, born from a previous long-standing, but not married, relationship. Although in line with Anglo-Norman practice, disinheriting Gruffudd was contrary to Welsh custom and law which did not distinguish between children born in or out of wedlock. Having suffered a stroke in 1237, Llywelyn tried to have all the Welsh lords swear homage to Dafydd in 1238. When the king intervened to remind them that homage could only be given to the king himself, the Welsh rulers swore an oath to uphold Dafydd as Llywelyn's heir, thus giving fealty but not homage.

When Llywelyn died in 1240 his legacy was best summed up by the moniker that he became known by, Llywelyn 'Fawr' (the Great). He had seized opportunities to win territory from his rivals when the timing was right, but was just as astute at recognising when he should compromise and peace was the better option. His son was duly appointed his successor, but soon found out that having a title was far short of having the mastery to live up to it, particularly as many supported the rights of Gruffudd.

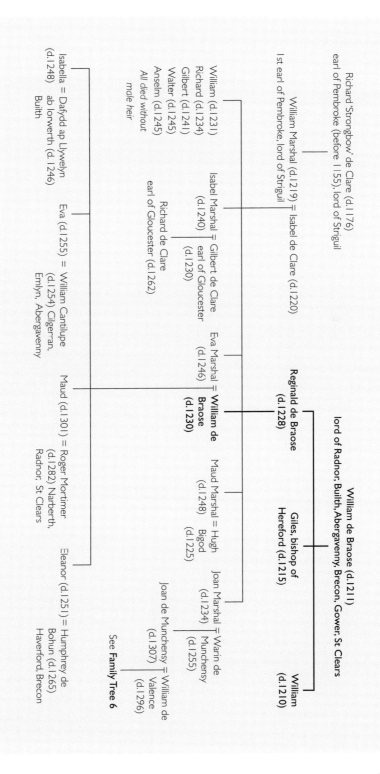

Family Tree 5 Select descendants to the Marshal/ de Braose inheritance

Richard 'Strongbow' de Clare (d.1176)
earl of Pembroke (before 1155), lord of Striguil

William Marshal (d.1219) ⊤ Isabel de Clare (d.1220)
1st earl of Pembroke, lord of Striguil

William (d.1231)
Richard (d.1234)
Gilbert (d.1241)
Walter (d.1245)
Anselm (d.1245)
All died without
male heir

Isabel Marshal ⊤ Gilbert de Clare
(d.1240) | earl of Gloucester
     (d.1230)

Richard de Clare
earl of Gloucester (d.1262)

Eva Marshal ⊤ **William de**
(d.1246) | **Braose**
    (d.1230)

Isabella = Dafydd ap Llywelyn
(d.1248) ab Iorwerth (d.1246)
Buillth

Eva (d.1255) = William Cantilupe
    (d.1254) Cilgerran,
    Emlyn, Abergavenny

Maud (d.1301) = Roger Mortimer
    (d.1282) Narberth,
    Radnor, St Clears

William de Braose (d.1211)
lord of Radnor, Builth, Abergavenny, Brecon, Gower, St Clears

Reginald de Braose
(d.1228)

Giles, bishop of
Hereford (d.1215)

William
(d.1210)

Maud Marshal = Hugh
(d.1248) | Bigod
    (d.1225)

Joan Marshal ⊤ Warin de
(d.1234) | Munchensy
    (d.1255)

Joan de Munchensy ⊤ William de
(d.1307) | Valence
    (d.1296)

Eleanor (d.1251) = Humphrey de
Bohun (d.1265)
Haverford, Brecon

See **Family Tree 6**

101

During the 1230s, although Gilbert was able to re-establish the Marshal influence at Court following his brother's rebellion, he had been unable to take Cardigan from Welsh hands. However, the death of Llywelyn brought about another rapid change of circumstances. A short time after his father's death, Dafydd gave homage to Henry III at Gloucester for his ancestral rights in Gwynedd, but was forced to concede to the king the homage of the other Welsh rulers; the southern rulers then travelled to Windsor in June of 1240 to swear their fealty. Furthermore, he had to agree that the lands in the Marches that had been seized from the barons by his father would be subject to arbitration. Conscious of the changing circumstances, an army led by Gilbert's brother, Walter, moved on Cardigan, which he was able to win back swiftly.

When Dafydd did nothing to proceed with the agreed arbitration over the lands that had been seized from them, the Crown tried to settle the matter in court; however, Dafydd remained uncooperative, refusing to attend several arranged meetings. When his patience ran out, Henry organised a campaign into north Wales in 1241. The chronicles report that it was unseasonably dry, allowing Henry's army to move at speed. Dafydd, losing support from the rulers in Wales who supported Gruffudd, was nearly cut off from the safety of his mountain stronghold as he was retreating. Forced to come to humiliating terms with Henry, Dafydd agreed the return of all lands without arbitration and handed his brother, Gruffudd (who he had imprisoned), over to the King, agreeing that a legal arbitration of the brothers' inheritance could happen in the king's court.

Gilbert Marshal was now in a very strong position. One of his first acts was to remove Cynan ap Hywel from Emlyn, to replace him with a new favourite, Maredudd ap Rhys (d.1271), the son of Rhys Gryg. Gilbert also allowed Maredudd to hold Kidwelly as a reward for his loyalty and support, despite the claims of the

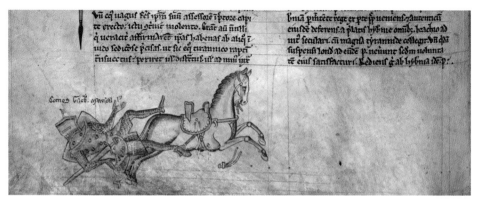

Matthew Paris' *Chronica Maiora II* (MS 016II): depiction of the death of Gilbert Marshal
(© Parker Library, Corpus Christi College, Cambridge)

de Londres heiress. He also extracted an oath of fealty from another Welsh ruler in Ceredigion, that he held his lands from Gilbert and not the king, to the displeasure of Henry. Whilst this had the potential to become a crisis, this was averted when Gilbert, who was not the most skilful competitor at tournaments, given his earlier clerical career, was killed in June 1241. His foot became stuck in a stirrup as he fell from his horse during a tournament that he had attended in defiance of a ban decreed by the king, and he was dragged a considerable distance to his death. His titles of earl of Pembroke and Lord Marshal passed to his younger brother Walter, but not for several months after Gilbert's death, because of the king's anger at Walter's disobedience of royal orders, as Walter had also attended the tournament. When Walter did come to receive his inheritance, it did not include Carmarthen and Cardigan. The king demanded that these two key castles were returned to the Crown, and from then on they were never again granted away.[9] Walter himself lived only until 1245, and when he died his brother Anselm, the last of the sons of William Marshal, would have become the new earl of Pembroke, but he too died within a month without male heirs. Thus, despite having five sons, the Marshal's inheritance failed to pass to a third generation, with the lands divided between his five daughters and the families that they married into, whilst the great Marshal earldom of Pembroke died out and returned to the Crown.

The lightning quick royal campaign of 1241 had restricted Dafydd to his ancestral land of Gwynedd, and, with Gruffudd now held in confinement in the Tower of London, Henry had leverage over Dafydd. Across the central and southern Marches, the dispossessed Marcher lords seized back the lordships that they had lost to Llywelyn ab Iorwerth. In Cemais, Nicholas fitz Martin (d.1296) reaffirmed a grant to the burgesses of Newport in 1241, that had been made by his father before 1216.[10] In Kidwelly, Hawise de Londres finally came into her inheritance in around 1243 when it was restored to her and her third husband, Patrick de Chaworth.[11] Also, Guy de Brian, who would turn out to be a very capable warrior and often present in the south-west, became the lord of Laugharne in 1244.[12]

With the king now holding Tegeingl in north-east Wales, and Carmarthen and Cardigan in the south-west, there was a noticeable increase in the exactions of aggressive royal agents, with consequent Welsh unrest growing at the burdens being placed on them. When Gruffudd, exasperated by his forced confinement in the Tower, fell to his death in 1244 whilst attempting an escape, the threat that the king could use his brother against him was removed from Dafydd. With the shackles of royal administration biting, Dafydd took up arms, starting to style himself 'Prince of Wales' – the first use of the title. Unlike in 1241, when many of the southern Welsh rulers joined the king on his campaign, this time they were united with Dafydd against the overbearing actions of the Crown. Furthermore, there was no powerful earl of Pembroke to exert control. Maredudd ap Rhys Gryg, Maelgwn Fychan ap Maelgwn and Maredudd ab Owain ap Gruffudd all joined the uprising. Patrick de Chaworth and Guy de Brian were two of the Marcher lords in active royal service, but there are scant records of any significant military action by either side in the south.

In summer 1245, Henry assembled a formidable army and moved along the north Welsh coast to quell the rebellion. However, in an exact replica of his father's campaign 34 years earlier, unable to progress into Snowdonia, and with the troops suffering from hunger and persistent skirmishing from the Welsh, Henry was forced to withdraw without achieving a conclusive outcome. The matter was settled, though, when Dafydd died suddenly in February 1246. His death left Gwynedd forfeit as he had been in rebellion as well as dying childless, thus fracturing yet again the alliance of Welsh rulers. In a devastating show of English strength, the king ordered one of his captains, Nicholas de Molis, to dispossess Maelgwn Fychan of his lands in northern Ceredigion, as he had not returned to the loyalty of the king following the death of Dafydd. Nicholas was joined by Maredudd ap Rhys Gryg and Maredudd ab Owain ap Gruffudd, who had again sworn allegiance to the Crown. This combined host moved quickly through northern Ceredigion, which forced Maelgwn Fychan to seek refuge in Gwynedd.

CONCLUSIONS

This chapter started with the Lord Rhys at the height of his powers (though the signs had already set in that these were starting to crumble away), and has described how the violent feuds between his sons and grandsons destroyed forever a united polity of Deheubarth. Although the advent of the Marshal earls of Pembroke brought a new powerful Marcher lord into the region, the chief disruptor was Llywelyn ab Iorwerth, ruler of Gwynedd. He was able to exploit the weakness of the English Crown on the one hand, and on the other the disunity caused by the squabbles between the descendants of the Lord Rhys, to establish his own hegemony over much of the lands of Deheubarth.

As with his ancestors in the tenth and eleventh centuries, Llywelyn's political and military domination depended on his own skills and character. With no formal structure to sustain it, the basis of his power and influence rapidly disappeared after his death. Even so, the opportunity for independent native rule in south-west Wales had become extremely limited: for the best part of 30 years, the descendants of the Lord Rhys had had a choice between accepting the authority and overlordship of the ruler of Gwynedd or giving homage to the English king.

The circumstances and choices made by the grandsons and great-grandsons of the Lord Rhys influenced the course of events over the next 50 years.

The descendants of the Lord Rhys remained fragmented, only uniting when they were in alliance with either the Crown or the ruler of Gwynedd. They fell back on their own power-bases, with the descendants of Gruffudd ap Rhys in northern Ceredigion and the descendants of Rhys Gryg maintaining a hold over Ystrad Tywi and Cantref Bychan. The descendants of Maelgwn ap Rhys were the biggest losers, as the Marcher lords reclaimed their lands following Llywelyn's death. They were pushed back to southern Ceredigion and parts of Cantref Bychan, slowly losing influence until they almost disappear from the records. It is the descendants of Rhys Gryg who would go on to play the more significant role in the events of the region.

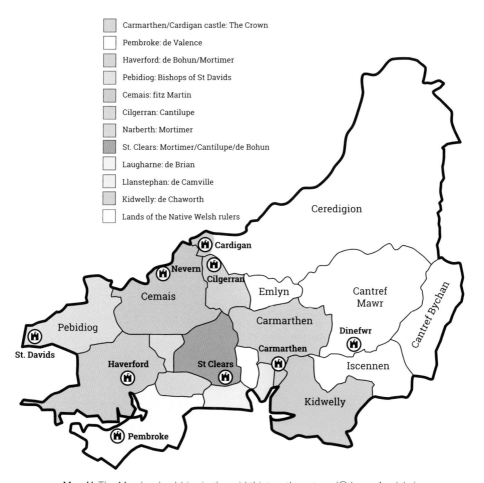

Map 11 The Marcher lordships in the mid thirteenth century (© Jason Appleby)

Llywelyn's domination across Wales had also limited the scope of the Marcher lords. With his death, followed by the subsequent extinction of the Marshal dynasty, the Marcher lords were able to regain their lordships as well as becoming key royal servants in the region. The fitz Martins in Cemais, the de Chaworths, through marriage to Hawise de Londres, in Kidwelly, the de Brians in Laugharne and the de Camvilles at Llanstephan would all play a role in the defence of south Wales in the years leading up to the final conquest in 1283. Furthermore, William de Valence, the king's half-brother, was married to Joan de Munchensy, who was a granddaughter of William Marshal. Through this marriage, he became the lord of Pembroke, which resulted in him attempting to have all the lordships subordinated to him as they had been under the Marshals.

CHAPTER SIX

Llywelyn ap Gruffudd and the end of native rule in Wales

THE RISE OF LLYWELYN AP GRUFFUDD

WHEN Dafydd ap Llywelyn died childless and in rebellion, his nephews responded quickly in an attempt to forestall King Henry III from taking Gwynedd into his own hands, which would have been his right. The eldest two sons of Gruffudd ap Llywelyn, Owain Goch and Llywelyn ap Gruffudd, on the advice of their counsellors, agreed to divide between themselves the ancestral lands of Gwynedd to the west of the River Conwy, together with an offer to cede to the Crown all the lands to the east, the Perfeddwlad. Henry accepted the offer, which was confirmed at the Treaty of Woodstock in 1247. In the south, all the rulers eventually returned to the loyalty of the king. Maelgwn Fychan did come off worse for holding out, losing some of his territory in Cantref Bychan, but he eventually received several *commotes* in Ceredigion as compensation.

Wall painting, possibly Henry III, in Westminster Abbey (© Dean and Chapter of Westminster)

After some six years of comparative peace, the Woodstock agreement was disrupted in 1253 when Henry III supported the claims made by Dafydd, a younger brother of Owain and Llywelyn, to a share of the inheritance according to Welsh custom. Not only did this attempt to further fragment Gwynedd come to naught, but it also provoked a strong response from Llywelyn ap Gruffudd. He initially suggested a compromise whereby Dafydd be given the lands to the east of the Conwy, the Perfeddwlad, now controlled by the Crown; but when the compromise was rejected and negotiation failed in 1255, the brothers took up arms against each other with Llywelyn decisively defeating Owain Goch and Dafydd.

Llywelyn ap Gruffudd now reigned supreme in Gwynedd. At the same time resentment was growing at the harsh nature of the rule imposed by the agents of the Lord Edward in the lands that had been taken under royal control (the king had granted rule of all the Crown lands in the Marches and Wales to his son and heir, the Lord Edward, together with the earldom of Chester). When the Lord Edward visited his Welsh possessions in the Perfeddwlad in 1256, any hope that he would ease their burden and exercise a more balanced lordship was soon dashed. The only course of action the Welsh felt was open to them was to entreat Llywelyn ap Gruffudd to come to their aid, for '... *they preferred to be slain in battle for their liberty than to suffer themselves to be trampled upon in bondage by men alien to them.'*

Llywelyn moved quickly, successfully taking control of the Perfeddwlad within a week, with the support of Maredudd ap Rhys Gryg. Eager to maintain the momentum, Llywelyn headed south, proceeding to take the lands of Meirionnydd for himself, whilst granting the portion of Ceredigion held by the Lord Edward to Maredudd ab Owain, who was again back on the side of the Welsh. After that, Llywelyn moved on Ystrad Tywi where he forced out the English ally, Rhys Fychan, replacing him with Rhys's uncle, and ally of Llywelyn, Maredudd ap Rhys Gryg. To complete his circular rampage across Wales, Llywelyn had time to seize possession of the *commote* of Gwerthrynion from Roger Mortimer on his way back to the north.

The following year, 1257, Llywelyn moved south again, ravaging the English settlements in Kidwelly and Gower, which spurred the royal authorities into action. Stephen Bauzan, an experienced agent of the Crown, was put at the head of a large army which included several Marcher lords, with the goal of restoring Rhys Fychan, an ally of England, to the head of Deheubarth. The chronicles report how the army set out from Carmarthen without deploying scouts. Consequently, as they moved up the valley, they were constantly harassed by Welsh skirmishers from the woods. Matters took a turn for the worse for the English when their ally, Rhys Fychan, fled from the camp to make his way to Dinefwr on his own. Realising that they were in a desperate situation, they moved back towards the safety of English territory. They didn't make it. The rout was the worst defeat of a foreign army in Wales since the battle of Crug Mawr in 1136. With the English presence in Ystrad Tywi destroyed, the Welsh were able to maraud at will. The castle at Carmarthen was still too strongly defended to take. However, nothing could stop the Welsh raiders from ravaging the countryside, destroying the castles of Llanstephan, Laugharne and Narberth.

Later in the year, with Llywelyn himself now in full military array in Cemais, he brokered a reconciliation between Rhys Fychan and Maredudd ap Rhys, who together attacked Newport Castle and sacked it. They were now joined by Maredudd ab Owain before moving south to attack the Marcher lands in Rhos.[1] Nicholas fitz Martin and Guy de Brian, lords of Cemais and Laugharne respectively, had been taken prisoner after the disaster in the Tywi valley. They were held captive for a while but were eventually released on payment of a ransom.[2] In response to these setbacks, Henry III led an army across north Wales as far as Deganwy. It was late in the campaigning season and, unable to make headway into the mountains and with provisions running out, he was forced to withdraw back to Chester.

In 1258, Llywelyn took action to consolidate his gains when he summoned all the other rulers of Wales, including the leading members of the house of Deheubarth, to an assembly to give an oath of allegiance to him on pain of excommunication. Llywelyn was now the undisputed leader of all the Welsh. However, the supremacy of Gwynedd was not something that sat well with everyone. Within a matter of months, Maredudd ap Rhys defected to the English, renouncing the oath he had pledged to Llywelyn. This was because the latter had restored Dinefwr and Carreg Cennen to Rhys Fychan after he had returned to Llywelyn's side – having granted them to Maredudd in 1256, when they were taken from Rhys Fychan as punishment. Maredudd allied himself with the leading royal agent in the area, Patrick de Chaworth, the lord of Kidwelly. When hostilities broke out in the Tywi valley, a series of battles and skirmishes ensued, that resulted in the town of Kidwelly being burned up to the castle gates by the forces led by Maredudd ab Owain and Rhys Fychan. With further fighting near Cilgerran, it was agreed that a meeting should be made to agree a truce. Maredudd ap Rhys and Patrick, acting as seneschal of the king, went with an army to meet senior Welsh representatives. However, the meeting didn't go as planned as, for some reason, the English contingent felt they could surprise the Welsh and so launched an attack:

> When Maredudd and Patrick saw the other men, they broke the truce and rushed upon them. And then Patrick was slain and many knights and foot soldiers along with him.

Maredudd barely escaped but was captured by Llywelyn not long after. At a meeting of Welsh magnates in May 1259 Maredudd was found guilty of treason and taken to Criccieth Castle to be imprisoned.

Llywelyn had demonstrated that any recalcitrant Welsh ruler who dared go against his oath would be dealt with harshly. The truce with the English was renewed, but this did not prevent Llywelyn from the occasional military foray. For

Criccieth Castle: Maredudd ap Rhys (d.1271) was imprisoned here for not supporting
Llywelyn ap Gruffudd (© Crown copyright 2022 Cadw)

example, when he sacked Tenby near Pembroke whilst William de Valence, the
lord of Pembroke, was in exile, having been forced to leave the country following
a violent confrontation with the leading baronial rebel, Simon de Montfort.
Llywelyn's position was strong enough now that he allowed Maredudd to return
to his castle at Dryslwyn, but only upon handing over his eldest son as a hostage
and relinquishing his claim to other castles, including Dinefwr. Llywelyn sought
a permanent treaty with the English Crown to confirm his gains and cement his
legitimacy as ruler of all Wales, but a permanent treaty remained elusive. Instead,
the truce that had been agreed was renewed annually.

Baronial reform and rebellion in England

Meanwhile, in England, another crisis between the Crown and disaffected
barons, led by Simon de Montfort, was emerging, with concerns mounting
over the king's over-generous patronage of his foreign relations (which included
William de Valence), coupled with a vain attempt to put his younger son on the
throne of Sicily, which nearly bankrupted the country. The parliament held at
Oxford in 1258 had forced upon Henry III a series of reforms – the Provisions
of Oxford – and a Council of 24 men (12 nominated by the barons, 12 by the
king) was established to advise the king. Shortly after, the size of the Council
was reduced to 15. With Marcher lords sitting on the Council, there was no
desire to reach a settlement with Llywelyn, that would formalise his gains and
his position. Although Henry III rejected the Provisions of Oxford in 1261, he

continued to resist further negotiations with Llywelyn. Hostilities broke out in both 1262 and 1263. On each occasion the focus was the central Marches, with Llywelyn seizing the *cantref* of Maelienydd from the Mortimers. After this, as a sign of how he perceived his own position, Llywelyn began to use the title 'Prince of Wales and Lord of Snowdon'.

Eventually, the divisions in England moved towards open war when the baronial opposition, led by the charismatic Simon de Montfort, broke out in full rebellion. In early 1264, Llywelyn allied with Simon de Montfort, possibly out of frustration at the lack of progress in securing a permanent treaty from the Crown, and in the hope that Simon would prevail. He was also exasperated by the support given by the Lord Edward to his own rebellious brother, Dafydd.

Events came to a head in England in May 1264 at the battle of Lewes. In a brilliant military action, de Montfort routed the king's forces, taking the king, the Lord Edward and the royal family captive. Simon de Montfort now controlled the government, using King Henry as a puppet, granting charters in the king's name but strictly according to his own will. Llywelyn's bet paid off when, in June 1265, he finally obtained the treaty he had sought. The Treaty of Pipton granted to Llywelyn, by right of his sovereignty as Prince of Wales and to the heirs of his body, his rights in all the lands he held, including several of his annexations in the Marches, and the fealty of all the rulers in Wales. The treaty was witnessed by Rhys Fychan, Hywel ap Rhys Gryg and Maredudd ab Owain ap Gruffudd, leading men of Deheubarth, thus confirming their subordinate role to the dominant Llywelyn, Prince of Wales.[3]

Battle of Lewes memorial on the site of the ruins of Lewes Priory, East Sussex

Llywelyn had finally achieved the recognition that had been sought by both his grandfather and himself. In reality, however, the treaty was worthless as the administration of Simon de Montfort was already collapsing. A few weeks earlier, the Lord Edward, aided by Roger Mortimer (d.1282), had escaped his captivity in Hereford to plan a campaign to defeat de Montfort. The two armies met at Evesham on 4 August 1265, with the battle resulting in the death of Simon de Montfort and the slaughter of the rebel troops. Following Evesham, the English government focused on restoring peace to the divided country, and thus two years passed before the Crown was able to give attention to Wales. When it did, the resultant Treaty of Montgomery, signed on 29 September 1267, confirmed much of what Llywelyn had received in the now obsolete Treaty of Pipton. Finally, the undivided English Crown recognised by treaty Llywelyn's rights to the title 'Prince of Wales'. The agreement accorded to Llywelyn, and not to the English Crown, the homage of all the other native rulers in Wales, with one exception – Maredudd ap Rhys of Dryslwyn (d.1271). In recognition of his support, Maredudd was allowed to hold his lands from the Crown and not from Llywelyn; however, Maredudd ap Rhys's vassalage was bought by Llywelyn for 5,000 marks (both the possibility and the amount had been stipulated in the Treaty) shortly before his death in 1271, thus bringing all the Welsh lords into his fealty. As John Lloyd has pointed out in his *History of Carmarthenshire*, it also demonstrated how little the English were concerned about Llywelyn accumulating more power in south-west Wales – and, indeed, there followed a period of relative peace.[4]

TRIUMPH LEADS TO FURTHER CONFLICT

The Treaty of Montgomery undoubtedly represented a high point in Llywelyn ap Gruffudd's life and career. However, within ten years the treaty had unravelled, and within 16 years, when Llywelyn had been hounded to his death and his brother executed, native rule in Wales was effectively extinguished. The key aspects that contributed to this dramatic reversal were:

- the treaty itself contained several ambiguities, particularly with regards to rights over lands within the central region of the Marches, which created increasing friction between Llywelyn and the Crown, together with areas of localised conflict. Furthermore, arbitration that had been agreed never happened.

- the treaty required Llywelyn to pay 25,000 marks to the Crown in instalments, which rose to 30,000 when he purchased the homage of

Maredudd ap Rhys. This was an enormous amount that severely over-stretched his resources, resulting in late payments of the annual amount owed from as early as 1270, and later defaulting on the payments. Not only did this cause tension between Llywelyn and the Crown, but also between Llywelyn and the people of Wales who greatly resented the methods used by Llywelyn to raise the money, leading to hostility and loss of support in Wales.

- if the political status-quo in England had remained, the ambiguities, irritations and local conflicts might easily have been resolved; instead, a seismic change took place, which began to lead to outright conflict. In 1270, the Lord Edward left England to go on Crusade, leaving his lands and children in the care of a council of five custodians. When Henry III died in 1272, with the Lord Edward still absent, the council of custodians (including Roger Mortimer, d.1282, of Wigmore) acted as regents until his return in 1274. During this period, Llywelyn's relationship with the Crown began to deteriorate. Not surprisingly, with Roger Mortimer to the fore, the regency government was unsympathetic to Llywelyn's complaints that the terms of the treaty were not being fulfilled. Another point of friction between Llywelyn and the regency government arose when he built a new castle on his lands at Dolforwyn, but within sight of the royal castle at Montgomery. When the Lord Edward finally returned in 1274 to be crowned Edward I, for the first time in three-quarters of a century the throne was occupied by a monarch who was an experienced war leader and administrator; one with a strong personality and the personal authority to impose his will on others. Furthermore, given the loss by his grandfather of most of the Angevin empire on the Continent, his energies would be directed to his lands north of the English Channel.

- during 1274, Llywelyn became aware of a plot to kill him, which had been instigated by his own brother, Dafydd, and Gruffudd ap Gwenwynwyn, the ruler of southern Powys. Enraged, Llywelyn took up arms against them, but they fled to England, where the new king, Edward I, not only gave them refuge, but also tacit support to raid the border. Inevitably, these actions inflamed an already tense relationship

- whilst allied with Simon de Montfort, it had been arranged for Llywelyn to marry Simon's daughter, the 13-year-old Eleanor. After the battle of

Evesham, de Montfort's family fled to the Continent; however, in 1275, while Eleanor was still on the Continent, Llywelyn was legally married to her by proxy. Immediately, Eleanor set sail to join Llywelyn, but her ship was captured, and Eleanor held captive at Windsor for nearly three years (only being permitted to join Llywelyn one year after his defeat in 1277).

Henry III tomb effigy (© Dean and Chapter of Westminster)

It was against this background of tension and legitimate complaints on both sides that events spiralled to open conflict. Not surprisingly, Llywelyn chose not to attend the coronation of Edward I in August 1274. Twelve months later, in August 1275, Llywelyn was summoned to Chester to give homage to the new king, but Llywelyn refused to attend on the grounds that Edward I was sheltering his enemies, Dafydd and Gruffudd ap Gwenwynwyn, and the location was in hostile territory. When three more summonses were issued and ignored, armed conflict was becoming inevitable. In November 1276, war was declared, and Edward I made plans for a three-pronged attack in the southern, central and northern Marches, with the goal to bring all of Wales to submission.

By the campaigning season of 1277, the armies were assembled and ready. Edward I himself led the northern army; the earl of Lincoln and Roger Mortimer, the central one; whilst the southern army was led by Payn fitz Patrick de Chaworth, lord of Kidwelly. The southern army met with little opposition, particularly as the descendants of the Lord Rhys either quickly allied with the English or fled to join Llywelyn in Gwynedd. Rhys ap Maredudd, reverting to his old allegiances, submitted to Payn early, enabling him to keep Dryslwyn; while Rhys Wyndod, the heir to Rhys Fychan (d.1271) and the great-grandson of Rhys Gryg, held out a bit longer. He signed a treaty that kept him in the king's peace, but he had to give up the ancestral home of Dinefwr, which was never recovered.

When the army in the central region captured Llywelyn's new castle of Dolforwyn after a siege of two weeks, and the army led by the king progressed across the north, building castles at Flint and Rhuddlan and capturing Anglesey, Llywelyn was forced to submit and agree a humiliating settlement. Although the Treaty of Aberconwy, sealed in November 1277, allowed Llywelyn to retain the title of 'Prince of Wales', it was now a hollow title. He was confined to his ancestral lands of Gwynedd Uch Conwy, which he could hold for his lifetime, but had to agree to Dafydd's hereditary right to part of the land after his death. He was forced to cede other land to the king, and retained the homage of only five minor lords, with the rest reverting to the king. These included Rhys ap Maredudd and Rhys Wyndod, descendants of Rhys Gryg, who both travelled to pay homage to the king in person in the autumn of that year.

In January 1278 a commission was established with the aim of determining the rightful owners of the disputed territory in Wales, comprised of the bailiffs of many of the Marcher barons. During the enquiries in 1279, John Giffard (d.1299) claimed the lordship of Cantref Bychan, with the castle of Llandovery, against the already diminished Rhys Wyndod, by right of his wife Matilda Clifford. The Commission deliberated for a couple of years, finding in favour of Giffard in 1281, who was one of

Edward I: conquered Wales in 1282–83 and established the Principality to govern the lands annexed to the Crown
(© National Portrait Gallery, London)

the king's favourites. By the end of the proceedings, the Welsh ceased attending the meetings, probably because they were preparing to dispute ownership via different means, which became clear in 1282.[5]

The settlement imposed by the Treaty of Aberconwy lasted for only five years. With grievances mounting about the harsh rule of the royal administration in the Perfeddwlad, on Palm Sunday (22 March) 1282 Dafydd attacked Hawarden Castle, killing the garrison and taking captive the commanders. Almost at once, several rulers across Wales rose in support. In the south-west, Rhys Wyndod and several descendants of the Lord Rhys rose in rebellion. They sacked the castles that had been taken from them in 1277 at Llandovery and Iscennen. Rhys ap Maredudd ap Rhys Gryg, though, would remain loyal to the Crown throughout the events of 1282–83, supporting the royal army.

Llywelyn did not join the rebellion immediately, but as the uprising grew, he was left with little choice - he either took command, or ceded authority to his brother Dafydd. The conflict in 1282 was not as straightforward as it had been in 1277, given the element of a popular revolt against the harsh rule of the English overlord. An English army suffered a heavy defeat near Llandeilo in eastern Cantref Mawr, with the heir to William de Valence, lord of Pembroke, William, killed in the action. The English resources, however, were too great and soon the situation was back under their control. Edward again led an army into Gwynedd. Attempts to agree a peaceful resolution failed when the terms offered by the king were deemed too humiliating – Llywelyn to be pensioned off in exile in England, while Dafydd would be required to go on Crusade to the Holy Lands, never to return. Not surprisingly, the conflict continued.

Encircled within Snowdonia, in a desperate move to break out, Llywelyn led a force into the central Marches, where he was ambushed and killed near Builth on 11 December 1282. The instigator of the rebellion, Dafydd, now styling himself 'Prince of Wales and Lord of Snowdon', became a fugitive in his own lands. He evaded capture for several months, but with his pleas for mercy falling on deaf ears, he was eventually captured in June 1283, tried for treason at Shrewsbury and sentenced to an horrific death.

THE STATUTES OF WALES (OR RHUDDLAN) 1284

The deaths of Llywelyn and Dafydd resulted in the forfeiture of their lands to the king, together with the lands of the other Welsh rulers who had adhered to them. *Pura Wallia* was now annexed to the Crown, and Edward I created a new dispensation, with the majority of the lands retained under the control of the Crown. Although these lands, previously under native Welsh rule, were

Carmarthen Castle: a royal administrative centre for south Wales (© Neil Ludlow)

annexed by the king, and were to be administered along English lines, they were not integrated into the administrative and judicial structures of England, but rather remained the private domain of the English king, becoming known as 'The Principality of Wales'.

The Statute of Wales, issued at Rhuddlan in 1284, set out the laws and governance structures for the new territories. The ancestral lands of Gwynedd to the west of the River Conwy were divided into four counties (Conwy, Anglesey, Caernarfon, Merionnydd). In west Wales, as the king was already in possession of Carmarthen and Cardigan – and, since 1277, the lordship of Llanbadarn – he attached to these castles the newly acquired territories for purposes of administration. The new shire of Carmarthenshire was formed by attaching Cantref Mawr, with its castles of Dinefwr and Dryslwyn, to the existing lands that belonged to the castles; while Cardigan Castle formed the basis for the new shire of Cardiganshire. The two new shires constituted the Crown lands of west Wales, administered on behalf of the king by the Justice of west Wales, with the centre of government at Carmarthen Castle. The Statute of Wales did not impose

English law wholesale on the Principality, but rather blended English and Welsh, with English law pertaining to criminal cases, but Welsh law retained for other aspects, including partible inheritance. While Edward I stamped his authority in stone across the north and centre of Wales, with an enormous building programme of majestic and dominant castles, there was no need in the south and west with the royal castles of Carmarthen and Cardigan already in place, supported by the host of castles of the Marcher lordships, such as Pembroke, Cilgerran, Kidwelly and Laugharne.

The Principality of Wales and the Marcher lordships

The Statute of Wales thus formalised the distinction and division that had developed in south-west Wales during the previous two centuries – the areas that lay along the coast where Marcher lordships had been formed, and which had mainly remained in the control of the Marcher lords, continued as such. The lands that had remained mainly under native rule were annexed to the Crown, with the exception of Iscennen, where a new Marcher lordship was formed from a *commote* in southern Cantref Bychan, which had previously been under the control of the ruler of Deheubarth. It was granted to John Giffard in 1284, who, as the heir of the Cliffords, was also confirmed in Cantref Bychan. It should be noted that this happened more extensively elsewhere. In north-east Wales, three of the four *cantrefi* of the Perfeddwlad, and the lands of the rulers of northern Powys, were granted to Edward I's commanders and favourites as new Marcher lordships. Meanwhile, in recognition of his own and his predecessors support for the Crown, the ruler of southern Powys, Gruffudd ap Gwenwynwyn, was allowed to keep his lands, though these were now held from the king as a baron of England, thus forming Powys into a new Marcher lordship.

The Statute of Wales did not apply to the Marcher lordships. By default, therefore, it institutionalised the Marcher lordships' independent status, with their own laws and jurisdictions, lying between the realm of England and the king's lands in the west and north of Wales. After two centuries of conflict and fluctuation, although there would be some minor changes, the structure of the Marcher lordships in the south and west, that had evolved over that period, remained in place for the next 250 years until the Laws in Wales Acts of 1536 and 1542 abolished the Principality and the powers of the Marcher lords.

Conclusions

Unlike his predecessors, Edward had decided to end native rule in *Pura Wallia*, but what prompted him to do so? The answer can be found by examining the circumstances that had changed by 1282–83. As the previous chapters have shown, from well before the arrival of the Normans, Welsh rulers had accepted, and at times sought, the overlordship of the Anglo-Saxon kings of Wessex and England. With lands that spanned the Channel, (which, during the reign of Henry II, extended to the Pyrenees) creating problems and priorities elsewhere, the Norman and Anglo-Norman kings were happy to use their overlordship to exert their will in Wales. When Welsh rulers threatened the stability of the region, military campaigns gave a sharp reminder of where power lay, while the barons were permitted to take lands on the fringes and in areas with a vacuum in local leadership. (The previous two chapters have illustrated how this balance of power changed.)

The loss of Normandy and most of the Crown's possessions on the Continent by King John in 1204 switched the focus of the Crown onto the British Isles for the first time in nearly a century and a half. However, the distractions experienced during the reign of King John, with the rebellion by his barons that led to Magna Carta, quickly followed by the minority of Henry III and the later baronial wars, severely weakened the authority and capacity of the English Crown.

The polities created by Llywelyn ab Iorwerth and Llywelyn ap Gruffudd, which spanned most of Wales, now posed more of a threat to England than the warring rivalries of the disparate kingdoms of the eleventh and twelfth centuries. However, this supremacy of a single ruler also contained within it a twin-threat. Firstly, by the thirteenth century concepts of overlordship, fealty and homage had become much more formalised; whereas, in earlier centuries accepting the overlordship of the Anglo-Saxon kings could have a fairly loose meaning, and was dependant on the strength of individual rulers, this was no longer the case. A consequence of the agreements made by Llywelyn ab Iorwerth, Dafydd ap Llywelyn and Llywelyn ap Gruffudd with the English Crown was that the feudal relationship that had been established meant that the lands of the princes of Gwynedd reverted to the Crown if they committed treason or died without heirs. After the Treaty of Montgomery in 1267 – in which Llywelyn ap Gruffudd was granted the fealty of the other rulers in Wales and he in turn gave fealty on their behalf to the Crown – the other Welsh rulers were also subject to the lands being forfeit if they rebelled. Secondly, a single larger polity could be easier to defeat than numerous smaller ones.

There were times when both King John and Henry III could have invoked the forfeiture of the princes of Gwynedd, but didn't have the strength, resources or desire to do so. In contrast, Edward I came to the throne, at the age of 33, as an experienced administrator, warrior and commander of men, with the strength of personality to unite the barons. As noted above (and clearly illustrated by Professor David Carpenter)[6] Edward was not burdened by the question of the lost Norman lands of 1204. That matter had been settled and his only concern in France was the English hold over Gascony. He also had enormous sums of money at his disposal, and was not afraid to spend it where necessary.

Even so, it would be wrong to use the benefit of hindsight to create the view that it was inevitable that Edward I would end native rule in Wales. We can identify the factors that were moving things in that direction, not least the stand-off that developed between Llywelyn ap Gruffudd and Edward I; but it was still not inevitable. Even in 1277, although Edward I was in a position to annex all of Wales, the Treaty of Aberconwy showed that he had not yet resolved to do that; he was content to humiliate Llywelyn ap Gruffudd by confining him to the heartlands of Gwynedd. In the end, it was something that was both impulsive and personal that pushed the King to impose the final solution that ended native rule. Exasperated by the further rebellion in 1282, he felt a deep personal betrayal and great anger that this had been instigated by Dafydd ap Gruffudd. Edward had protected and supported him when Dafydd had been exiled, and had set him up with large estates. The personal anger was reflected in the cruel death meted out to Dafydd when he was finally captured.

POSTSCRIPT: THE REBELLION OF RHYS AP MAREDUDD 1287–92

The preceding chapters have shown how, after the death of Rhys Gryg in 1234, the control of Ystrad Tywi split between two branches of Rhys's descendants: the lords of Dinefwr (the principal castle) were Rhys Gryg's son, Rhys Mechyll (d.1244), his son Rhys Fychan (d.1271), followed by Rhys Wyndod (d.1302); whilst the lords of Dryslwyn were Rhys Gryg's son Maredudd ap Rhys (d.1271), followed by his son, Rhys ap Maredudd (d.1292). The first branch, the lords of Dinefwr, generally remained loyal to Llywelyn ap Gruffudd after he had asserted his supremacy across Wales. In contrast, the second branch, the lords of Dryslwyn, tended to ally with the English king. In 1277, with war approaching, Llywelyn ap Gruffudd made determined efforts to win the support of Rhys ap Maredudd, but to no avail with Rhys remaining loyal to Edward I. Although Rhys Wyndod, lord of Dinefwr, initially sided with Llywelyn, he made his peace with Edward I in time to avoid losing all his lands. However, the king took over control of the symbolically significant castle of Dinefwr.

Although he had not received the rewards that he might have expected after 1277 (in part because his influence had led to other rulers in the south supporting

Dryslwyn Castle: from here, Rhys ap Maredudd ap Rhys Gryg broke into rebellion in 1287
(© Crown copyright 2022 Cadw)

the English Crown), Rhys ap Maredudd again remained on the English side during the wars of 1282–83. Again, Rhys Wyndod supported Llywelyn, but this time he was captured and imprisoned in England until his death 20 years later. With Rhys ap Maredudd being the only lord of the lands of Deheubarth who was loyal to the king, there was more scope for him to be rewarded. Accordingly, Rhys received further lands, becoming the lord of all of Cantref Mawr except for one *commote*, which significantly contained the castle of Dinefwr, which was still held by the king. Despite this, with the addition of two *commotes* in Cardigan, Rhys was well placed.

Yet, a few years later, Rhys rebelled against the English. In the summer of 1287, he and his followers, catching the English by surprise, seized the castles of Llandovery, Dinefwr and Carreg Cennen, raiding as far as Swansea and Aberystwyth. However, the rebellion soon lost momentum, and by September a royal army led by Earl Edmund of Cornwall, having recaptured the castles, moved on to take Rhys's own castles of Dryslwyn and Newcastle Emlyn. Rhys, though, escaped to raise a force that in November retook Newcastle Emlyn and raided into the lands of Llandovery. As in September, Rhys was defeated by another English army, becoming a fugitive until he was betrayed, and sent captive to Edward I in York, where he was convicted and executed as a traitor in 1292.

It is possible to identify some of the factors that built up resentment in Rhys and probably caused him to turn against Edward I. His hopes of operating as an independent lord were severely curtailed when the king took personal control of the lands of Carmarthen (Rhys had been promised exemption from attendance at royal courts except those on royal lands, but Edward's acquisition of Carmarthen meant that Rhys could now be held to account in those courts). The creation in 1280 of the powerful position of Justiciar in south and west Wales, answerable only to the king, further restricted Rhys; and from 1281 the Justiciar was an assertive official, Robert Tibetot, who clashed frequently with Rhys. Although Rhys was undoubtedly feeling more and more constrained, the interesting question is why he chose to rebel, given the way in which Llywelyn and Dafydd ap Gruffudd, with far greater resources, had been crushed only five years earlier. While the answer to this lies in part in Rhys's thwarted ambitions to become a significant ruler in south Wales, the other aspect lies in the complexity of the relationships that had developed between Welsh rulers, Marcher lords and the English Crown. Rhys may well not have fully realised that, although he had been useful to the king while Llywelyn ruled in Gwynedd, the destruction of Llywelyn had effectively lessened his usefulness. Furthermore, in 1285, Rhys had married Ada, the sister of John Hastings, lord of Abergavenny and Cilgerran. Related by marriage now to a great Marcher lord, it is possible that Rhys began to identify himself with them and the independent powers that they exercised. If he did so, he was to become swiftly disillusioned.

CHAPTER SEVEN

Consolidation, decline and the abolition of the Marcher lordships

THE governance of the Principality of Wales and the independent powers of the Marcher lords survived for a further 250 years after the 1284 Statute of Wales. The Principality of Wales, and the powers of the Marcher lords, were removed by the Laws in Wales Acts of 1536 and 1542 – sometimes later referred to as the 'Acts of Union' [of England and Wales]. The focus of this book has been the circumstances that shaped the formation of the Marcher lordships, and the unique powers wielded by the lords; however, it is necessary briefly to outline later developments to show why those powers were eventually dissolved.

The structure of the Marcher lordships in south-west Wales was complicated by the two powerful centres at Pembroke and Carmarthen (the latter being an administrative and judicial centre for the southern part of the Principality of Wales after 1284). The lord of Pembroke claimed jurisdiction at his court over every lordship in Pembrokeshire with mixed success. This made for a complicated political picture in most of the lordships. For example, in 1376 the lord of Cemais complained that his subjects were being unjustly summoned to the court at Pembroke, and if they refused they would be imprisoned.[1]

Another development in the south-west was the steady trend through which the ownership of the lordships changed. The extinction of a family through death without a male heir, such as that befalling the Marshals and the de Braoses, resulted in their lands being distributed between the families that the heiresses married into. Across the whole of the March the turnover was such that, of the leading families in 1284, only three survived at the end of the fourteenth century, and these all had their power-bases in the middle March. Consolidation was the dominant theme, with the overall number of Marcher lords reduced from 25 to 15 by 1400.

Map 12 (overleaf) illustrates the concentration of lordships across the March into the control of fewer families. One aspect that stands out from the map is that this trend is slightly less pronounced in the south-west. This was probably caused by a number of factors: the control by St Davids of two of the lordships;

the dominance of Pembroke; the proximity to the Crown lands of the Principality and the administrative centres of Carmarthen and Cardigan; and complicated inheritances that led to divided ownership.

A strong factor in the south-west was the increasing influence of the Crown. When the families of the hereditary Marcher lords died out, or their lands were forfeited through treason, the lordships passed into the ownership of the Crown of England – or, in the case of two lordships, became the private property of the monarch. The lordships of Iscennen and Kidwelly had become part of the Duchy of Lancaster. After Henry Bolingbroke, duke of Lancaster, seized the Crown in 1399, one of his first acts as king was to decree that the lands of the duchy should be held separately from all other Crown possessions, and should descend through the monarchy as a private estate. Around the beginning of the fifteenth century, only the lesser lordships of Cemais, Narberth, Laugharne and Cantref Bychan were not held by the Crown, with Cemais and Cantref Bychan held by the same family.

The composition of the families also changed after 1284. In 1200, Pembroke was the only lordship held by an earl, William Marshal. In 1300, that number had risen to seven of the ten earls in England holding Marcher lordships. In 1400, that number was still over half, with nine of the seventeen earls holding the title of Marcher lord. Naturally, these powerful men had interests throughout the realm. Not only did they have extensive land holdings elsewhere, but they were also active on the political stage of England. Although it had little impact on the south-west directly, the Despenser wars during the reign of Edward II involved most of the lords in the region, and resulted in the extinction of the Giffard line in Iscennen. Later still, the Hundred Years War of Edward III's reign occupied the major barons of England for much of the fourteenth century and early fifteenth century; indeed, the Hastings earls of Pembroke were invested with their earldom whilst in France, upon attaining their majority. The Marcher lordships were also fertile recruiting ground for the soldiers required for the expeditions to the Continent.

Another result of the concentration of ownership, and the establishment of the absentee lord, was that the economics of the lordships changed in the fourteenth and fifteenth centuries, as the lords stopped farming their own demesne lands, instead establishing tenants who then paid rent. This was an easier system to administer from afar, with a steward or other official appointed to collect the rents, or indeed to pay a flat fee to manage the lordship themselves. It was not just rents that provided revenues for the lord. Fines for all manner of items were still a key earner. As one example, *Amobr*, a traditional tax on Welsh tenants, that was originally paid when a woman lost her virginity, became institutionalised and lost its original purpose, becoming a tax on marriage and also sexual activity outside

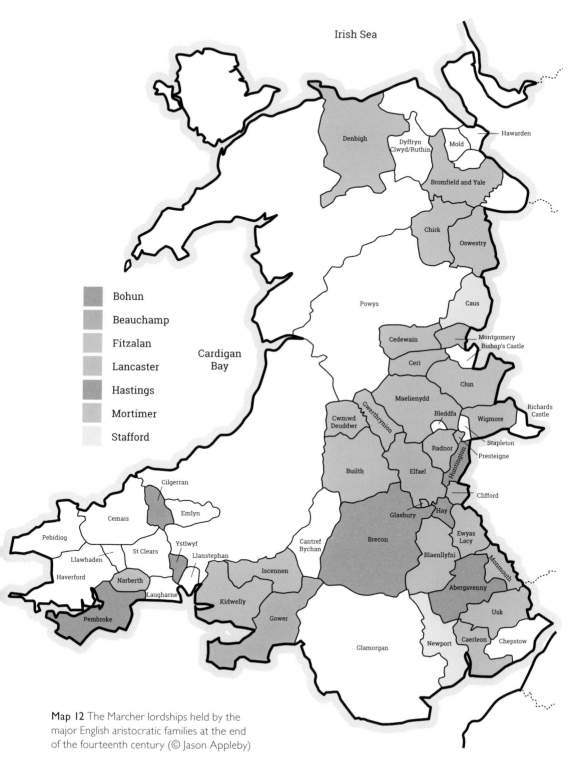

Map 12 The Marcher lordships held by the major English aristocratic families at the end of the fourteenth century (© Jason Appleby)

of marriage. In fact, while the virginity tax could only be levied once, the new tax could be levied for any proven sexual activity, until a woman was declared a common prostitute and no longer had to pay! This tax raised more than £21 in 1395 in Kidwelly, a significant sum.[2] These sources of revenue were not confined to individuals either. Fines for the general misbehaviour of a community – for example, hunting in forests or using the wood without consent – could result in a significant financial penalty. With the management of lordships left to local officials, they often 'franchised' their office by paying a flat fee and then extracting as much as they could from the lord's subjects.[3] This could lead to an abuse of power in the lordship, with an unscrupulous agent extorting the maximum amount from the tenantry with little regard for the well-being of the lord's subjects.

A good lord would try to make sure that there was a balance between revenue and the well-being of his subjects. This was difficult to manage when a lordship was spread across the entire March. An example of how one powerful family, the Mortimers, did so was that of their receiver-general Walter Brugge. The Mortimers were the largest landowners in the March by 1400. Because of this, it was necessary to use an officer like Walter to visit their estates and perform audits. He travelled by horse from the Mortimer's main residence at Ludlow Castle, riding as far as their lordship at Narberth. He even stayed in the friendly confines of Laugharne Castle on his return to Ludlow, a journey that took nearly a month and covered 300 miles.[4] It should be noted that revenues from a Marcher lordship often formed a meaningful portion of a lord's overall revenue. The Hastings revenues from their Marcher estates were valued at over £1,000 per annum at the end of the fourteenth century, a significant sum. The Duchy of Lancaster also received over £1,000 annually in revenues, of which £650 was raised in Kidwelly and Iscennen.[5]

Significantly, with an absentee lord, justice could be farmed out to powerful local landowners. With little central authority to assure fair practice, justice could be bought and sold, which contributed to the growing reputation that the March of Wales was a lawless place. In the middle of the fifteenth century, that abuse of power could also come from the royally controlled Principality, as happened at Carmarthen in the middle of the fifteenth century.

When native rule of Wales was extinguished in 1282–84, many Marcher lordships, including those in the south-west, lost their strategic significance as a defensive region or a staging post for attacks against the Welsh. However, there were exceptions in the south-west. The miles of exposed coastline meant that there was always a fear of French attack during the many years of war. This fear became heightened during the most significant rebellion of the post-conquest era, that of Owain Glyn Dŵr. The rise of the absentee landlord and the subsequent aggressive management of Marcher estates had created discontent amongst the local populations. This combined with the usurpation of Richard II by the Lancastrian, Henry Bolingbroke, to further divide loyalties.

The rebellion began as a local dispute between Glyn Dŵr and the Marcher lord Reginald Grey (d.1440) of Ruthin in north Wales. However, Pembroke became embroiled when Glyn Dŵr's forces moved south in 1401, defeating a local army raised from the non-Welsh tenants of the south-west. Over the ensuing years the rebellion affected all parts of Wales. In 1403, when many of the leading local inhabitants defected to the rebel cause, it was only a crucial military action by Thomas of Carew that defeated a large Welsh contingent near St Clears, which prevented further gains. In 1405, Glyn Dŵr struck an alliance with France, creating the threat of an imminent French invasion. Indeed, the French did land in August with a contingent of troops, and they and the rebel army destroyed many of the towns of the south-west, including the castle of Carmarthen. It was only on payment of a fine of £200 that the locals were able to secure a truce to prevent further destruction; something which harked back to the days of Llywelyn ab Iorwerth in the early thirteenth century. Although such a local deal was forbidden by the Crown during the rebellion, the need for self-preservation outweighed the threat of a royal sanction. In the end it was a wise move, as the rebellion began to falter from 1406, and was finished by 1410. However, the damage that was caused to many of the towns and lordships in the region was significant, resulting in economic decline.

As noted above, management of estates was increasingly placed in the hands of local people. One such was Gruffudd ap Nicholas (d.c.1460), who was the deputy-justiciar of the southern part of the Principality based at Carmarthen. Gruffudd and his sons had a reputation for ruthless management, once securing the Marcher lordship of Newcastle Emlyn by preventing, through intimidation, the appointed lord from ever trying to take possession – thus keeping the lordship in their family, which was never challenged. Another example of this lawlessness was the raids into Pembroke in 1451 by armed men loyal to

Monument to Llywelyn ap Gruffudd Fychan of Caeo, in the castle bailey at Llandovery. During Glyn Dŵr's War of Liberation, Henry IV led an army through Llandovery in search of Glyn Dŵr. Llywelyn was publicly hung, drawn and quartered before the king for refusing to betray Glyn Dŵr and the cause of Welsh freedom
(© Philip Hume)

Gruffudd, from Carmarthen and Ceredigion, extorting and kidnapping leading locals for profit. The king sent men to deal with this disorder, but the machinations of local justice were controlled by Gruffudd with the result that he was pardoned – although this did stop the raiding.[6]

The Crown was not oblivious to Gruffudd's abuse of power in Carmarthen. One aspect of the attempt to restrain him was the appointment in 1452 of an influential earl of Pembroke, Jasper Tudor (d.1495), Henry vi's half-brother through their mother Catherine of Valois. Unlike many of his predecessors, Jasper was often at Pembroke and took a direct interest in bringing order back to the south-west, which he achieved with some difficulty. The Tudor connection with Pembroke was to have profound significance.

In 1457, a young Henry Tudor (d.1509) was born at Pembroke Castle to Edmund Tudor, Jasper's brother, and Margaret Beaufort (d.1509). Although, as the sons of Catherine of Valois (the widow of Henry v), Jasper and Edmund were half-brothers to Henry vi, their father was a commoner, Owen Tudor, thus they had no English royal blood. Margaret Beaufort, though, could claim descent from Edward iii, albeit a tenuous claim as her grandfather had been one of the children of the relationship between John of Gaunt and Katherine Swynford: born illegitimate, her grandfather and his siblings had been legitimised when Gaunt was able to marry Katherine, following the death of his wife. Although, as Margaret's son, it was an extremely tenuous link to the throne, a combination of circumstances, luck and perseverance would bring Henry Tudor to the throne.

Henry's father, Edmund, had died three months before his birth at Carmarthen Castle, following his capture in the disturbances of the early years of the Wars of the Roses. In this way, Jasper played a key role in protecting and ensuring the survival of his nephew. South-west Wales had been a Lancastrian stronghold, following many years of patronage by the Lancastrian kings to promote local supporters. Accordingly, when Edward iv (d.1483), a Yorkist rival, came to the throne in 1461, he appointed one of his most loyal servants, William Herbert (d.1469) to be earl of Pembroke. With only a brief interlude in 1470–71, Edward iv and the Yorkists were in power until 1485. Significantly, however, the sudden death of Edward in 1483, followed by the accession of his brother, Richard iii, at the expense of the dead king's son, Edward v – presented Henry Tudor with an opportunity to make his own move for the Crown.

Jasper Tudor and his nephew, Henry, had fled into exile in Brittany when the Yorkists were in control. They now recognised that the disputed succession presented them with an opportunity to stake Henry's claim to the throne. Sailing to Wales in 1485, they landed near Haverfordwest (the 'west' was added to

Henry Tudor: the future Henry VII was born at Pembroke Castle in 1557 (© Philip Hume)

differentiate it from Hereford), then marched through Pembroke, gathering forces as they went. One key ally to Henry Tudor was to be Rhys ap Thomas (d.1525), the grandson of Gruffudd ap Nicholas. However, he did not commit straight away, having been an ally of Richard III. When the Tudor army met the king's army at Bosworth Field in 1485, Rhys, though, *did* side with the Tudors and their Lancastrian heritage. It is even claimed that he struck the fatal blow that killed Richard.

Henry Tudor was duly crowned Henry VII, thus bringing in the Tudor age. Jasper Tudor was reinstated as the earl of Pembroke until his death in 1495. Jasper's position as the king's main agent in south Wales was then taken by Rhys ap Thomas, who was now able fully to exploit the benefits of having supported Henry VII. He became one of the most prominent figures in south Wales over the next years. He was able to operate supreme in the region, even becoming a Knight of the Garter in 1507, which he celebrated lavishly at his residence, Carew Castle, which had also come into his hands. The death of Henry VII in 1509 did not diminish his career, and he continued to play a significant role in Wales and the security of the south-west until his death in 1525.

The loss of such a powerful figure in south Wales led to some significant changes. Rhys's heir was his grandson, Rhys ap Gruffudd; however, he was not accorded the status and titles of his grandfather, which instead went to Walter Devereux, Lord Ferrers. Frustrated and disappointed, Rhys's conduct turned increasingly lawless, culminating in 1529 in armed conflict with the men of Lord Ferrers at Carmarthen. In a sign that times had changed in the March and of the growing intolerance of the power exerted by his family, Rhys was imprisoned in the Tower where he was executed in 1531 on charges of treason (which were probably trumped up by Henry VIII).

At the same time, the body of regional governance that became known as the Council in the Marches of Wales, had been gradually growing in importance. Its origins lay in the household council created by Edward IV in 1471, to administer the considerable lands and estates of his infant eldest son and heir, Prince Edward. Two years later, the council was enlarged when the three year-old Prince was established at Ludlow with his own court and with responsibility for the Principality, the county of Chester and most of the Crown-controlled Marcher lordships. Although its primary purpose, as a household council, was to manage the prince's affairs and estates, its royal connection and local presence created opportunities for it to be used in other ways, and it began to acquire further ad hoc political and judicial roles. Although the Council lapsed during the reign of Richard III, it was recreated by Henry VII, when he gave a similar role to his seven-year-old eldest son, Prince Arthur. Although it was still a prerogative body (one that existed purely on the instruction of the king), it continued to be given more judicial powers over the Principality and the Marcher lordships, particularly in 1534 when an Act of Parliament gave the Council a range of statutory powers.

To many people, a key cause of the perceived lawlessness and criminality in Wales and the Marches was the outdated anachronism of the large number of separate judicial structures

Henry VIII c.1520 by unknown Anglo-Netherlandish artist (© National Portrait Gallery London)

– the 50 or so Marcher lordships, plus the jurisdictions of the Principality. Henry VIII took a personal interest in the matter but was somewhat reluctant to upset the Marcher lords who were naturally opposed to anything that would cause them to relinquish the power that they held in their lordships. Henry was reminded that 'your grace hath half the lord marchers in your hand or more. If your grace and Counsaill wold commande the reformacion to be had who durst saie the contrarie.'[7] Thus over the next few years, a series of reforms were driven through by Thomas Cromwell, the chief adviser to Henry VIII. These reforms culminated in The Laws in Wales Acts of 1536 and 1542 – sometimes later referred to as the 'Acts of Union' [of England and Wales] – which abolished the governance and judicial structures of the Principality of Wales and removed the powers of the Marcher lords. The purpose of the Act of 1536 was spelled out in its title: 'An Act for Laws and Justice to be Ministered in Wales in like form as it is in the Realm'. The Act established a new structure of county governance throughout Wales, with the Principality subsumed into the newly-created counties, which also took over many of the administrative and judicial powers of the Marcher lords.

The Act of 1536 followed the traditional boundaries of pre-1066 Wales, placing all the districts of Dyfed, the lands to the west of the River Tywi, into the new county of Pembrokeshire: Cemais, Cilgerran, Narberth, Pebidiog, Haverfordwest, Pembroke, Llanstephan, Laugharne, Ystlwyf and St Clears.

The lands to the east of the Tywi (those of Ystrad Tywi), were allocated to the new county of Carmarthenshire: Cantref Bychan, Iscennen, Kidwelly and Emlyn.

This dispensation, however, was soon changed when the 1542 Act removed Llanstephan, Laugharne, St Clears and Ystlwyf out of Pembrokeshire and into Carmarthenshire, recognising the administrative ties that had developed over the preceding centuries.

Wales was now administered in a similar way to England, with a judicial structure based on shires. The few remaining independent Marcher lords were stripped of many of the powers that had defined them as such. As it pertained to Pembrokeshire and Carmarthenshire, the change would only have been felt in some parts, as most of the lordships of the two counties were in royal hands. One consequence of the economic downturn following the outbreaks of the plague in the fourteenth century, and then the destruction caused by the Glyn Dŵr rebellion, was that Pembroke did not recover as a town. In contrast, Haverfordwest had benefitted from grants of trade that it had received, making it a flourishing place to live and do business. Consequently, when the county of Pembrokeshire was created, it was Haverfordwest that became the county town and not Pembroke.

Map 12 The traditional Welsh counties created by the Laws in Wales Acts of 1536 and 1542

CHAPTER EIGHT

The Lordships of Pembrokeshire

PEMBROKE, HAVERFORD, CEMAIS, CILGERRAN/ EMLYN, NARBERTH, PEBIDIOG/ LLAWHADEN

THE lordships that were grouped around the powerful castle of Pembroke were mainly carved out of the *cantrefi* and *commotes* of the early Welsh kingdom of Dyfed. As described in chapter two, Dyfed lay to the south of the River Teifi, and the west of the River Tywi, and much of the territory was incorporated in 1536 into the 'new' county of Pembrokeshire. Dyfed's neighbouring kingdom, Seisyllwg, comprised the lands to the north of the River Teifi (medieval Ceredigion, or the traditional county of Cardiganshire), together with the lands of Ystrad Tywi on the eastern side of the Tywi river. It was as late as the first half of the tenth century that Dyfed and Seisyllwg became a single polity known as Deheubarth. It appears

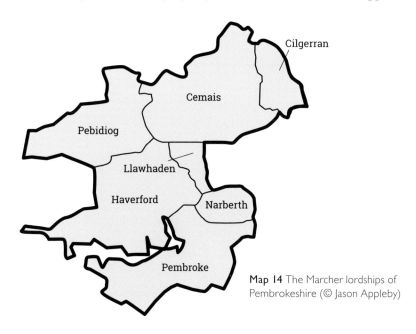

Map 14 The Marcher lordships of Pembrokeshire (© Jason Appleby)

that Hywel Dda, the son of Cadell ap Rhodri Mawr, having married the sister of
the king of Dyfed, became the ruler of Dyfed before his father died. Following
his father's death in *c*.911, Hywel inherited Seisyllwg, initially as joint ruler with
his brother, Clydog, but as sole ruler after his brother died in 920. It was this
combined area of Seisyllwg and Dyfed that became known as the kingdom of
Deheubarth. Thus, the concept of Deheubarth was only a little over 100 years old
by the time the Normans arrived in England, which goes some way to explaining
the subsequent forces for fragmentation amongst the Welsh rulers.

After the arrival of the Normans in England, one might have expected the
most likely threats to Dyfed to come from the coastal access routes across south
Wales or from the sea. However, when the first significant Norman incursions did
arrive in 1093, it was from a different direction completely. Roger of Montgomery,
1st earl of Shrewsbury, had been gradually moving along the uplands of the Severn
Valley from his base at Montgomery/ Hen Domen to secure the strategic route
into and out of central Wales. Following the vacuum created by the death in
battle of the ruler of Deheubarth, Rhys ap Tewdwr, in 1093, a force led by Roger
and his sons swept over the uplands, and down into Ceredigion. From here they
turned south into Dyfed, founding the castle at Pembroke. Strategically located
in a loop of the river, at the end of a ridge with water on three sides, the castle was
virtually impregnable. Moreover, with easy access to the coastal reaches of the

Pembroke Castle (© Philip Hume)

Cleddau river, supplies could be maintained. Consequently, Pembroke was never taken by the Welsh and became the anchor around which the other lordships could develop. Inevitably, its strength attracted royal interest and for periods it was the property of the Crown.

As described elsewhere, the dynamics within the region were fascinating and often singular. When the steward of Pembroke Castle, the Norman Gerald of Windsor, married Nest, the daughter of Rhys ap Tewdwr, their children and grandchildren were to play key roles in the establishment of Marcher authority, but also were closely related to the native Welsh rulers in the region. The influx of Flemish settlers in *c.*1107 resulted in the establishment of several smaller lordships, as well as the Marcher lordship of Haverford. Their settlement was so thorough that they forced the Welsh out of the far south-west entirely. The appointment of the Lord Rhys as Henry II's Justiciar of south Wales, created a unique dimension, whilst the bloody feuds between his sons destroyed a united polity of Deheubarth. During the period when the Lord Rhys was dominant, many of the Marcher families turned their attention to gaining lands in Ireland because the potential rewards were far greater in the newly-conquered territories. The arrival of the powerful Marshal family as earls of Pembroke created another dynamic; whilst the disunity amongst the descendants of the Lord Rhys led to the opportunities for two powerful rulers from Gwynedd – Llywelyn ab Iorwerth and Llywelyn ap Gruffudd – to assert their ascendency over south-west Wales.

Across these tumultuous years, the two lordships in the far north of the region, Cilgerran and Emlyn, were, for much of the time, held by the native Welsh rulers (although the latter later became part of the county of Carmarthenshire, it is included here as its history was entwined with Cilgerran). Elsewhere, although there were periods of war and raiding across the lands of the lordships, and sometimes the castles were taken (though not Pembroke), the Welsh were not able to sustain control for long.

The Lordship of Pembroke

The Marcher lordship of Pembroke was the dominant lordship in south-west Wales, claiming superiority over the other lordships in the region. Inevitably, therefore, the history of Pembroke is bound up in the history of the wider region (described in Chapters 3–6). This section provides a brief summary of the details that can be found in those chapters. The claim to superiority of the Pembroke lordship was based on the conquests made by the Marshal family in the early thirteenth century. After the last Marshal died without a male heir, the lords of Pembroke fought legal battles in the king's court, in order to have their authority recognised – particularly when it came to where justice was to be dispensed. As a large Marcher lordship, Pembroke had several minor lordships within it, that were held of the lord of Pembroke, for example Carew and Manorbier. The lordship is bordered by Narberth and Laugharne to the east. Pembroke is surrounded by water on the other three sides, with Milford Haven to the west and the Bristol channel to the south and east. The pre-eminent position of the lordship owes its status to the mighty fortress that was built on the rocky outcrop above a tidal inlet. Pembroke Castle, once established in 1093, was never taken by the Welsh.

Manorbier Castle looking west, with Manorbier Bay beyond. Manorbier was a barony of the lordship of Pembroke, and the birthplace of Gerald of Wales (© Paul Davis)

The lords of Pembroke

Arnulf of Montgomery (d.c.1120); Crown control from 1102–38; **Gilbert fitz Gilbert 'Strongbow' de Clare** earl of Pembroke (d.c.1149); **Richard fitz Gilbert 'Strongbow' de Clare** 2nd earl of Pembroke (d.1176); **William Marshal** 1st earl of Pembroke, 2nd creation (d.1219); **William Marshal the younger**, 2nd earl of Pembroke (d.1231); **Richard Marshal** 3rd earl of Pembroke (d.1234); **Gilbert Marshal** 4th earl of Pembroke (d.1241); **Walter Marshal** 5th earl of Pembroke (d.1245); reverted to **the Crown** until 1247; **William de Valence** 1st earl of Pembroke, 3rd creation (d.1296); **Aymer de Valence** 2nd earl of Pembroke (d.1324); **Laurence Hastings** 1st earl of Pembroke, 4th creation (d.1348); **John Hastings** 2nd earl of Pembroke (d.1375); **John Hastings the younger** 3rd earl of Pembroke (d.1389); reverted to **the Crown** until 1414; **Humphrey, duke of Gloucester** 1st earl of Pembroke, 5th creation, 1st duke of Gloucester (d.1447); **William de la Pole** 1st earl of Pembroke, 6th creation, 1st duke of Suffolk (d.1450); **Jasper Tudor** 1st earl of Pembroke, 7th creation, 1st duke of Bedford (d.1495); **William Herbert** 1st earl of Pembroke, 8th creation (d.1469); **William Herbert** 2nd earl of Pembroke (d.1491) until 1479 when he ceded it to **the Crown**; **Prince Edward** 1st earl of Pembroke, 9th creation (d.c.1483), merged with **the Crown** again in 1483; **the Crown** until 1485; **Jasper Tudor** (d.1495); reverted to **the Crown** until 1532; **Anne Boleyn** Marquess of Pembroke (d.1536)

BRIEF HISTORY

As already outlined, the history of the lordship of Pembroke begins with the Norman incursions into south-west Wales by the Montgomery family in 1093, following the death of Rhys ap Tewdwr, the ruler of Deheubarth. Having built a castle at Pembroke, the responsibility for the operation was given to the youngest son, Arnulf, who would have had few prospects in England given that he had elder brothers. There are no records that tell us of the other castles built by the Montgomery family and their followers, but we know there were several, as in 1094 the *Brut* states:

> *The Britons threw off the rule of the French, being unable to suffer their tyranny ... And at the close of that year the Britons destroyed all the castles of Ceredigion and Dyfed except two, that is, Pembroke and Rhyd-y-gors* [near present-day Carmarthen].

The Norman hold over south Wales remained tenuous. Often away at his other land-holdings in England, Arnulf entrusted the defence of Pembroke Castle to Gerald of Windsor, another younger son who sought to make his way on the frontier of Wales. When the castle of Rhyd-y-gors was abandoned in 1096, Pembroke became more vulnerable, with a great host of Welsh rulers moving against the castle; however, they were unable to destroy it. Writing nearly 100 years later, Gerald's grandson, Gerald of Wales, described that it was only the ingenuity of Gerald of Windsor that frustrated the Welsh attackers and encouraged them to head home with the spoil they had taken.[1] This Norman outpost held out through the following few violent and turbulent years of Norman and Welsh conflict.

When the Montgomery rebellion at the start of the reign of Henry 1 failed, with Arnulf exiled, this provided the opportunity for the new king to take the strategic lordship of Pembroke into his own hands, appointing his own stewards. Gerald of Windsor was replaced (possibly because he had been too close to Arnulf of Montgomery) by a knight called Saer; however, Gerald was reinstated in 1105. Gerald was now married to Nest ferch Rhys ap Tewdwr, who had previously been the mistress of Henry, with whom she had had a son who would later become a Marcher lord himself. It is unclear how the marriage arrangement was made, but Nest proved an invaluable asset to the Norman occupation. Firstly, she produced at least three sons for Gerald and, after his death, at least another two sons with other men. These children would form the backbone of the Norman occupation. Secondly, her background meant that her children were half-Welsh, of royal stock, thus close relatives of the native Welsh rulers of Deheubarth.

Henry 1 demonstrated a flexible but commanding approach to affairs in Wales, balancing Norman barons and Welsh rulers to achieve his aims of a secure region. In central and northern Wales, he used his overlordship of the Welsh rulers to influence affairs, backed by shows of military strength when required. In contrast in the south, where there was a vacuum in Welsh leadership, he was content to allow the barons to consolidate the gains made in the reign of his predecessor, and indeed extended them by putting in place leading Normans in strategic lordships. One important factor that contributed to a different approach in the south-west was Henry's personal control of Pembroke, which gave him a special interest in the region. Indeed, the Crown's influence increased when the royal castle was built at Carmarthen. An effect of this was that Pembroke was now the administrative centre solely for western Dyfed, a division of the region that would remain permanent.

Gerald of Windsor took advantage of Henry's dominance to expand his own interests, building a castle at Carew (to be held of Pembroke) which would remain the lordship of Carew for centuries. Gerald then built a castle at Cenarth Bychan,

Carew Castle, originally established by Gerald of Windsor (© Philip Hume)

which is now presumed to be present-day Cilgerran, possibly to create his own Marcher lordship. It was here in 1109 that Gerald's wife, Nest, was abducted in the famous crime of passion described in Chapter 3. This resulted in Gilbert de Clare (d.1117) securing control of Ceredigion, which provided even further security to the new settlements of south-west Wales.

Apart from a short rebellion in 1115–16 by the son of Rhys ap Tewdwr, which never seriously threatened Norman authority, the early twelfth century was a time when the Marcher lordships developed and flourished, with Pembroke remaining in royal hands throughout. The Pipe Roll of 1130 shows the royal accounts for that year as accounted for by the sheriff, who was a Flemish immigrant by the name of Hait.[2] There was also a royal mint at Pembroke, producing silver pennies. Overall, Pembroke was administered as an English county and produced a respectable revenue for the royal coffers.

The death of Henry 1 was followed by uprisings across all of Wales, which resulted in many of the lands lost to the Norman barons being regained, although not Pembroke. The response of the new king, Stephen, was limited and ineffectual, in part due to his nature, but also because of his insecurity in England. To broaden his support, in 1138 Stephen increased the number of earldoms, which he distributed to his most faithful allies. One was the earldom of Pembroke, which he granted to Gilbert fitz Gilbert de Clare (d.c.1149). Gilbert initially had little involvement with Pembroke as he was soon completely preoccupied with the civil war that erupted in 1139 between Stephen and the daughter of Henry 1, Matilda. He finally made a military expedition into south Wales in 1145. It is unclear whether he ventured as far as Pembroke, but he is on record as having fortified Carmarthen Castle and building a new castle near Pencader in Ceredigion.[3] Gilbert died sometime around 1149, leaving his son Richard fitz Gilbert de Clare (d.1176), who assumed the title of earl of Pembroke upon his father's death. He witnessed several charters using that title, as well as his inherited title of the lord of Striguil (Chepstow) in eastern Wales (see Family Tree 3, p. 69).

When Henry II came to the throne in 1154, with the objective to restore royal authority, one of his early acts was to eliminate the earldoms that had been created by Stephen, including the earldom of Pembroke, which thus reverted to royal control. Richard did maintain his Marcher status by retaining the lordship of Striguil, but it was a diminished role to that of his father. Richard's prospects were also reduced by the rise of the powerful Welsh ruler, the Lord Rhys, who was in near-constant strife with the Marcher lords. When an opportunity arose to marry the daughter of the king of Leinster, Richard took it on the condition that he would become the king of Leinster upon his father-in-law's death. The Norman invasion of Ireland, which brought Henry II to Ireland to assert royal authority, was incredibly successful. He came to an agreement with Richard, that he could hold his lands in Ireland, but directly from the king of England. After his death, Richard's heir, Gilbert, was still a minor when he died in 1185. For this reason, he never inherited his titles; instead, Richard's daughter, Isabel de Clare, became one of the most prized heiresses in the kingdom as the heir to Striguil and Leinster.

William Marshal (d.1219) was a medieval celebrity. He had gained fame on the tournament circuit, where he earned a handsome living, and secured a place in the household of Henry II, holding various roles for several different family members. His main sponsor was the eldest son of Henry II, Henry 'the young king', but when he died before his father, William Marshal went on Crusade. Upon his return, he joined the household guard of Henry II, in the final troubled years of Henry's reign. William remained steadfastly loyal to the king, even as Henry's enemies were closing in on him. The king had promised to reward William with the hand of Isabel de Clare, but Henry died before the grant could be fulfilled. Henry's successor, Richard I, honoured the promise that his father had made, and William married Isabel de Clare at a hastily arranged wedding at the Tower of London, receiving the de Clare lordships of Striguil and Leinster. When Richard met a premature death, struck by a crossbow bolt in France, William Marshal was part of the contingent who supported Richard's younger brother, John, when he claimed the throne ahead of his nephew by an elder brother. Grateful for William's support, John recreated the earldom of Pembroke for William Marshal,[4] who was also granted the *commotes* of Velfrey (which became attached to Narberth) and

Ystlwyf until he could recover his lands in Emlyn, which were still held by a son of the Lord Rhys. William was mainly active on the Continent with John in the turbulent early years of the thirteenth century, but this all changed after the French conquered Normandy in 1204. William returned to Pembroke after the defeat in France, from where he immediately launched a strike north, which recovered the *commote* of Emlyn, Cardigan Castle and almost certainly restored Cemais to the fitz Martins.

William Marshal was one of the few barons who was permitted to keep his lands in Normandy, where he swore fealty to the French king for them. Although he was very close to King John, he fell out of favour in 1205 when he advised against sending an army to France to recover Normandy. The military expedition never took place, which made John furious. With the king blaming William's lack of support for the campaign's failure, William went to Ireland to lay low for a few years. In 1210, John pursued William de Braose, the leading Marcher baron who had become a fugitive, to Ireland, where he also sought to deal with several barons who he felt had aided de Braose, one of whom was William Marshal. William, however, was somehow able to stay on good enough terms that their relationship was never completely broken. When John returned to England, he continued to concentrate on Welsh affairs, launching a military campaign against Gwynedd, that nearly ended in total defeat for the Welsh in 1211. This represented a high point in John's leadership, though, as from 1212 the barons of England slowly started to move towards open rebellion against his harsh rule. With John in search of all the support he could get, he turned to the ever-loyal earl of Pembroke and brought him back into favour. In 1213, he granted Haverford to William Marshal for a modest fine, and with this the earl of Pembroke now exerted some control over every secular lordship in the region.

Pembroke Castle: the great tower, constructed by William Marshal (© Philip Hume)

After the barons broke into open revolt in 1215, William Marshal was mainly active in England. Llywelyn ab Iorwerth, ruler of Gwynedd, recognising an opportunity, launched a devastating winter campaign in 1215. Most of the Marcher lordships in the south-west were taken into Welsh hands except for Pembroke and Haverford. The spoils were divided between the sons and grandsons of the Lord Rhys, with the Marshals being the biggest losers. Following the death of King John, William Marshal was appointed regent of the country and was entirely focused on supporting the young King Henry III, who was crowned in 1216. William Marshal, with the support of several other loyal senior barons, was able to establish his authority through battle and diplomacy. The 1218 Treaty of Worcester between the Crown and Llywelyn ab Iorwerth, however, confirmed the gains made by the latter in south-west Wales.

When William died in 1219, his successor, William Marshal the younger (d.1231), resented the concessions that his father had made in the interests of stability in England. Despite the treaty, Pembroke was invaded by Llywelyn again in 1220, which further underlined the superiority of the Welsh position. William Marshal agreed a truce that stopped the fighting for a time, but also meant that the Welsh were confirmed in their gains. Although there was correspondence imploring Llywelyn to return the Marcher territory that he'd seized, the reality was that nobody was in a strong enough position to force him to do so. When the truce that had been renewed at Easter of 1222 expired in 1223, William Marshal took matters into his own hands. He landed near Pembroke with an army that he had raised in Ireland, quickly moving through his territory, taking Cardigan Castle and all the lost territory in Dyfed. In the region of Carmarthen, he was initially held to a stalemate; however, later in the year he launched a second campaign that restored most of the Marcher lordships in western Carmarthenshire to Anglo-Norman control. This time it was Llywelyn who was not able to respond to the strength of the earl of Pembroke.

When William Marshal died childless in 1231, his brother and heir, Richard (d.1234) was in France holding the Marshal lands there. To receive his English inheritance, he had to renounce his loyalty to the French king and forfeit the family's Norman estates. Richard paid his homage to Henry III in August of 1231, thus becoming the earl of Pembroke at a time of division within the royal court. The seizure by the king's new Justiciar of a manor owned by the baron Walter Bassett, a close associate of the Marshals, caused particular consternation; indeed, it was against the fundamental principles of Magna Carta. The king did nothing to reverse the confiscation of the lands, and this pushed Richard Marshal into revolt in 1233.

The movement did not gain widespread baronial support, but it became a major issue for the Crown when Richard secured an alliance with Llywelyn ab Iorwerth, the family's former bitter rival. The conflict ended with Henry III removing the unpopular foreign ministers, and also agreeing a truce with Llywelyn, that would secure peace in Wales until the latter's death in 1240. Before the conflict had been finally resolved, Richard Marshal went to Ireland with a force of knights, to stabilise the situation there, as his Irish estates were under pressure from royal agents. He was able to achieve some initial success, primarily with the help of local Irish allies; however, in early April 1234, he was wounded in battle and captured. He died two weeks later in captivity.

Richard's heir was his brother, Gilbert (d.1241), who was given safe passage to swear his loyalty. Although the king was suspicious of Gilbert and the Marshals, he allowed Gilbert to gain his lands, granting him also Carmarthen and Cardigan as compensation for the lands in Normandy that the family had given up on Richard's accession. Cardigan was an empty gift though, as it was still held by the Welsh who had taken it in an uprising in 1231. With the truce that had been agreed between the king and Llywelyn in place, the boundaries that had been established were maintained by both sides for the rest of the decade.

Although peace did prevail during this period, Earl Gilbert was not able fully to gain the trust of Henry III. This mistrust turned out to be well-founded when Gilbert, following the death of Llywelyn in 1240, sent his brother Walter to seize Cardigan Castle. He further demanded the homage of several Welsh tenants, to the fury of the king. Gilbert also deposed Cynan ap Hywel in Newcastle Emlyn,

Cardigan Castle was taken back into royal custody in 1241 along with Carmarthen

to replace him with his own supporter, Maredudd ap Rhys Gryg. It took an angry letter from the king to bring Gilbert to court where it was affirmed that no Welsh ruler should pay homage to anybody other than the king. Gilbert was fined and forced to concede an earlier grant of Pevensey back to the Crown in order to restore the king's good graces.[5] It is unclear whether this would have been the end of the matter; however, Gilbert died in a riding accident at an unlicensed tournament in June 1241. The king delayed conferring the earldom on Gilbert's brother and heir, Walter (d.1245), until after his summer campaign in Gwynedd. When he did summon Walter to him, the king demanded the return of both Cardigan and Carmarthen. Walter had no choice but to agree and the two strategic castles were once again in Crown hands, never to be relinquished.

Walter's time as earl of Pembroke was short as, on a visit to Pembroke in 1245, he was ill, or soon taken ill, and died without a male heir. His brother, Anselm, who was to be the last remaining Marshal male heir, died childless shortly thereafter and before inheriting the earldom. Thus, the vast Marshal inheritance, which had seemed secure when the first earl had five sons that survived to adulthood, ended abruptly, as it was divided between the daughters and granddaughters of William Marshal (d.1219).

The earldom of Pembroke, which had been created for William Marshal, was discontinued; however, in 1247 the king granted to his own half-brother, William de Valence, marriage to Joan de Munchensy, a granddaughter of William Marshal (d.1219), through whom de Valence became the lord of Pembroke. The rest of the land holdings in England, Wales and Ireland were split amongst the many other heirs (see Family Tree 5, p. 101).

William de Valence was one of the half-siblings whom Henry III invited to England in April 1247,[6] all of them sharing Isabelle d'Angoulême (the second wife of King John and later wife of Hugh de Lusignan) as their mother. They were all bestowed with gifts and titles which created a great deal of resentment amongst Henry's barons. In fact, it was one of the key grievances that later led to the baronial reform movement (1258–65) that culminated in a royal victory at the battle of Evesham.

William de Valence was a key supporter of the royal family, accompanying Edward on Crusade in 1270. He was also a military leader for Edward I in his Welsh and Scottish wars as well as an ambassador to France. In the first Welsh war in 1277, he was part of the Marcher army under the leadership of Payn de Chaworth of Kidwelly, that secured a rapid victory for the English. In the final war of 1282–83, William was made the leader of the army of west Wales. The comprehensive victory that was achieved led to the creation of the Principality, with its administrative centres at Carmarthen and Cardigan. His wide-ranging service to the Crown meant that he was an absentee lord, leaving Pembroke to be administered by appointed officials. However, his agents stayed active on his behalf, filing suits against other Marcher barons who would not recognise the supremacy of the lord's court at Pembroke over their own local justice.[7] When William de Valence died in 1296, his heir was a younger son Aymer (d.1324), who came into his inheritance after his mother died in 1307.

Aymer continued the tradition of dependable royal service. Throughout the turbulent reign of Edward II (d.1327) and during the uprising in 1322 against Edward and his favourite, Hugh Despenser (d.1326), Aymer fought on the side of the king, despite many senior barons joining the rebellion. The rebels were defeated at the battle of Boroughbridge in 1322, with Aymer granted the lands of some of the executed barons. He continued to be active in the king's service, dying in France in 1324. His near continuous royal service meant that he too was an absentee lord, leaving the administration of Pembroke to prominent local men. Having died without a male heir, Aymer's estates were divided between his two sisters, with the Pembrokeshire estates (but not the earldom, which lapsed) inherited by the descendants of Isabel de Valence (d.1305), who had been married to John Hastings, lord of Abergavenny (d.1313). Their eldest son, John, died in 1325 before he could inherit, and thus the lands passed to his infant son, Laurence.

Laurence was born in 1320 and entered military service for Edward III's war with France in 1338. He was bestowed a further new creation of the earldom of Pembroke in October 1339 whilst campaigning in France, which was appropriate as his career was defined by the military service that he provided. He thus became the 1st earl of the 4th creation of the title. Laurence died suddenly in 1348, with his son and heir, John, only one year old on his death. John (d.1375) came into his inheritance in 1368 at the age of 20. He too was active in military service during Edward III's campaigns in France.

The succession to the Hastings lands became complicated when John had a falling out with a potential heir to his estates. If John were to die childless (which looked increasingly possible), Reginald, second lord Grey of Ruthin, would become the rightful heir by right of his descent from John Hastings (d.1313) and Isabel de Valence. Hastings used a legal mechanism known as *feoffees* to position his cousin, Sir William Beauchamp, as his heir for some of his estates, granting that the Crown should receive Pembroke should he die childless. As John set sail for Aquitaine as the lieutenant of that region in 1372, he would have felt assured that his plan was securely in place. His small fleet, however, met disaster near La Rochelle, where he was taken captive by Spanish mercenaries and sent to a

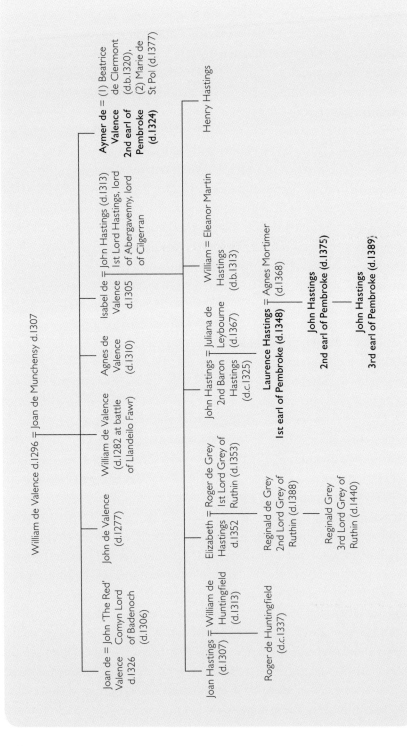

Family Tree 6 Select descendants to the de Valence/ Hastings inheritance

Spanish prison, where he was kept for over two years. He finally managed to arrange a ransom but died of an illness on his way home in 1375.

John did not know at the time of his departure from England, that his wife was pregnant, only learning of the birth of an heir when he was in captivity. This meant that all his well-laid plans appeared to be invalid; however, circumstances were to bring them back into play. His son, another John, was born in 1372 (although he never attained his majority, he was considered to have been the earl of Pembroke). When he died childless in 1389, killed whilst practising for a tournament, the plans that his father had put into action were revived. Lord Grey and Beauchamp came to an agreement over Abergavenny; however, the lands in west Wales, Pembroke and Cilgerran came into royal hands, because the last Hastings had died without an heir, thus bringing an end to the 4th creation of the title.[8]

During the tumultuous years that followed John Hastings' death, the king appointed trusted men as stewards. Following the Glyn Dŵr rebellion, which caused a great deal of destruction in the lordship, the Lancastrians sought to solidify their power-base in south-west Wales. Henry v made his younger brother Humphrey, duke of Gloucester, 1st earl of Pembroke (of the 5th creation) in 1414. He, together with the Justiciar of south Wales, James, Lord Audley (lord of Cantref Bychan and Cemais) made a formidable administrative duo in the region. They were also active in the wars in France, so often relied on local people to manage the lordship. Humphrey died in 1447, with the title lapsing again, and another staunch Lancastrian, William de la Pole, the duke of Suffolk, became 1st earl of the 6th creation; however, he was blamed for the loss of the war with France and tried to flee the country to save himself. As he tried to make his escape he was seized by an angry mob and beheaded in 1450. The ineffectual King Henry vi chose his half-brother by his mother Catherine of Valois, Jasper Tudor, to be the next earl (of the 7th creation). Dependent on his royal relation, he remained a staunch supporter of the Crown, being given the wardship of the young Henry Tudor, his nephew, who was born at Pembroke in 1457. Defeat at the hands of the Yorkists in 1461, however, sent Jasper Tudor into exile also.

The new Yorkist king, Edward iv, aware that south-west Wales was a Lancastrian stronghold, made one of his closest allies, William Herbert, the new earl of Pembroke (of the 8th creation) in 1462. Herbert worked hard to gain the loyalty of prominent local men, but was killed in battle in 1469, during the successful Lancastrian uprising against Edward iv. This saw Jasper Tudor restored to the earldom; however, the Lancastrian recovery was short-lived, with Edward iv retaking the Crown in 1471. William Herbert's son, William (d.1491) was restored to the earldom, but in 1479 he surrendered the title to Edward iv, receiving in lieu the earldom of Huntingdon. The king immediately granted Pembroke and the earldom (the 9th creation) to his son and heir, Prince Edward. The king's sudden death in 1483 and the short-lived accession of Edward v resulted in the earldom merging once again with the Crown.

When Edward iv's brother, Richard iii, seized the Crown instead, he imprisoned Edward v and his younger brother in the Tower of London. Richard's resultant unpopularity in some quarters presented an opportunity to the Tudors. They landed near Haverford in 1485 with a small, armed retinue, with the purpose of removing Richard from power. As they moved through Wales, they gained more support and finally met the king at the battle of Bosworth Field, where Richard iii was mortally wounded. Henry Tudor, who had been born at Pembroke, assumed the throne as Henry vii, the first Tudor king. He reappointed Jasper Tudor to the earldom of Pembroke, which remained in his hands until his death in 1495. Following Jasper's death, the earldom was not revived. The revenues of Pembroke were granted to a series of royal favourites, including by Henry viii, who granted it in 1532 to his mistress, Ann Boleyn. After her execution in 1536, it reverted again to the Crown.[9]

When the powers of the Marcher lords were abolished through the Laws in Wales Acts of 1536 and 1542, Pembroke was incorporated into the new county of Pembrokeshire.

Carew Castle: owned by Sir Rhys ap Thomas, a favourite of Henry VII (© Philip Hume)

Castles and Abbeys, etc.

Pembroke Castle: the castle has been heavily restored after falling into disrepair over the centuries. Key features of the castle are the great round keep built in stone by William Marshal in the early thirteenth century, and the large cavern that lies under the castle, Wogan's Cavern. The castle is privately owned and has been managed by a Private Charitable Trust since 1969, but is open to the public for most of the year (see pp. 12, 48, 129, 134 & 141).

Carew Castle: the impressive current castle ruin was built by Rhys ap Thomas after he acquired it in the fifteenth century. The original castle was built by Gerald of Windsor in the early twelfth century for his family. It is open to the public. The extremely fine Carew Cross, an intricately-carved four-metre-tall standing Cross dating from the eleventh century, stands a short distance away (see pp. 24, 36, 39 & 148).

Manorbier Castle: the original castle dates from around 1100 and was built by Odo de Barri who held it from the lord of Pembroke. It was the birthplace of Gerald of Wales in 1147, from whom we know so much about the medieval history of Wales. It is hard to disagree with his biased assessment that, 'It follows that in all the broad lands of Wales Manorbier is the most pleasant place by far'[10] (see pp. 136 & 149).

Lamphey Palace: the impressive country retreat of the bishops of St Davids, primarily built by bishop Henry de Gower between 1328 and 1347. The ruins are now managed by Cadw.

Tenby: little remains of the stone castle that replaced an earthwork structure in the thirteenth century. However, the town walls that were constructed around the same time, on the orders of the earl of Pembroke, William de Valence, are some of the best preserved in Britain. Tenby belonged to the lordship of Pembroke and benefitted from its location to become an important trading centre (see p. 66).

Manorbier Castle: '... the most pleasant place by far', according to Gerald of Wales (© Philip Hume)

THE LORDSHIP OF HAVERFORD

The Marcher lordship of Haverford was established during the royally-sponsored Flemish immigration into the area in the early 1100s. There is some debate as to who built the first castle at Haverford, but it was most likely one of the leading Flemish settlers. We know that one senior figure in that region was a certain Tancred. We also know from Gerald of Wales, in his *Journey through Wales* in 1188, that Tancred's son was confirmed as the lord of Haverford at that time, indicating that Tancred was indeed the original lord. The castle was built in a strong defensive position above the Cleddau river at a point that was fordable and navigable. Haverford Castle benefitted from being situated deep within the area that the Flemish had settled. It was therefore seldom attacked, in contrast to other castles that were nearer large Welsh settlements. This relative security from attack, and the fact that the local traders received several privileges that allowed them favourable trading terms, fostered a rate of growth that made Haverford one of the largest medieval cities in Wales. Its name was changed to Haverfordwest in the fifteenth century to distinguish the town from Hereford.

The lords of Haverford

Tancred (d.c.1159); Richard fitz Tancred (d.c.1188); Robert fitz Richard (d.1211); the Crown 1210–13; William Marshal 1st earl of Pembroke, 2nd creation (d.1219); William Marshal the younger 2nd earl of Pembroke (d.1231); Richard Marshal 3rd earl of Pembroke (d.1234); Gilbert Marshal 4th earl of Pembroke (d.1241); Walter Marshal 5th earl of Pembroke (d.1244); Humphrey de Bohun (d.1265); William de Valence 1st earl of Pembroke (d.1296), 3rd creation, until 1273 during minority of de Bohun heir; Humphrey de Bohun 3rd earl of Hereford, 2nd earl of Essex (d.1298); Queen Eleanor (d.1290); the Crown until 1308; Aymer de Valence 2nd earl of Pembroke, 3rd creation (d.1324); reverted to the Crown, granted to Queen Isabella (d.1358) in 1327, passed to Edward 'The Black Prince' duke of Cornwall (d.1376); property of the Crown.

BRIEF HISTORY

The castle at Haverford was built in the early years of the Flemish settlement in the region in around 1107, and was certainly there no later than 1110, with the first reference to the castle appearing in the records as having been founded by the Fleming, Tancred (d.*c.*1159). Haverford was one of several castles built by the Flemish immigrants to the region of Rhos and Daggledau, with the defence of the

Roch Castle, built on a rocky outcrop by Flemish immigrants; it is now a luxury hotel

area relying on the network of castles that supported each other in times of trouble.

Tancred chose an excellent strategic position: a precipitous rock outcrop close to the lowest fordable point on the river, the Western Cleddau, yet accessible to the sea-going vessels of his day. There are very few early records from Haverford, other than those relating to the Flemish settlement and displacement of the native peoples, which was a further contributing factor in securing Norman and Flemish control in the region. It is noteworthy that other Norman and Flemish castles that were situated nearer to concentrations of Welsh inhabitants, such as Narberth and Wiston, were recorded as having been sacked regularly during Welsh uprisings, whereas there is no mention that Haverford suffered the same fate before the thirteenth century, lying much deeper in Flemish-controlled territory. At times, though, the surrounding lands were briefly occupied, such as following the disastrous battle of Crug Mawr in 1136, when the Welsh ravaged Dyfed before returning to their own homes.

Tancred's choice of spouse was characteristic of the interrelationships that the local settlers used to establish themselves. He himself married a daughter of Gerald of Windsor and Nest, whilst two of Tancred's daughters married the lords of Manorbier and Carew, who were prominent local lords. Although neither family was from the major Norman aristocracy, the descendants of Gerald of Windsor and Tancred were key players in south-west Wales for many years.

We get a first-hand account of the son of Tancred through Gerald of Wales's *Journey through Wales* in 1188. He was full of praise for Richard fitz Tancred (d.c.1188), who was of course his first cousin, calling him 'a great and mighty man in his own day and in his own land'. However, Gerald was not so flattering of Richard's sons. Indeed, he even questioned whether Richard had sired one of them (and that was the more positive remark of the two!).[11] Despite his alleged character flaws, Robert fitz Richard (d.1211) was in royal service under King John, being confirmed in the lordship of Haverford by the king in 1204 and 1207. He was also entrusted with keeping Cardigan Castle for a time, which was in royal hands.

It was in the early thirteenth century that the Augustinian priory was founded by Robert fitz Richard slightly downstream from the town. He granted to the new priory three churches, an indication that Haverford was already a relatively large settlement for Wales at that time. Robert fitz Richard was granted a Sunday market and an annual fair by John in 1207 which also contributed to its standing and position as a leading market town in the region.

For reasons unknown, Robert was deprived of all his holdings by King John when the king returned from Ireland in 1210, with John taking them into his own hands and Robert sent into exile, where he died a year later. As King John came under further pressure in England from his disaffected barons, he rewarded the loyal William Marshal, earl of Pembroke, with Haverford in October 1213.[12] Haverford thus became part of the demesne lands of Pembroke and a key staging-point for the earl of Pembroke's journeys to Ireland. During William's lifetime, he granted Haverford a charter that bestowed several significant benefits on the

Haverford Castle: grants made to the town by the Marshals ensured that it would become a major trading centre in the region (© Paul Davis)

inhabitants of the town, including the right to become a free man if one were to live in the town for a year and a day without being challenged. Further, he granted the burgesses the right to sell their property without the lord's permission and decreed that an heir coming into his inheritance need only pay 12 shillings in order to succeed his parents. This charter, which was witnessed by many of the great and the good of Pembroke (including Henry fitz Gerald, William de Barri and William de Brian amongst others) was so generous that it would have contributed significantly to the desire to live there and, therefore, to the growth of the town.[13] The burgesses were also given other favourable benefits that would have assured that Haverford remained a centre for commerce for years to come.

When the Welsh allied against King John in 1215, their leader Llywelyn ab Iorwerth rampaged through Dyfed, burning as he went, though Haverford was spared in that year. However, in 1217, when Llywelyn undertook another campaign through Wales, including Dyfed, he did turn his attention towards Haverford. The townspeople sought a truce which was finally brokered by the Welsh bishop of St Davids, whereby they offered hostages and a ransom of 1,000 marks to spare the town. Llywelyn withdrew, but not before ravaging the surrounding country-side. The new royal government, with William Marshal as regent for the child Henry III, sought peace with Llywelyn which was confirmed by the Treaty of Worcester in 1218. Although the Marshals were the biggest losers in Llywelyn's campaigns, William, as Regent for the still-precarious government of Henry III, put the national interest before that of himself and his family. When William Marshal died in 1219, he was succeeded by his son William Marshal the younger (d. 1231) who inherited his lands and titles immediately. One of William's first acts was to reaffirm the charters and liberties that his father had granted to Haverford.

The following year, 1220, Llywelyn again campaigned south with an army. Although there was supposed to be a truce, he claimed that the Marshals and the Flemish had continually 'broken the peace' by staging attacks against the Welsh. He burned both Narberth and Wiston castles and moved against Haverford, where he was able to burn the town right up to the castle gates, however the castle was strong enough to withstand the assault. The damage to the town, though, was extensive, and the records of grants show there must have been a substantial amount of rebuilding required. The Marshal campaign of 1223 re-established the earl of Pembroke's authority in the region, with the surprise invasion quickly sweeping through the south-west, retaking all the castles including Carmarthen and Cardigan, placing Haverford once again in a far more secure position. The ravages of war, which sometimes flared up over the next 40 years, did not encroach upon that corner of Wales and the town prospered and grew.

Each son of William Marshal (d.1219) died childless with the inheritance passing to his younger brother. Finally, in 1245, the last son Anselm died without a male heir, and the vast Marshal estates were split between the first earl's daughters and granddaughters. Haverford was apportioned to Eva, who had married William de Braose (d.1230), but she was already dead. Therefore, the lordship was divided between her three surviving daughters and the families that they had married into, with Haverford split between the Mortimers, the de Cantilupes and the de Bohuns, who were all powerful Marcher families. Shortly after the partition, the de Cantilupes gave their portion of Haverford to the de Bohuns. Thus, Humphrey de Bohun (d.1265), who had married Eleanor de Braose, became the majority holder of Haverford with his two-thirds share in 1248. Humphrey, who was the son of Humphrey de Bohun, 2nd earl of Hereford (d.1275), sided with the rebel barons in the Barons' War of 1264–65, dying in captivity of wounds sustained in the battle of Evesham in 1265, thus predeceasing his father. During the rebellion, Haverford was seized by William de Valence (d.1296), lord of Pembroke in 1265. As Humphrey's father, the 2nd earl of Hereford, had fought in the victorious royal army at Evesham, de Valence was to hold the lordship only until Humphrey's (d.1265) son (another Humphrey), came of age. Although this occurred in 1273, de Valence did not hand the castle over to him immediately, requiring an intervention by the new king, Edward 1, to settle the matter. De Valence conceded the castle to Edward 1, who granted it in 1275 to Humphrey (d.1298) when, on the death of his grandfather (the 2nd earl of Hereford), he acceded to all the lands and titles of the de Bohun family.

Haverford Castle: acquired by Queen Eleanor in 1288, who spent vast sums improving it (© Paul Davis)

It was around this time that Edward I's queen, Eleanor, fell in love with Haverford whilst making a pilgrimage to St Davids. Meanwhile, de Bohun and de Valence continued to have a contentious relationship, with de Valence claiming that Haverford be held of him and de Bohun arguing that it was a separate lordship held directly from the king. De Bohun was also involved in various other struggles throughout the March, particularly with Gilbert de Clare (d.1295), the earl of Gloucester. With these other pressing matters, and the fact that he only held a two-thirds portion, he exchanged his share of Haverford with Queen Eleanor in 1289. She promptly put her own men in charge and spent large sums of money on improving the castle, though she was not able to enjoy the fruits of the labour as she died in 1290. After the queen's death, William de Valence claimed again that the burgesses of Haverford owed suit at his court in Pembroke. However, Edward I decided against de Valence, and the townspeople of Haverford were able to hold their own court, with a bailiff chosen from three honest men from the town. King Edward also confirmed that the residents of Haverford were free from toll throughout the realm. The town remained under royal control until Edward's death in 1307. The following year, the two-thirds of Haverford controlled by the Crown were granted by Edward II to Aymer de Valence (d.1324). Aymer, a younger son of William de Valence, had become earl of Pembroke after his mother's death in 1307. He was a loyal and active servant of the Crown, particularly in France and Scotland, though his extensive travels meant that he was an absentee lord.

As Aymer was the earl of Pembroke, the matter of whether Haverford was part of the lordship of Pembroke was again not a point of conflict. However, after Aymer's death (childless) in 1324, when his two-thirds reverted to the Crown, the one-third portion that had gone to Roger Mortimer (d.1282) through his marriage to Maud, the daughter of Eva de Braose, became significant. He would, most likely, have been denied any revenues while it was in the hands of his baronial enemy, Humphrey de Bohun (d.1265), but he would have received revenue thereafter. The revenues that were made up of burgage rents on his third amounted to £6 10s at his death in 1282.[14] After Roger's death, as it was part of Maud's inheritance, the one-third share formed part of her dower, which she granted to a younger son, Roger Mortimer of Chirk (d.1326). Although Roger of Chirk was a loyal administrator and commander throughout his career, the threat posed by Hugh Despenser to the Mortimers pushed him into the faction that took up armed opposition to the Despensers, and thus against Edward II. Captured in 1322, Roger of Chirk was imprisoned in the Tower of London, where he died in 1326.

The nephew of Roger of Chirk, Roger Mortimer of Wigmore (d.1330), who had been imprisoned in the Tower with his uncle, escaped to flee into exile in France, where he forged an alliance with Edward II's wife, Queen Isabella, who was also in exile at the French court. Returning to England in 1326, Roger and Isabella forced Edward II to abdicate in favour of his teenage son, who became Edward III. During the minority of the new king, Roger Mortimer was the de facto ruler of the country, alongside Queen Isabella, becoming the 1st earl of March. During his ascendancy, Mortimer took all of Haverford for himself (disinheriting his uncle's son) and granted it to the Queen. When Mortimer was executed for treason in 1330, Edward III agreed that his mother, Isabella, could keep Haverford for herself. When she died in 1355, it reverted to her grandson, the Black Prince, who was the eldest son of Edward III and therefore the heir to the throne. After his death it passed to his son, Richard, and on his coronation it thus merged with the Crown, Haverford remaining a royal possession to be managed by agents of the Crown.

The Laws in Wales Acts of 1536 and 1542 incorporated Haverford as the county town into the new county of Pembrokeshire.

Castles and Abbeys

Haverfordwest Castle: originally built in the first wave of Flemish settlement by Tancred the Fleming on a strategically important site above the Cleddau river. The remains of the castle we see today originate from the works carried out by Queen Eleanor of Castile, the wife of Edward I, who fell in love with Haverford and acquired it for herself in 1289 (see pp. 152 & 154).

Haverfordwest Priory: the Augustinian Priory was built downstream of Haverford Castle in the time of the Fleming, Robert fitz Richard (d.1211). The current priory site features a restored medieval garden that was uncovered during excavations in the 1980s. It is the only surviving medieval ecclesiastical garden in Britain. The site is managed by Cadw.

~

The Lordship of Cemais

The Marcher lordship of Cemais was formed from one of the seven existing *cantrefi* of Dyfed in western Deheubarth. The lordship was established during the early part of the reign of Henry I and, remarkably, was in the hands of one family, the fitz Martins, for over 200 years. Cemais is bounded to the north by the River Teifi with its strategic castle of Cardigan. To the east is Cilgerran/ Emlyn, with, to the south and west, the lordships of the bishops of St Davids, Pebidiog and Llawhaden. The Irish Sea forms its western border.

> ### The lords of Cemais
>
> Robert fitz Martin (d.c.1159); William fitz Martin (d.1209); William fitz Martin (d.1216); Nicholas fitz Martin (d.1282); William Martin (d.1324); William Martin (d.1326); James Audley (d.1386); Nicholas Audley (d.1391); John Tuchet (d.1408); James Tuchet (d.1459); John Tuchet (d.1491); James Tuchet (d.1497), lordship forfeited to the Crown.

Brief History

A great deal of the early historical work on Cemais was carried out by George Owen of Henllys, who himself was a lord of Cemais, although it was no longer a Marcher lordship by then. His work *A Treatise of Lordshipps Marchers in Wales* was the definitive book on the subject from the time of its publication in around 1595, and remained so for several hundred years. Ironically, he set out to prove that Cemais had been a Marcher lordship held directly from the king, but in fact found that it had been held of the earls of Pembroke. It is now accepted that the first Norman to conquer Cemais was Robert fitz Martin (d.c.1159). As a younger son of a Norman magnate from Devonshire and Somerset, he had to look for advancement elsewhere: the March of Wales provided such an opportunity in the early reign of Henry I. Although the details of Robert's early life are obscure, he married the widow of Robert Peverel, which brought lands in Devon as her dowry. Robert fitz Martin was one of the early *Conquistadors* of Wales, building Nevern Castle on high ground a few miles inland, on the remains of an existing ancient fortification. By 1110, there were two other Norman castles nearby, that would have provided some security during the establishment of the lordship, but which also became a focal point of the political conflict in that region. Firstly, Gerald of Windsor built his castle at what is now Cilgerran by 1109 and secondly the de Clares built a castle at Cardigan as part of their occupation of Ceredigion after 1110.

St Dogmael's Abbey founded by Robert fitz Martin in the early twelfth century
(© Crown copyright 2022 Cadw)

We know that Robert must have felt secure enough in his position, and held high enough status, to establish a religious house at St Dogmael's in 1113, just downstream from Cardigan Castle and on the southern bank of the Teifi. He travelled to France to the abbey of Tiron, and brought back the original 13 monks to populate his newly-established religious house. This was followed by another 13 monks and an abbot which elevated St Dogmael's to abbey status.[15]

Following the death of Henry I, there was a sudden shift in the balance of power. The Welsh rebellion which followed came right to the doorstep of Cemais. When a large Welsh army marched south towards Cardigan Castle in 1136, destroying Norman outposts as it went, Robert fitz Martin was part of the group of local settlers that met the Welsh just north of Cardigan at the battle of Crug Mawr, where the Norman, English and Flemish army suffered a comprehensive defeat. Although Robert survived the battle, his lordship was in a precarious position. There is no record that the Welsh sacked his castle at Nevern, nor is there any evidence that they tried. Robert was most likely rarely present in Cemais over the next few years; indeed, the area may have been in Welsh hands. He was active in the civil war that ravaged England, siding with the Empress Matilda against King Stephen, as many other Marcher barons did. Robert was dispossessed of some of his lands in England for his support of the Empress, but when her son Henry II ascended to the throne, his lands were restored.

Robert's first wife predeceased him without producing an heir. Robert's second wife, Alice, bore two sons and a daughter. The eldest son, William fitz Martin (fitz Martin had become a family name), was a minor when his father died at around the age of 70 in *c*.1159, and little is known about the history of Cemais during William's minority. When William (d.1209) did come into his inheritance in 1176, he married Angharad, a daughter of the Lord Rhys. Cemais bordered the *cantref* of Emlyn, which Rhys had occupied in 1165, and Henry II had confirmed to him in 1171 when he was made Justiciar of south Wales; so this marriage acted as mutual security for both William and the Lord Rhys.

When Henry II died in 1189, the Lord Rhys mounted a campaign throughout south-western Wales, sacking several Marcher castles in the process. In 1191, despite his oath of loyalty to his son-in-law, he sacked Nevern Castle, transferring the castle to his own eldest son, Gruffudd. During the strife amongst the sons of the Lord Rhys, Gruffudd lost Nevern to his elder brother and arch-rival, Maelgwn, who, working with the help of another brother, Hywel Sais, dispossessed him. The two brothers also had a disagreement with their father, which resulted in the capture and imprisonment of the Lord Rhys in the very castle that he had treacherously taken from his son-in-law. With the political situation in Deheubarth so fluid in the mid 1190s, in the absence of Maelgwn, Hywel took control of Nevern and decided that it was prudent to release his father from prison, without the consent of Maelgwn. In 1195, the tide began to turn when William de Braose (d.1211) waged

Nevern Castle: the first castle built by the Norman occupiers of Cemais (© Paul Davis)

a campaign of conquest through Deheubarth in which he took St Clears from Hywel, which was also held by him. The fear of losing Nevern forced Hywel to destroy the castle in order to keep it from falling into Marcher hands. In 1204, Hywel ceased to play any further role when he was treacherously killed by the men of his brother, Maelgwn. The same year William Marshal took Emlyn and Cilgerran back for the Anglo-Normans and restored all Cemais to fitz Martin.

Towards the end of the twelfth century, William fitz Martin, who had clung on to parts of his lands, abandoned Nevern Castle after Hywel had slighted it, as it was outdated and becoming too difficult to defend. Although he received a loan from the government in 1197–98 to repair his castle at Cemais, it seems likely that he took this money to build a new castle rather than repair Nevern. He chose a headland, which he still held, at the mouth of the River Nevern as the best place to establish a new residence. A settlement quickly grew around it, named Newport, which was in existence no later than 1198. Although William was actively looking after his other estates in the south-west of England, he devoted enough of his time to get the castle and church built quickly.

When William fitz Martin died in 1209, he was succeeded by his son, William (d.1216), who was married to the sister of one of King John's key agents, Fawkes de Bréauté (d.1226). William was fined 300 marks to succeed to his inheritance by King John, a sum that was considerably larger than the 100 marks that was the accepted norm for such a fine. He would not have held Cemais for long, as Llywelyn ab Iorwerth took advantage of the turmoil surrounding the Barons' War that engulfed England. In a winter campaign of 1215, he overran most of Deheubarth, sacking the castle at Newport. In the following year Llywelyn granted it to Maelgwn, a son of the Lord Rhys, as part of his extensive holding in western Dyfed. William died in 1216, leaving an infant son, Nicholas, who was placed in the wardship of his uncle. Although Fawkes de Bréauté gained possession of the fitz Martin lands in Devon and Somerset at that time, he was still not in possession of Cemais in 1222, as there is a record of King Henry III reminding Llywelyn of his obligation to return Marcher lands taken in 1215.[16] The matter was settled by force in 1223 when William Marshal (d.1231) launched his invasion which re-took Cilgerran and Cardigan castles (amongst others) from the Welsh, thus re-establishing the authority of the earl of Pembroke in the region. An inquisition by the king followed, to determine whether Cemais was to be held directly from the king or from the earl of Pembroke. The king determined that Cemais was to be held of the earl of Pembroke, which probably dated back to the original re-conquest of William Marshal in 1204.[17] Cemais continued to be held by William Marshal the younger until Nicholas (d.1282) came of age in 1231.

Newport Castle, home of the lord of Cemais, the ruins now incorporated within a stately home
(© Crown copyright: Royal Commission on the Ancient and Historical Monuments of Wales)

The next years were generally peaceful, as Llywelyn ab Iorwerth saw out his last days under a truce. This period of stability was a time of growing power for the Marcher lords of the south-west, who became more active in key administrative and military roles for the Crown. However, when the Welsh, led by Llywelyn ap Gruffudd, rose against the harsh rule of the English in 1257, Nicholas was part of the English army comprehensively defeated in the Tywi valley that year. The leader of the expedition was killed, with Nicholas fitz Martin and other Marcher lords captured and held for ransom. With the English army in tatters, the resurgent Welsh destroyed Newport Castle amongst many others. Nicholas's tenants in Cemais were urged to raise the money to ransom him. This was eventually done and he returned to royal service, becoming, at various times, custodian of Cardigan and Carmarthen castles.[18] As his son had predeceased him, when Nicholas died in 1282, he was succeeded by his grandson William Martin (d.1324), the usage of 'fitz' having dropped out of fashion.

William Martin also had an active career in royal service, serving on Edward I's campaigns in Wales, Scotland and Gascony. Summoned to parliament in 1295, thus becoming Lord Martin, he was politically active in the turbulent reign of Edward II, remaining loyal to the king against the failed rebellion of the earl of Lancaster in 1322. When William Martin died in 1324, his heir (another William, who was married to the daughter of John Hastings) survived for only two years, dying childless in 1326. The lordship of Cemais was, therefore, divided between William's two sisters, Eleanor, the wife of Philip Colombers, and Joan, the wife of Nicholas, Lord Audley. Nicholas had died in 1316 leaving an underage son, James (d.1386), who was a ward of the king. When Roger Mortimer, 1st earl of March, had control of the royal government, he gained the wardship of James in 1328, marrying him to his daughter Joan. The other half of the inheritance also came to James in 1342 when his aunt Eleanor died childless. James had an active career in military service. He granted Cemais to his son, Nicholas, no later than 1370 (some 16 years before his death). Nicholas fell out of favour with the king for a time, as he continued to dispute the jurisdiction of the earl of Pembroke over Cemais. Once again, the lord of Cemais was reminded that he held from Pembroke and owed suit in the court there, and received a hefty fine for his efforts. He had, though, managed to get back in favour before he died childless in 1391, having arranged that his widow Elizabeth would hold Cemais for the rest of her life. When she and another sister died childless in 1401, Cemais passed to the sister of Nicholas Audley, Joan, who was married to Sir John Tuchet. With the Tuchets becoming the lords of Cemais from this point and summoned to parliament as 'Lord Audley'. (The Tuchet descent is described in more detail in the lordship section under Cantref Bychan.) Cemais passed into royal hands when the last lord of Cemais was beheaded in 1497 for rebelling against King Henry VII.

The Laws of Wales Acts in 1536 and 1542 incorporated Cemais into the new county of Pembrokeshire.

Castles, Churches and Abbeys

Newport Castle: built at the end of the twelfth century when the fitz Martin lords moved their home castle to the safer location near the sea. The castle is now incorporated into a private residence and is not open to the public (see p. 161).

Nevern Castle: built on the high ground above the Nevern river by the fitz Martin family in the early twelfth century, the motte and bailey castle was taken and occupied by the Lord Rhys and his sons in 1191. This forced the fitz Martins to move their main castle downstream to Newport. The remains of the bailey and motte are still clearly visible to the visitor who is prepared to hike up from the village to see them (see p. 159).

Church of St Brynach: the church is a Norman structure which occupies a site said to have had a church on it originally dating back to the sixth century. The impressive **Nevern Cross** can be found in the churchyard and is similar to the more famous Carew Cross. It also dates from the late tenth or early eleventh century.

St Dogmael's Abbey: founded in the early twelfth century by the lord of Cemais, St Dogmael's Abbey was started by 13 monks brought from France. The ruins of the abbey lie just downstream from Cardigan Castle. The site is open to the public and admission is free (see p. 158).

~

The Lordships of Cilgerran and Emlyn

The Marcher lordships of Cilgerran and Emlyn were formed from the *cantref* of Emlyn, which was one of the seven *cantrefi* in Dyfed. The lordships are combined here as they comprised a single polity until their formal separation in 1240, though Norman control of Emlyn was piecemeal and sporadic in the twelfth century and early thirteenth century. The two lordships were formed within the boundary of the *cantref* of Emlyn, with the *commote* of Emlyn Is-Cych becoming Cilgerran, and the lordship of Emlyn formed from Emlyn Uwch-Cych, with the two separated by the River Cych. Indeed, the Laws in Wales Act of 1536 placed Emlyn in the county of Carmarthenshire with the Cych forming the boundary with Pembrokeshire; however, Emlyn is included here due to its earlier association with Cilgerran.

The lords of Cilgerran and Emlyn

Gerald of Windsor (d.c.1116); **William fitz Gerald** (d.1173); from 1165 to 1204 under the control of **the Lord Rhys and his sons**; **William Marshal** 1st earl of Pembroke, 2nd creation (d.1219); from 1215 to 1223 held by **Maelgwn ap Rhys**; **William Marshal** the younger 2nd earl of Pembroke (d.1231); **Richard Marshal** 3rd earl of Pembroke (d.1234); **Gilbert Marshal** 4th earl of Pembroke (d.1241).

Cilgerran Castle by J.M.W. Turner 1798 (© Tate)

The lords of Cilgerran

From 1240: **Gilbert Marshal** 4th earl of Pembroke (d.1241); **Walter Marshal** 5th earl of Pembroke (d.1245); **George de Cantilupe** (d.1273); **John Hastings** (d.1313); **John Hastings** (d.1325); **Julia de Leybourne** (d.1367); **John Hastings** 2nd earl of Pembroke, 4th creation (d.1375); **John Hastings the younger** 3rd earl of Pembroke (d.1389); reverted to **the Crown** until 1414; **Humphrey** 1st earl of Pembroke, 5th creation, 1st duke of Gloucester (d.1447); **William de la Pole** 1st earl of Pembroke, 6th creation, 1st duke of Suffolk (d.1450); **Jasper Tudor** 1st earl of Pembroke, 7th creation, 1st duke of Bedford (d.1495); **William Herbert** 1st earl of Pembroke, 8th creation (d.1469); **William Herbert** 2nd earl of Pembroke (d.1491) until 1479 when he ceded it to **the Crown**; **Prince Edward** 1st earl of Pembroke, 9th creation (d.c.1483); merged with **the Crown** again in 1483; **the Crown** until 1485; **Jasper Tudor** (d.1495); reverted to **the Crown** until 1532.

The lords of Emlyn

From 1240: **Mareudd ap Rhys Gryg** (d.1271); **Rhys ap Mareudd** (d.1292); from 1288, possession of **the Crown** until 1340; **Richard la Bere** (d.1382); **Simon de Burley** (d.1388); John Hastings the younger, earl of Pembroke (d.1389); **John de Burley** (d.1428); **William Burley** (d.1446); **Thomas Hopton** (d. not known); **Gruffudd ap Nicholas** (d.1461); **Thomas ap Gruffudd** (d.1474); **Rhys ap Thomas** (d.1525); **Walter Devereux**, Lord Ferrers, 1st viscount of Hereford (d.1558).

BRIEF HISTORY

It is likely that the first Norman castle in the region was built by Gerald of Windsor, the steward of Pembroke Castle. The *Brut* retells how he built the castle of Cenarth Bychan, which is generally considered to be latter-day Cilgerran in 1108, and he, *'Placed there all his possessions and his wife and his offspring and all his nearest kin.'*

Gerald clearly intended to establish his own Marcher lordship; however, his position was not as secure as he had hoped. As described in Chapter 3, Owain ap Cadwgan of Powys and his men dug their way into the castle in order to abduct Gerald's wife Nest, with Gerald escaping through the latrines. After sacking the castle Owain raped Nest before taking her and the children away. This incident caused outrage and set in motion the events that led Henry I to grant Ceredigion to the de Clare family. Gerald was to get his revenge in 1116, when Owain was spotted near Carmarthen Castle by a group of Flemish fighters who were on royal business with Gerald. They pursued Owain, who is said not to have run because he too was on royal business. However, the memory of the abduction of Nest still burned, and they chased him down and killed him. It is likely that Gerald died shortly thereafter, as he no longer appears in any records, with his son, William fitz Gerald (d.1173) succeeding him as lord of Cilgerran.

Gerald's security would have been greatly enhanced by the strong Norman presence to the north in Ceredigion, established by the de Clares. That safety barrier, however, was shattered following the death of Henry I. William and his brother Maurice were in the Anglo-Norman and Flemish army that was routed at Crug Mawr in 1136, with both fortunate to escape the slaughter of the battle.

When Henry II came to the throne in 1154, the castle was still held by William fitz Gerald. Although he had some difficulty keeping the young Rhys ap Gruffudd in check, in general the early reign of Henry II was a time for a resurgence of Marcher authority. Indeed, the ruler of Deheubarth was forced to concede some lordships that had been gained during the reign of King Stephen – most notably Carmarthen, Ceredigion, Cantref Bychan and Llanstephan. However, Henry II's failed military campaign of 1165 led to another Welsh resurgence. With royal authority weakened in Wales, Rhys ap Gruffudd went on the offensive after Henry II returned to the Continent. Rhys sacked Cardigan Castle and captured its castellan, Robert (also a son of Nest by a different father, Stephen, a former castellan of Cardigan in the 1130s). He then moved on to Cilgerran Castle which he took, imprisoning the unfortunate Robert there. The following year, an army of Flemish fighters (and we must assume William) twice failed in their attempts to retake the castle by force; with Rhys in the ascendency, they lacked the resources to dislodge him. Indeed, in 1167, Robert was allowed by the Lord Rhys to join the campaign to Ireland, provided he swore never to return to west Wales.

Cilgerran Castle and Emlyn remained in the hands of the Lord Rhys until after the end of the century. In fact, when William fitz Gerald died in 1173, his heir, Odo, was compensated with lands in Devon by Henry II for the loss of 'the castle and land of Emlyn'.[19] Rhys now held territory adjacent to William fitz Martin in Cemais. As part of a treaty between the two, Rhys married his daughter to the lord of Cemais and promised to provide joint-security.

With the accession of King John to the throne, William Marshal was made the earl of Pembroke. He was granted the *commote* of Velfrey and the lordship of Ystlwf 'until he might regain Emlyn'. He was mainly active in France in the early 1200s, engaged as a military commander for the king in the failed defence of Normandy. Upon returning from France in 1204, William Marshal travelled to south-west Wales and, in a royally-sponsored campaign, swept north from Pembroke in a surprise attack to take Cilgerran and Cardigan castles from the sons of the Lord Rhys. Both remained in Marshal hands until 1215, when they were lost to Llywelyn ab Iorwerth, who invaded south-west Wales during the time of the baronial rebellion against King John. At a council

Cilgerran Castle: construction of the stone castle was begun by William Marshal the younger (d.1231) (© Philip Hume)

summoned by Llywelyn at Aberdyfi in 1216, Emlyn was granted to Maelgwn, a son of the Lord Rhys. It remained with Maelgwn until William Marshal the younger (d.1231) recovered it in his campaign at Easter 1223. Maelgwn was replaced as leader of Emlyn by Cynan ap Hywel, a grandson of the Lord Rhys and the son of the murdered Hywel (d.1204), and supported the Marshals in the recovery of Emlyn. This is another example of how the descendants of the Lord Rhys would ally themselves with whomever they believed would give them the best advantage for gain.

Following the Marshal campaign of 1223, William began to build a strong stone castle at Cilgerran, the remains of which we see today. Cynan ap Hywel remained in charge but was subject to the earldom of Pembroke until the death of Llywelyn in 1240. Following the death of the great ruler of Gwynedd, his heir, Dafydd, was not able to hold the gains his father had made through conquest, with the Marshals regaining lands. At the same time, they removed Cynan ap Hywel from Cilgerran/ Emlyn, who they claimed had supported the Welsh against them. This time, they retained the western *commote* of Emlyn Is-Cych (Cilgerran) in their direct control, installing Maredudd ap Rhys Gryg, a staunch ally of Gilbert Marshal in the eastern *commote* of Emlyn Uwch-Cych (Emlyn). This arrangement backfired when Maredudd complained to the king that he was being forced to pay homage to the Marshals; that is, he did not hold of the Crown. Following an enquiry, it was adjudged that Maredudd did indeed hold from the Crown, thus formally splitting Emlyn into a separate lordship. It was a short time after the division in 1240 that Newcastle Emlyn Castle was constructed by the Welsh on the strategic loop in the Teifi river, to provide a castle in the new lordship.

~

THE LORDSHIP OF EMLYN

On the death of Maredudd in 1271, Emlyn passed to his son, Rhys ap Maredudd, who supported the English in the final conquest of Wales in 1282–83. His main castle was at Dryslwyn where he harboured expectations that his loyalty would lead to Marcher status; however, he soon found that he was under the strict guidance of the local royal official, Tibetot, and subject to the royal court at Carmarthen. With his powers curtailed, he rebelled in 1287, taking several Marcher castles; however, he was soon pinned back in his castle of Newcastle Emlyn. When the English brought up a large siege engine, he knew the game was up and went into hiding, but was captured and executed. After Rhys's rebellion, Emlyn was forfeited to the Crown, and despite attempts by the earls of Pembroke to have it granted back to them, the

Crown maintained its hold over it. The Marcher lordship of Emlyn was then managed by various stewards for the Crown until 1349. It was during this period that the castle was repaired and rebuilt. The ruins that we see today are from this time. There followed a succession of lords appointed by Edward the Black Prince, including his close associate and tutor to the future King Richard II, Simon de Burley. He was condemned to death by the 'Merciless Parliament' in 1388 for treason, along with many other of the king's close associates. Following a brief interlude during which the lordship was held by Pembroke, the lordship was granted back to the brother of Simon de Burley after the Glyn Dŵr rebellion. It was sometime after his heir and brother died in 1446, that the lordship was seized by Gruffudd ap Nicholas, who was the sheriff of Carmarthenshire and used his position to amass large estates in Carmarthenshire. His grandson, Rhys ap Thomas, was a key supporter of Henry Tudor, helping him to victory at the battle of Bosworth and to the throne. Rhys would have found the castle in a state of disrepair, as a result of which he renovated it and turned it into a Tudor hunting lodge.

~

THE LORDSHIP OF CILGERRAN

Cilgerran remained in Marshal hands until the last of the male line died without an heir in 1245, becoming part of the great Marshal inheritance that was divided between the daughters and granddaughters of William Marshal (d.1219). The Cilgerran portion went to a granddaughter, Eva, who married William de Cantilupe (d.1254). When Eva died a year after her husband, the heir to the lordship was her son George who was not of age. His custody was entrusted to Nicholas fitz Martin of Cemais, and then to Guy de Brian of Laugharne. George Cantilupe came into his inheritance in 1273 but died that same year. The lordship then passed to the son of George's sister, John Hastings (d.1313), who came of age in 1283 after having been a ward of the earl of Pembroke, William de Valence. John Hastings was a loyal servant of the Crown, taking a leading role in the efforts to quell the uprising of 1287 by Rhys ap Maredudd, and serving in Scotland and Gascony. In 1309, he granted Cilgerran to his son, another John (d.1325), who inherited all the Hastings estates on the death of his father in 1313. John died in 1325 and his heir by his first wife, Juliana de Leybourne, was Laurence, who was a minor. In 1325 Laurence's wardship was granted to King Edward II's favourite, Hugh Despenser the younger; however, the lordship of Cilgerran was granted back to Juliana and her second husband Thomas Blount in dower. Laurence Hastings died in 1347, before his mother, so he never came into the lordship of Cilgerran (though he had inherited from his grandmother, Isabel de Valence, the earldom of Pembroke). When Juliana died in 1367, Cilgerran passed to her grandson, John Hastings (d.1375), earl of Pembroke. He was confirmed in his lordship when he came of age a year later in 1368. When John died in 1375 the lordship passed to his son, John Hastings the younger, who also became earl of Pembroke. When he was accidently killed practicing for a tournament in 1389, the lordship passed to the Crown, after which it continued to be granted as part of the earldom of Pembroke.

The Laws in Wales Acts of 1536 and 1542 incorporated Emlyn into the county of Carmarthenshire, whilst Cilgerran became part of Pembrokeshire.

Castles and Abbeys

Cilgerran Castle: the remains of the stone castle sit prominently above a gorge on the Teifi river in the far north of Pembrokeshire. The castle was built by William Marshal (d.1231) after his re-conquest of Dyfed in 1223. The castle is open to the public and managed by Cadw (see pp. 74, 96, 164, 166 & 170).

Newcastle Emlyn Castle: an example of a stone castle that was built by a Welsh lord in west Wales. The original castle dates from around 1240, but the features of the ruins of the castle that one can see today are from around 1500, when the lordship was in the hands of Rhys ap Thomas, a favourite of King Henry VII. The castle is open to the public (see below).

Newcastle
Emlyn
Castle

Reconstruction of Cilgerran Castle
(© Chris Jones-Jenkins)

The lordship of Narberth developed in close association with that of Pembroke. It is likely that there was an early Norman castle on the site as part of the incursion by the Montgomery family in 1093. Early references to the castle are often in association with it being burned down during a Welsh uprising. The first recorded lord of Narberth was Henry fitz Henry, a son of Nest ferch Rhys ap Tewdwr, from her affair with Henry I. He was the half-brother of many of the leading early Norman settlers, who were also the offspring of Nest. They formed a tight group who took key positions in the early days of the conquest. Narberth is landlocked and lies just to the north of Pembroke. The masonry castle that we see today was most likely built in the mid to late thirteenth century when it was in the hands of the powerful Mortimer family.

The lords of Narberth

Initially unclear, possibly part of the royal demesne of Pembroke; **Henry fitz Henry** (Roy) (d.1157); no formal records, see text; **the Marshals** (last Marshal d.1245); **Maud Mortimer** (d.1301); **Roger Mortimer of Chirk** (d.1322); forfeited to **the Crown**; 1322–26 controlled by **the Crown** (**Rhys ap Gruffudd**, d.1356, steward 1326–30); **Roger Mortimer** 1st earl of March (d.1330); 1330–54 controlled by **the Crown** (**Rhys ap Gruffudd**, steward 1332–37); controlled by the diocese of St Davids on behalf of **the Crown** 1337–54; from 1354, **Roger Mortimer** 2nd earl of March (d.1360); **Edmund Mortimer** 3rd earl of March, 5th earl of Ulster, 2nd creation (d.1381); **Roger Mortimer** 4th earl of March, 6th earl of Ulster (d.1398); 1397, granted to **Sir Edmund Mortimer** (d.1409), forfeited in 1402; **Crown** control from 1402–13; **Edmund Mortimer** 5th earl of March, 7th earl of Ulster (d.1425); **Richard Plantagenet** 3rd duke of York, 6th earl of March, 8th earl of Ulster (d.1460); York descent to **the Crown**.

BRIEF HISTORY

The history of Narberth as a Marcher lordship began with the Norman invasion of Dyfed in 1093 by the Montgomery family. Arnulf of Montgomery, a son of Roger of Montgomery, was given the castle that was built at Pembroke to the south-west. It is possible that a castle was built at Narberth around this time or shortly thereafter by one with an affinity to the Montgomery family, although no record survives of such a castle. We do know, from the chronicle sources, that all the castles of Dyfed were destroyed and burned in the Welsh fight-back of 1094, apart from Pembroke itself, suggesting an array of castles in the area. The first known record in the written sources of the castle at Narberth is in 1116, when it was sacked and burned by Gruffudd ap Rhys during his brief uprising. The rebellion was short-lived, and the castle would have been rebuilt while Henry I kept the province in royal hands until his death in 1135.

It is unclear precisely when, but the son of Henry I by his mistress Nest (the sister of Gruffudd ap Rhys) became the lord of Narberth – Henry fitz Henry (Roy), who was styled 'Lord of Narberth'. It seems likely that the grant of the lordship occurred sometime during the reign of Henry I, but it could have happened later, when Pembroke was made into an earldom and granted to Gilbert de Clare in 1138. In any case, Henry would immediately have been on the defensive as the Normans and Flemish suffered a catastrophic defeat in battle near Cardigan in 1136. Although the settlers in the region had suffered a severe setback, the fact that there is no mention of the castle being sacked in the *Brut*, most likely indicates that it was not attacked at that time. Henry was also the first steward of the Marcher lordship of St Davids, and thus in charge of the secular responsibilities. His local connections and his relationship to the king would have been instrumental in his appointment. Henry fitz Henry most likely held the lordship until his death in Anglesey in 1157, when he was part of a seaborne force of knights sent from Pembroke to aid Henry II's invasion of Gwynedd. Unfortunately, with the lust for battle and plunder getting the better of the attackers, they made a brief stop in Anglesey; after plundering several churches they paused, allowing the local Welsh to quickly counter-attack with Henry killed while retreating to the ships.

It is also unclear who held the lordship following Henry's death. Gilbert de Clare had died in c.1149, to be succeeded as earl of Pembroke by his brother Richard. When Henry II abolished many of the new earldoms, Pembroke went back into royal hands, and it is not certain that there was a lord of Narberth at that time. There was certainly a castle, as it was sacked and burned in 1159 during the revolt by Gruffudd's son, Rhys. There is a late twelfth-century charter that mentions a William of Narberth, who may have been the lord, but this is unclear.[20]

Narberth was bordered by the *commote* of Velfrey to the east, which had been part of the lordship of St Clears that had reverted to the Crown. Velfrey was granted to the Lord Rhys in 1171 by Henry II, along with several other grants when he was made Justiciar. It seems, though, that Narberth remained in Anglo-Norman hands throughout this period. When Henry II died, the Lord Rhys went on the offensive against the Marcher lords of Dyfed, and it is probable that Narberth would have been caught up in the attacks.

The ruins of thirteenth-century Narberth Castle (© Philip Hume)

When William Marshal became earl of Pembroke, he had a claim to Emlyn; however, this was in Welsh hands at the time and, in 1201, King John granted him Velfrey (which had reverted following the death of the Lord Rhys) and Ystlwyf until he could regain Emlyn. William Marshal launched a successful attack on Emlyn/Cilgerran in 1204, establishing him firmly in the wider region, whilst also stabilising the area for the Anglo-Norman settlers. There is still no mention of a 'lord of Narberth' in the records in the early thirteenth century, and therefore it was most likely part of the lands of the earl of Pembroke. William Marshal's hold over the lordships around Pembroke remained strong through the early years of John's reign. Despite this, as the pressures grew on King John (leading to the Barons' Revolt and Magna Carta in 1215), circumstances changed for Marshal. Seizing the opportunity presented by the weakness of the English Crown, the ruler of Gwynedd, Llywelyn ab Iorwerth, launched an invasion with the support of most of the Welsh rulers of Deheubarth, including Maelgwn and Rhys Gryg, sons of the Lord Rhys, and two grandsons, Rhys and Owain. They swept through Dyfed with ease, with Narberth, and several other Marcher castles, burned. With the royal government in no position to counter the Welsh attacks, Llywelyn decreed that the lands of Ystrad Tywi, Carmarthen and Ceredigion be divided between the descendants of the Lord Rhys. Although Narberth was threatened, it remained in the hands of the Marshals.

When William Marshal died in 1219, his son and heir William Marshal the younger (d.1231) became the earl of Pembroke. With the royal government still rebuilding and the new earl of Pembroke in place, the Welsh went on the rampage again in 1220. This time, Narberth, along with Wiston, was burned, and the town of Haverford was also destroyed up to the castle gates. Such was the damage to

Narberth, an order went out in 1220 to the locals to assist William Marshal (d.1231) in repairing the castle.[21] Despite these setbacks, William agreed a truce with the Welsh; however, he took advantage of the ensuing period of peace to go to Ireland to raise an army. On the day the truce expired, Easter 1223, Marshal landed at Dale at the head of the army. He swept up through Dyfed and Carmarthenshire and was able to reassert Marshal authority over the region. He regained control of most of the Marcher lordships which had been lost during the Welsh attacks of 1215–20. It was probably at this time that he annexed Velfrey into Narberth, thereby significantly increasing the size of the lordship.

Narberth remained in the hands of the sons of William Marshal, earls of Pembroke, until the line died out without a male heir in 1245. The landholdings of the earl of Pembroke were divided between the daughters and granddaughters of William Marshal (d.1219). Narberth passed to Roger Mortimer of Wigmore (d.1282) through his marriage to Maud de Braose, the daughter of Eva de Braose (née Marshal). The Mortimers also received a third of Haverford and a third of St Clears.

Narberth had not been in Mortimer hands for long when another Welsh invasion in 1257 saw the castle destroyed, with many of the garrison slain, including its constable, Henry Wingan. Evidence suggests that it was following the sacking of the castle in 1257 that the Mortimers set about rebuilding it in stone. The stone upgrade was most likely finished by the time that Roger Mortimer died in 1282.

The lordship of Narberth, which now included the *commote* of Velfrey, was held by Mortimer from the Crown directly. The first lord of Pembroke after the Marshals was William de Valence, the half-brother of Henry III. He sought to re-establish the authority of the earldom of Pembroke over Narberth by claiming jurisdiction in legal matters, insisting that suits of court in Narberth be held at the court of the earl of Pembroke. Roger Mortimer did acquiesce to this claim in 1272, ordering his tenants to hold suit at the county court of Pembroke; however, it is difficult to know to what extent they complied with this agreement, as there were later complaints from Pembroke that this was not being implemented.[22]

After Roger Mortimer died in 1282, Narberth was part of the dower lands of

Narberth Castle: the stone castle was built by the Mortimers in the thirteenth century

Roger's widow Maud, who granted the lordship to a younger son, Roger Mortimer of Chirk (d.1326). The final Welsh wars did not impact upon Narberth. Despite this, the castle did suffer a further burning in 1299 when Roger of Chirk was away campaigning in Gascony.

Subsequently, Roger Mortimer of Chirk was one of the main rebels against Edward II and his favourite Hugh Despenser the Younger. He was with the rebels who surrendered in 1322 and was sent to the Tower, where he died in 1326. Forfeited to the Crown, Narberth was held by a constable, Rhys ap Gruffudd (d.1356), until 1326 when it became a grant for life. However, when Edward II was forced to abdicate in 1326 by another Mortimer, Roger (d.1330), the nephew of Roger Mortimer of Chirk, Rhys had to flee to Scotland. Roger Mortimer exercised his new powers to take large amounts of land into his possession, including Narberth, despite his own cousin, the son of Roger of Chirk, being the actual heir. When Roger Mortimer, now 1st earl of March, was executed in 1330, Narberth again reverted to the Crown, which set in train several lawsuits to gain possession.

In c.1331–33 the grandson of Roger of Chirk unsuccessfully petitioned Parliament for Narberth. At the same time Rhys ap Gruffudd, who had been granted Narberth for life in 1326, petitioned for the lordship as well as one third of St Clears and his suit was successful. Despite this, he never managed to gain possession and he relinquished his claim in 1337. The heir of the downfallen Roger Mortimer (d.1330), his grandson Roger (d.1360), gradually rehabilitated the family standing with King Edward III, becoming the 2nd earl of March. He was able to have Narberth and his third of St Clears granted to him in 1354, despite the fact that the rival claims of the Chirks and Rhys ap Gruffudd were still bubbling away. On his death in 1360 his lands were assigned to his widow Philippa, who retained Narberth until her death in 1382, outliving her son, Edmund, by one year. Thus, her heir became her grandson, Roger Mortimer (d.1398), a minor who received the lordship upon attaining his majority in 1394.

Though Roger died in Ireland in a skirmish in 1398, he had gifted Narberth to his brother Sir Edmund in 1397 who became caught up in the Owain Glyn Dŵr revolts. He was dispossessed of Narberth in 1402, and died fighting on the side of the Welsh. After a period in the control of the Crown, it reverted to Edmund Mortimer, 5th earl of March (d.1425), whose heir was his nephew Richard, duke of York, who held Narberth until he was killed in 1460 at the battle of Wakefield. Along with all the other Mortimer and York lands, Narberth passed to Richard's son, Edward, and when he was crowned Edward IV, it merged into the properties of the Crown.

The Laws in Wales Acts of 1536 and 1542 incorporated Narberth into the county of Pembrokeshire.

~

THE LORDSHIP OF PEBIDIOG/ LLAWHADEN

The Marcher lordship of Pebidiog/ Llawhaden, which belonged to the diocese of St Davids, was the sole ecclesiastical Marcher lordship in south-west Wales. Following the Norman Conquest, King Henry I used his authority to have the first Norman bishop installed there in 1115, confirming that the lands were held directly from the king, granting the bishop the right to hold his own law court, build castles and exert general dominion over his tenants. These were the same rights as those held by secular Marcher lordships.

The narrative of the bishopric after 1115 was dominated by the attempts of many of the bishops to make St Davids a metropolitan See on a par with Canterbury and York. Their attempts were thwarted by both the kings and the archbishops of Canterbury. The most famous candidate to the bishopric was Gerald of Wales. However, he was also a victim of the central authority's success in blocking a strong candidate with aspirations for the Church. That story is outside the scope of this study but is ever-present in the background of the narrative. The chief seat of the diocese was at the cathedral, with the lands surrounding it known as Pebidiog. The bishops later built a castle as an administrative centre at Llawhaden. They also held lands near Pembroke Castle where they built a palace at Lamphey in the fourteenth century.

St Davids Cathedral: seat of the bishops of St Davids (© Philip Hume)

The lords of Pebidiog/ Llawhaden

The **diocese of St Davids** held the lordship, which was normally administered through stewards, who paid the bishops an annual fee and kept the proceeds including from justice and rents for themselves.

BRIEF HISTORY

The bishops of St Davids were heads of the prime Church of Wales, but they were also active in the turbulent politics of Wales. A good early example was the involvement of Bishop Sulien (d.1090), who aided Rhys ap Tewdwr in 1081 to gain the leadership of Deheubarth. Following that victory, it may have been the bishop who negotiated the agreement with King William I, which made Rhys a client ruler of William's. Furthermore, Gerald of Wales noted in his retelling of the story of the early defence of Pembroke Castle in 1096, that Gerald of Windsor allowed a letter to slip into the hands of bishop Wilfred, knowing that the bishop would betray its contents to the Welsh, thus deceiving the besiegers into believing that the Norman defences were stronger than they were. Gerald of Windsor was subsequently recorded in the *Brut* getting his revenge for the bishop's lack of discretion:

> *The following year Gerald the steward, to whom the stewardship of Pembroke castle had been entrusted, ravaged the bounds of Menevia* [St Davids].

Bishop Wilfred remained in his position throughout the subsequent Norman incursions into Wales, struggling to hold some of his decentralised lands against the new invaders. When he died in 1115, the canons of St Davids were summoned to London to choose a successor. With the king promoting Bernard, the queen's chaplain, as his favoured candidate, the Welsh canons had little choice but to accept. With his appointment, Bernard also received a grant from the king that he would hold his lands directly from the Crown, administering them as a Marcher lordship. In a move that would be repeated by many subsequent bishops, Bernard chose a person with strong political connections to be his steward – Henry, the illegitimate son of Henry I by Nest, the Welsh princess.[23] Bernard remained bishop throughout the reign of Henry I and through the Welsh resurgence after 1135. Following his death in 1148 the bishopric was granted to the son of Gerald of Windsor and Nest, David fitz Gerald. This was most likely a reflection of the fact that large parts of the region were now under Welsh control, and that somebody with local credibility and authority (and who was half-Welsh) would be preferable to another candidate from the royal court. Bishop David chose his brother Maurice fitz Gerald to be the steward, which furthered the grip of that family's power in the region.

The Marcher rights of St Davids were confirmed by Henry II on his visit to the cathedral in 1171, on his way to Ireland.[24] When Bishop David died in 1176, he had been accused of granting church lands to his family members, which he was unable to deny. This perhaps influenced Henry II in the next appointment. The canons favoured Gerald of Wales, who was the nephew of Bishop David and also part Welsh. He was also a strong proponent of the metropolitan status of St Davids. Henry II was not interested in creating more problems and pushed for Peter de Leia, the prior of Wenlock Abbey, to succeed David. Henry had his way, and Peter was duly consecrated. Bishop Peter's greatest achievement was the rebuilding of St Davids Cathedral, which began during his bishopric. He clearly had insight into how the machinations of local power worked there, because he chose the son of Maurice fitz Gerald, William, as his steward.

Bishop Peter de Leia may have been the head of the Welsh Church, but he was often absent from Pebidiog and Llawhaden, preferring the comforts of England. However, he was also not immune to the conflict that raged towards the end of the life of the Lord Rhys, visiting the ruler of Deheubarth in 1197 to plead for peace, as his territory had suffered earlier when his castle at Llawhaden had been taken in 1192 and then destroyed in 1194. The sons of the Lord Rhys were in no mood for peace, so they took exception to his visit. They dragged him out of his bed half-dressed and into the woods. It was only the intervention of the men of William de Braose that saved him from their clutches and an unknown fate. Peter then exercised the most powerful weapon available to him: he excommunicated Rhys and his sons. Therefore, when Rhys died a few days later he was not allowed to have a church burial. The distraught sons begged for a reversal of the excommunication. Peter, upon receiving assurances of peace, readmitted the corpse of the Lord Rhys back into the church (after it had been purged through a ritual flailing) and he was duly buried in St Davids Cathedral.

The lordship continued to be governed by bishops who were the choice of either the king or the Archbishop of Canterbury until 1214, when Iorwerth (d.1229), the abbot of Talley Abbey, was chosen. There is little doubt that the powerful Llywelyn ab Iorwerth was instrumental in that choice, given that he was the first pure Welsh bishop since 1115. The early years of Bishop Iorwerth's tenure were marked by continuous warfare. He brokered the peace in 1217 that prevented the town and castle of Haverford from being burned or sacked. It is not clear why, but there

Llawhaden Castle: administrative centre of the Marcher lordship of Pebidiog (© Chris Jones-Jenkins)

are few records of any other actions by him. The next choice of bishop showed yet again where the power in the region lay, as he was the nephew of William Marshal (d.1219), Anselm le Gras (d.1247) – although a dispute between Henry III, who was in favour of his appointment, and the Archbishop of Canterbury meant that he was not appointed until 1231.[25]

In 1241, following the death of Llywelyn ab Iorwerth, Henry III reaffirmed that the bishop of St Davids was to pay homage only to the king directly. Although this was merely a reaffirmation of earlier grants, it was most likely directed at Gilbert Marshal, who was amassing more power in the region. He had already caused the displeasure of the king by demanding the fealty of one Welsh ruler. This grant must have been a move to stop the Marshals from exerting control over the bishop's secular interests. This clear demonstration by the bishops of St Davids of their Marcher status thwarted the few future attempts to subordinate St Davids by secular lords. During the rest of the thirteenth century another descendant of Gerald of Windsor and Nest was appointed as bishop, as well as the younger son of Nicholas Martin, the lord of Cemais.

St Davids Bishop's Palace (Crown copyright 2022, Cadw)

After the final conquest of Wales in 1283 another key difference between this ecclesiastical lordship and the other lordships became evident. A tax was levied by Edward I in 1292 to pay for a Scottish campaign, that the barons of the realm as well as the Marcher lords contributed to. The understanding from the Marcher lords was that the tax should not (and it did not) set a precedent for their future taxation. However, despite its status as a Marcher lordship, taxes were levied on St Davids on several occasions, being subject at times to the taxes levied on the other churches of the realm. The generally peaceful times that existed following the final conquest enabled the bishopric to acquire enough wealth to build lavish palaces. Under the leadership of Bishop Gower (d.1347) large parts of the Bishop's Palace at St Davids were built as well as the second hall at Lamphey Palace.

The bishopric suffered ups and downs through rebellion, plague and other events until the Dissolution. It should be noted that St Davids was spared the worst depredations of the Dissolution of the Monasteries, most likely because of Henry Tudor's connection to the region.

The Laws of Wales Acts in 1536 and 1542 incorporated Pebidiog/ Llawhaden, for administrative and judicial purposes, into the county of Pembrokeshire.

Castles, Cathedrals and Palaces

St Davids Cathedral: the seat of the head of the Welsh Church and a pilgrimage destination, St Davids Cathedral in its current form was begun during the tenure of Bishop Peter de Leia (d.1198) between 1180 and 1182. Subsequent bishops have made multiple additions to construct the cathedral that one sees today (see pp. 7, 40 & 176).

St Davids Bishop's Palace: built by bishop Henry Gower (d.1347) between 1328 and 1347 to create a home for the bishops, that matched the importance of the cathedral. Gower was also responsible for some of the most magnificent additions to the cathedral, including the site of his own tomb. The ruins are open to visitors and managed by Cadw (see p. 180).

Llawhaden Castle: this ruined castle/ palace lies in an area of central Pembrokeshire that also belonged to the bishopric of St Davids. A castle was originally built on the site by the first Norman bishop, Bernard (d.1148) to protect and administer the Marcher lordship that King Henry I created in 1115. After the Edwardian conquest the castle evolved into more of a fortified mansion, which offered protection and comfort to the visiting bishops. The site is open to the public and managed by Cadw (see p. 179).

~

OVERLEAF: The Welsh county of Carmarthenshire. Detail of the map by John Speed (by permission of Llyfrgell Genedaethol Cymru/ National Library of Wales)

CHAPTER NINE

The Lordships of Carmarthenshire

CANTREF BYCHAN, ISCENNEN, KIDWELLY, LLANSTEPHAN, LAUGHARNE,
YSTLWYF, ST CLEARS

THE lordships of Carmarthen were carved out of the southern part of the kingdom of Deheubarth that came into existence in the first half of the tenth century, when the kingdom of Seisyllwg joined with Dyfed during the reign of Hywel Dda (d.949). The kingdom of Seisyllwg was made up of the regions of Ceredigion and Ystrad Tywi, which became the counties of Cardigan and Carmarthen in 1536.

The lordships of Carmarthen were mainly formed from the southern *cantrefi* of Ystrad Tywi and eastern Dyfed which were taken by the Marcher lords in the late eleventh and early twelfth century. Cantref Mawr and Ceredigion remained in the lands of *Pura Wallia*. A number of areas that lay in eastern Dyfed (to the west of the Tywi) are included here as they came within the orbit of the castle at Carmarthen, and were incorporated into Carmarthenshire by the 1542 Laws in Wales Act; whereas the Act of 1536 had gone with the geography by including them in Pembrokeshire.

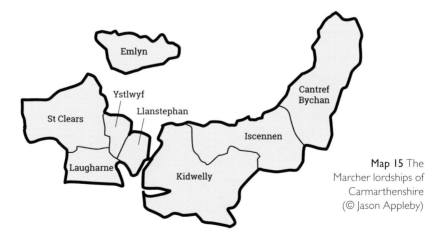

Map 15 The Marcher lordships of Carmarthenshire (© Jason Appleby)

The Marcher lordships of Carmarthenshire can be divided into three categories. Firstly, those where the main castle was within the protective sphere of the royal castle at Carmarthen, all of which had access to the sea. The second was the lordship conquered in the early reign of Henry I, but without access to the sea: Cantref Bychan. This proved difficult for its Marcher lords to hold; indeed, it was held by the Welsh more than by its Anglo-Norman lords for the first 200 years of its existence. The final lordship, Iscennen, was only created in 1283 from the Welsh *commote* in southern Cantref Bychan. It had been part of *Pura Wallia* until then.

The cluster of castles that were built near present-day Carmarthen can trace their roots back to the initial Norman conquest of eastern Dyfed by William fitz Baldwin in 1093. It was, however, Henry I's construction of the royal castle at Carmarthen between 1106 and 1109 that laid the foundation for the permanent settlements that become the Marcher lordships. This anchor of royal power was the military and administrative centre for the region, the fortunes of which set the tone for where the balance of power lay. Carmarthen was built near a previous Roman fort at the mouth of the Tywi river. All the Marcher castles lay to the east, south and south-west of Carmarthen, with the lands of *Pura Wallia* to the north. Thus, Carmarthen was often the first to come under attack in the event of Welsh campaigns. There were many examples of the castle and town suffering burnings and sackings. However, if the castle was able to withstand the assault, the Welsh hold in the region remained tenuous. There were two periods when the castle did fall or was destroyed: 1137 and 1215. In both instances, Carmarthen was occupied by the Welsh, which ushered in a period of native superiority.

Throughout the early thirteenth century the region was characterised by the struggle between Llywelyn ab Iorwerth – the mighty prince of Gwynedd and de facto ruler of Wales – and the powerful Marshal family, the earls of Pembroke. This period ended in the 1240s with the death of both Llywelyn and the last Marshal. With the rulers of Deheubarth fragmented politically since the 1190s, the period after 1240 was marked by a clear return to Marcher, and royal, supremacy. The lordships of Cemais and Kidwelly that had been seized, were granted back to the Marcher families who held them in hereditary right. The Marcher lords from these lordships were then active in military and administrative service during the final years of the reigns of Henry III and the reign of Edward I. When the king took Carmarthen and Cardigan castles back into royal hands in 1241, the ground was set for the formation of the Principality of Wales in 1284. This bastion of English administrative power controlled much of the region until the Laws in Wales Acts of 1536 and 1542.

The Marcher lordships of Carmarthenshire were different from those in the rest of the March. Tied to Carmarthen for security, the relationship was formalised by the bond that the Marcher lords owed. We know from several documents that the Marcher lords near Carmarthen held their lordship by the service of one knight's fee if needed in times of war. They were also bound to hold suit of court at the Carmarthen Crown Court for certain types of cases. So, it was not completely true that the king's writ did not run in this part of the March. That said, the lords still had their own courts and how much they respected this depended on the strength of the individual Marcher family.[1] An example of why this relationship to Carmarthen was more than just a formality is provided by Edward i's reaction to William de Valence's seizure of Ystlwyf following the failed rebellion of Rhys ap Maredudd in 1292. Edward sued de Valence in a royal court, arguing that the lordship pertained to Carmarthen. The king won the lawsuit and confiscated the lordship, although Edward did grant it back to de Valence within a year. However, he was to hold Ystlwyf from Carmarthen and not as part of his lordship of Pembroke. Clearly, it was more than just a casual historical link that bound Ystlwyf to Carmarthen; rather, it was a legal relationship bound by formal agreements.

This bond between Marcher lordship and the royal authority at Carmarthen, did become blurred over the centuries that followed. Indeed, the lordships of Kidwelly and Iscennen became part of the powerful Duchy of Lancaster, which withdrew those lordships entirely from royal administration. The other lordships maintained the administrative bond to varying degrees; though it is clear that by the time of the Laws in Wales Act of 1536 the bond had all but disappeared. When the county of Carmarthen was formed, those lordships that were in Dyfed – that is to the east of the Tywi river – became part of Pembrokeshire. The lordships of Llanstephan, Ystlwyf and part of St Clears had all become part of the holdings of the earl of Pembroke by the end of the fifteenth century. The pull of the historic bonds, however, led to an amendment in the updated Act of 1542, which transferred them back into Carmarthenshire (as well as Laugharne which had also been put with Pembrokeshire).

THE LORDSHIP OF CANTREF BYCHAN
The Marcher lordship of Cantref Bychan lies in the far north-east of present-day Carmarthenshire. It was a Marcher lordship by 1116, when it was recorded as the lands of Richard fitz Pons, with the castle at Llandovery which is situated on the old Roman road between Brecon and Carmarthen. It also lies strategically at the confluence of the Rivers Bran and Gwydderig, close to where those rivers run into the River Tywi. Unlike many Marcher lordships in the south-west, it was

landlocked and therefore could not be relieved from the sea. As it also lay very close to the centre of the power-base of the dynasty of Deheubarth at the castle of Dinefwr, all this combined to create a lordship that would prove hard to hold for its Norman lords. Indeed, it was in Welsh hands for over 100 years, becoming a flashpoint for the struggles between the heirs to the Lord Rhys.

Llandovery Castle: a flashpoint in the struggles for supremacy in Cantref Bychan

The lords of Cantref Bychan

Richard fitz Pons (d.1129); **Walter fitz Richard fitz Pons** – later styled Walter Clifford (d.c.1190); **The Lord Rhys** and his descendants until 1277; **John Giffard** (d.1299); **Katherine Giffard** m. Nicholas Audley (d.1299); **Nicholas Audley** (d.1316); **James Audley** (d.1386); **Nicholas Audley** (d.1391); **John Tuchet** (d.1408); **James Tuchet** (d.1459); **John Tuchet** (d.1491); **James Tuchet** (d.1497) beheaded – lordship forfeited.

BRIEF HISTORY

Cantref Bychan became a Marcher lordship during the reign of Henry 1 (d.1135) when Richard fitz Pons (d.1129) established himself there. Richard was a supporter of the conqueror of Brecon, Bernard de Neufmarché, who, in the late eleventh century, had steadily pressed along the Wye and Usk valleys, building castles as he went. By 1093 Bernard had reached Brecon, which forced the ruler of Deheubarth, Rhys ap Tewdwr, into a battle during which he was killed. Richard fitz

Pons was clearly instrumental in the conquest of Brecon as he was rewarded with the lordship of the *cantref* of Selyf, which he held from Bernard de Neufmarché. Richard expanded his influence downstream by building a castle at Llandovery in Cantref Bychan. With the son of Rhys ap Tewdwr, Gruffudd, in exile in Ireland in the early twelfth century, there would be little Welsh resistance. We know that the castle had been built by 1116 because it was one of the first to be attacked in Gruffudd's uprising of that year, following his return. The *Brut* states:

> *Thence he* [Gruffudd ap Rhys] *went to Llandovery, where was the castle of a certain leader called Richard fitz Pons, to whom king Henry had given Cantref Bychan, and he tried to breach it and to set it on fire, but he failed …*

It is interesting to observe a Welshman employed by a Norman as steward of a Norman castle. In this case it was Maredudd ap Rhydderch ap Caradog, a prominent local Welshman who was named by the *Brut* as the defender of the castle. The Welsh of Gruffudd ap Rhys had no suitable siege equipment, so the castle of Llandovery did not fall.

Following the death of Richard fitz Pons in 1129, his son Walter became lord of Cantref Bychan. Walter fitz Richard was also the steward of Clifford Castle and married to Margaret de Tosny, the daughter of the absentee lord of Clifford, Ralph de Tosny. With the de Tosny family mainly active on the Continent, Walter later began to style himself as lord of Clifford, and referred to himself as Walter Clifford, using that name in several charters. Although there was a de Tosny heir, Walter Clifford's bold usurpation of the name Clifford began to stick, thus displacing the de Tosny family to become the recognised lord of Clifford, which he combined with his holdings in Cantref Selyf and Cantref Bychan.

After the death of Henry I in 1135, Llandovery Castle was seized from Walter in the general Welsh uprising that broke out in 1136. There was no chance that Walter had the strength to retake the castle without royal assistance, which was not forthcoming. In fact, when a Norman relief party was sent to rescue the stranded wife of the lord of Ceredigion, who had been trapped in Cardigan Castle following the Anglo-Norman defeat at the battle of Crug Mawr, they were warned not to go via Llandovery as all roads were controlled by the Welsh. The castle of Llandovery and the lordship of Cantref Bychan remained in Welsh hands until 1158.

When Henry II came to the throne in 1154, one of his early aspirations was to re-establish royal control. The castle and lordship of Cantref Bychan were in the hands of the now head of the house of Deheubarth, Rhys ap Gruffudd (d.1197). Henry II forced Rhys to submit to his authority, making him return Cantref

Bychan to the Cliffords, as well as ensuring the return of several other lordships that Rhys held. However, the men of Walter Clifford somewhat overplayed their hand in 1158, as the *Brut* records that

> *In the meantime Walter Clifford carried off spoil from the territory of Rhys ap Gruffudd, and slew many of his men from the land next to him; for it was he who owned the castle of Llandovery.*

When Rhys approached the king for restitution and got no satisfactory response, he took matters into his own hands by sacking the castle of Llandovery as part of a general uprising against the new order. Henry came to south Wales again to quell the unrest, but his gains were temporary as he had to return to the Continent to deal with matters there. One can see from royal records that money was spent to repair Llandovery Castle in 1160 and 1161. However, the castle and lordship were finally lost to the Cliffords in 1163, as the records show that those expenditures ceased, indicating that they had given up trying to defend it.[2] After this loss, Cantref Bychan and Llandovery Castle stayed in Welsh hands for over 100 years.

The history of Cantref Bychan during the period the Lord Rhys was ruler of Deheubarth was generally a peaceful one. He had repairs carried out at the castle sometime before 1184. When a threat to his security in the area came, though, it was from his own family, members of which began violently to feud with one another, with his sons seeking control of the *cantrefi* and *commotes* where they could gain support. After Henry II died in 1189, the agreement between himself and Lord Rhys disintegrated, with the Lord Rhys attacking and sacking many of the Marcher castles in the south-west. However, whilst he was campaigning against the Marcher lords, his sons fought for their own gain. In 1195 the *Brut* records

> *And then Rhys and Maredudd, sons of the Lord Rhys, gained possession of the castle of Dinefwr by treachery and of the castle of Cantref Bychan with the consent of the men of the commote on every side.*

Rhys soon had the upper hand again though, imprisoning the two disloyal sons in a castle in northern Ceredigion.

The death of the Lord Rhys in 1197 set in motion the dynastic family feuds which were to dominate the history of Deheubarth for the next century. Maredudd ap Rhys had control of Cantref Bychan, but in 1201 he was killed by the Anglo-Normans of Kidwelly, and the lordship passed to his elder brother Gruffudd ap Rhys. When Gruffudd died later in 1201, his heirs, Rhys Ieuanc and Owain, became

Dinefwr Castle: family seat of the house of Deheubarth, which lies on the border of Cantref Bychan (© Philip Hume)

the rulers of Ystrad Tywi as well as Cantref Bychan. Despite the constant feuding between the sons of the Lord Rhys, the relationship between them was fluid, with the brothers forging alliances where they thought they could gain a territorial advantage. It would be too lengthy to recount here all the changes to the Welsh ownership of Cantref Bychan but, as an illustration of this, it changed hands between several of the Lord Rhys's sons and grandsons in 1202, 1203, 1204, 1210 and 1213. The constant infighting resulted in the loss of influence and power of the rulers of Deheubarth. In 1215, with King John (d.1216) embroiled in a civil war, the ruler of Gwynedd, Llywelyn ab Iorwerth, took advantage of the situation to establish his supreme authority throughout Wales. He marched south, uniting the separate rulers of Deheubarth on a campaign of conquest. The combined Welsh were able to take many of the Marcher lordships into their own hands. In 1216 Llywelyn was in such a strong position, and with royal power at its weakest, that he held a council to divide the inheritance of the Lord Rhys between his sons. Cantref Bychan was divided at this time, with the castle and *commote* of Hirfryn going to Maelgwn ap Rhys; the rest of Cantref Bychan was apportioned to his brother Rhys Gryg. This arrangement, however, did not last, with Llandovery Castle changing hands several more times between their descendants, until it was finally settled by the campaigns of Edward I in 1277 and 1282–83.

Following the first Welsh campaign of 1277 all the castles in the region were taken into the king's hands, and Edward I granted the castle of Llandovery to John Giffard of Brimpsfield (d.1299). After the second Welsh campaign, Giffard was confirmed in his grant of Llandovery Castle on 2 June 1282 by Edward I, and was also granted the nearby lordship of Iscennen. John Giffard was married to Matilda

Dryslwyn Castle: family seat of Rhys ap Maredudd, who rose in revolt in 1287 (© Crown copyright 2022, Cadw)

Clifford, the heir of Walter Clifford (d.1268), having managed to gain her hand by highly unconventional means. Widowed from her first husband, and a wealthy heiress after the death of her father, John Giffard abducted and raped her at his manor in Gloucestershire. She managed to get a message to the king to come and rescue her from her abductor. The king received the message and was on his way to secure her release when another messenger arrived. This one told the king that a rescue was no longer required as she had married her erstwhile captor! John Giffard thus became lord of Clifford with a right to Cantref Bychan (amongst others).

Although Giffard was clearly one of the king's favourites based on the royal favours that were bestowed upon him, he did lose Cantref Bychan and Iscennen for a time. In 1287, Rhys ap Maredudd, a local Welsh ruler from Dryslwyn, rose in rebellion against English rule. He had been a loyal supporter of Edward I throughout the two Welsh wars of 1277 and 1282, but he felt that he was not being treated by the king's officials in the way that he should, given the support he had provided. Rhys was able to score some stunning early victories, taking Llandovery Castle soon after the rebellion started. Although the rebellion was crushed within a year, with the defeated Rhys executed in 1292, John Giffard was blamed for the early setbacks that the English had suffered. In 1288, he was deprived of his lordships of Cantref Bychan and Iscennen on the grounds that he had garrisoned his castles with too few men, allowing them to be taken too easily; however, an order was given in 1289 to restore to him the lands that he had been deprived of following the rebellion. John Giffard was active in royal service for the last ten years of his life, dying in 1299 shortly after returning from Edward's Scottish campaign of 1298.

After his death, some of the lands that he held that pertained to the Clifford barony were divided between the four daughters of John and his wife, Matilda

Clifford. Cantref Bychan was granted to their second daughter, Katherine, and her husband Nicholas Audley (d.1299). As a side note, John Giffard had a son from a second marriage to Margaret Neville, also called John; however, John (d.1322) did not receive any lands pertaining to the Cliffords, though he did become the lord of nearby Iscennen, as that was not considered part of the Clifford barony.

Katherine's husband, Nicholas Audley, died in 1299, the same year in which they received Cantref Bychan. The heir was their son, Nicholas (d.1316), who was married to Joan Martin, the coheiress of Cemais, who also held vast estates in Devon. Nicholas died in 1316 leaving an underage son, James (d.1386), who inherited the lordship of Cemais as well as Cantref Bychan. He became a ward of Roger Mortimer, 1st earl of March, who had gained control of the government after forcing the abdication of Edward II in 1326. Roger arranged for James to be married to his own daughter, Joan, with James coming into his inheritance in 1329. James was part of the affinity of Henry, the earl of Lancaster, an extremely powerful and influential member of Edward III's regime. They would have been neighbours in the March, as Henry was the lord of Iscennen and Kidwelly. James died in 1386, having granted his Welsh holdings to his son Nicholas in 1374.

Nicholas (d.1391) was active in royal service in south Wales. He held various offices, culminating in his appointment as Justiciar in 1385, as well as constable of Carmarthen Castle. His period in office was controversial as the records show that he was accused by local juries 'of offences ranging from extortion and armed robbery to complicity in murder, apart from incompetence and oppression'.[3] Though he denied most of the charges, he was no longer in office after 1389. When he died childless in 1391, the lordship passed to Nicholas's sister Joan, whose son, John Tuchet, came of age in 1401 and held the barony until his death in 1408. Each of the Tuchets served in Parliament as Lord Audley, having been summoned as such. James Tuchet, the 5th Baron Audley was a staunch Lancastrian and dedicated local administrator in Pembroke, but was killed at the battle of Blore Heath fighting for the Lancastrian cause. James Tuchet, the 7th Baron Audley, was an active supporter of King Henry VII. For reasons that are not entirely clear, though, he rose in rebellion in 1497. He became the leader of a group of rebels that were protesting a tax that had been raised to fight the war in Scotland. They marched from Cornwall to London where they were defeated on Blackheath, at which time James was captured and beheaded. This marked the end of the Tuchet lordships and Cantref Bychan was taken into royal hands. It also spelled ruin for his family who were never to recover financially from his rash decision to rebel.

The Laws in Wales Acts of 1536 and 1542 incorporated Cantref Bychan into the new county of Carmarthenshire.

~

THE LORDSHIP OF ISCENNEN

The Marcher lordship of Iscennen came into existence when Edward I created new
lordships following the end of native rule of Wales in 1282–83. As shown on Map
3 (pp. 10–11), they were mainly in north-east Wales, with Iscennen being the only
one in the south. Iscennen was a Welsh *commote* that formed the southern half of
Cantref Bychan, and its early history was dominated by the struggles between the
rival rulers of Deheubarth. The castle of Carreg Cennen is the main feature of the
lordship, standing proudly on a limestone escarpment above the River Cennen.

Carreg Cennen Castle: the principal castle of Iscennen sits on a limestone outcrop

BRIEF HISTORY

Iscennen was the southernmost *commote* of Cantref Bychan, which was in the hands
of Richard fitz Pons from 1116 at the latest. It is impossible to know how much
control fitz Pons would have exerted in the early twelfth century over the region,
which was deep in Welsh territory. It isn't likely that he had a great amount of
influence as the castle of Llandovery, which was the centre of the lordship, lies some
15 miles to the north. The castle, which was the administrative and defensive centre
of Cantref Bychan, was sacked in 1136. It was then lost to the Anglo-Normans until
the reign of Henry II in 1157, at which time Walter Clifford became the lord.

Llandovery was destroyed by the Lord Rhys in around 1162 and remained under
the control of the Welsh princes of Deheubarth until 1277. After the Lord Rhys
had evicted Clifford, he or one of his sons held Cantref Bychan and, therefore,
also Iscennen until his death in 1197. Following the death of the Lord Rhys, all the
commotes and *cantrefi* in the environs of the family seat at Dinefwr were disputed
amongst the rival heirs, with the lands in a near-constant state of warfare and
flux. Initially, the eldest son, Gruffudd ap Rhys, held most of Ystrad Tywi, with
his brother Maredudd holding Cantref Bychan. When they both died in 1201 the
struggle for supremacy in the region intensified. The main factions contending for
Iscennen were the sons of Gruffudd, Rhys Ieuanc and Owain ap Gruffudd, and
their uncles, Rhys Gryg and Maelgwn.

In 1215, Llywelyn ab Iorwerth took advantage of the baronial revolt in England
to sweep south with an army to seize a great number of Marcher and royal castles.
Llywelyn confirmed his authority over the descendants of the Lord Rhys when he

held a conference at Aberteifi in 1216, at which he allocated to each their inheritance. Rhys Gryg was appointed the lord of Iscennen and much of Ystrad Tywi. Although there were regular conflicts and struggles for power, he managed to keep his control of Iscennen until his death in 1234.

In 1241, the son of Rhys Gryg, Rhys Mechyll, was made a tenant-in-chief to the Crown, owing his homage to the king only and holding his lands directly from him, the same status as that of a Marcher lord. When Rhys Mechyll died in 1244, his children were underage, with his son, Rhys Fychan, gaining Iscennen in 1248.

During the Welsh uprising of 1256 – this time led by Llywelyn ap Gruffudd, the grandson of Llywelyn ab Iorwerth – Rhys Fychan was initially on the side of the king. However, when a royal army came to support him, he switched sides, resulting in the rout of the English army in the nearby Tywi valley. Following this, Rhys was dispossessed of all that he held from the king. In contrast, Maredudd ap Rhys Gryg, Rhys Fychan's uncle, had deserted the Welsh rebellion, so was granted Iscennen and most other lands in Ystrad Tywi, as Rhys Fychan was now viewed as a traitor. In 1258, Maredudd ap Rhys was captured by his nephew, who treacherously attacked when they were supposed to be working towards a truce. Maredudd was taken prisoner and sent to Criccieth Castle. At a court arranged by Llywelyn ap Gruffudd, Maredudd was found guilty of treason and was dispossessed of all that he had gained apart from his main base at Dryslwyn Castle. After he had removed Maredudd from his holdings, Llywelyn granted Iscennen back to Rhys Fychan as a reward for his loyalty. As Henry III was embroiled in the domestic crisis caused by the second Barons' Wars, he was unable to provide support to his Welsh ally in Deheubarth, Maredudd ap Rhys, who consequently swore his fealty to Llywelyn to be allowed to go free.

When Rhys Fychan died in 1271, it is possible that his sons were minors, as the ownership of Iscennen becomes unclear. When war broke out in 1276 between Llywelyn ap Gruffudd and Edward I, with Llywelyn's rule becoming increasingly unpopular, many of the native rulers of Deheubarth swore their allegiance to the Crown. After his victory, Edward I took all the castles in the region into royal hands, with the goal being to determine the rightful owner of each lordship. Whilst Cantref Bychan was granted to John Giffard of Brimpsfield, Rhys Wyndod, the eldest son of Rhys Fychan, claimed Iscennen. However, no settlement was agreed while the various claims were contested in the courts, with bailiffs of the Crown appointed to run the castle of Carreg Cennen.

This stalemate ended when war broke out again in 1282. This time, all the native rulers of Deheubarth, including Rhys Wyndod, but excepting Rhys ap Maredudd ap Rhys Gryg, allied with Llywelyn ap Gruffudd and his brother,

Carreg Cennen Castle prominently sitting atop the hill above the River Cennen

Dafydd. The Welsh scored an early victory near Llandeilo in 1282, during which several prominent English lords were killed. Despite this, they were soon isolated and surrendered later that same year.

With the deaths of Llywelyn ap Gruffudd in 1282, and Dafydd in 1283, the war was over, and this time Edward 1 was determined to end native rule in Wales. Rhys ap Maredudd, who had stayed loyal, was allowed to maintain his chief castle at Dryslwyn as well as his lordship of Newcastle Emlyn, but as a baron of the Crown. All the other native rulers were dispossessed, with many imprisoned in England – including Rhys Wyndod who languished in captivity in England until his death in 1302. John Giffard was reinstated in Cantref Bychan, and the king created a new Marcher lordship in Iscennen, which he also granted to Giffard in 1283. The terms were the same as those for the other Marcher lordships in the sphere of Carmarthen Castle. That is, it was held for the service of one knight's fee as long as the men and the bailiff of the *commote* gave their service for three days if summoned.[4] Earl Humphrey de Bohun (d.1298) made a failed attempt to have Iscennen granted to him on the basis that he had received the personal surrender of Rhys Wyndod. As the lord of Gower, which borders Iscennen to the south, he would have benefitted from the addition to his lands.

Giffard's ownership lasted until 1287 when Rhys ap Maredudd, despite his years of loyalty, rose in revolt against the king. The rebels quickly took several castles, including Carreg Cennen, and burned several key towns of which Carmarthen and Swansea were the most significant. Although the revolt was soon crushed, as mentioned earlier, the lordships of Iscennen and Cantref Bychan were taken from Giffard on the grounds that he had not defended them adequately, and granted to earl Humphrey de Bohun, though both lordships were returned to Giffard in 1289. John Giffard was a regular in royal service, including taking an active role in quelling another Welsh revolt in 1294, for which he received many gifts from the king. In one of his last acts of service, he took part in the king's Scottish campaign of 1298.

When John Giffard died in 1299, the estates that pertained to the Clifford barony were divided between the daughters of John and Matilda Clifford. However, as Iscennen had never been part of the Clifford barony, the heir was his

Carreg Cennen Castle (© Crown copyright 2022 Cadw)

son, another John Giffard of Brimpsfield (d.1322), who came into his majority in 1308 when he was confirmed as lord of Iscennen as well as Brimpsfield. John Giffard served the new king, Edward II, and was one of the nobles captured at the defeat against the Scots at Bannockburn, where he had to be ransomed. Trouble began to brew for John Giffard when Hugh Despenser the Younger, a favourite of Edward II, was granted Dinefwr and Dryslwyn castles in 1317. The proximity of the two castles to one another meant that their tenants were often violently at odds. As Hugh Despenser was regularly in conflict with many other Marcher families, a great number of them rose in rebellion in 1321, demanding that the Despensers be banished from the kingdom. After some initial success the rebellion crumbled. John Giffard surrendered with the last of the rebels and was hanged in 1322. Hugh Despenser the Younger was granted all of John's lands, including Iscennen. Interestingly, the castle was granted to him with all rights, including quit of suit at the royal county court of Carmarthen. This meant that all matters of law were to be settled in the lord's local court and none at the royal court. This was a grant that none of the other lordships attached to Carmarthen received. Iscennen was now a completely independent Marcher lordship.

Hugh Despenser was not able to enjoy his success for long as he was executed in 1326 following the forced abdication of Edward II. Though John Giffard's forfeiture of 1322 was reversed at around this time, he had died childless. Therefore, Iscennen remained in Crown hands until 1330 when it was granted to John Mautrevers (d.1364), a close associate of Roger Mortimer, 1st earl of March (d.1330), who controlled the government at that time. When Mortimer fell from grace, Mautrevers was forced into exile and Iscennen was granted to Maurice de Berkeley (d.1347) for life in 1331. In 1337, Berkeley surrendered it to Edward III so that he could grant it to John Wylington, a cousin of John Giffard, in 1337 to hold by hereditary right. However, in 1340 his son, Ralph Wylington, gave the lordship to Henry of Grosmont, the 4th earl of Lancaster and the lord of Kidwelly. When Henry became the duke of Lancaster in 1350, the lordship of Iscennen became part of the Duchy of Lancaster.

Henry died without a male heir in 1361 and the lordship passed to his sister Blanche who was married to the son of Edward III, John of Gaunt. Their son was Henry Bolingbroke who became Henry IV in 1399. One of Henry's first acts as king was to stipulate the conditions under which the Lancaster inheritance should be held, specifying that it should be held separately from all other Crown possessions, and should descend through the monarchy as a private estate. Thus, Iscennen was held personally by the monarchs through the Duchy of Lancaster rather than the Crown.

As an aside, there was a suit filed by Gilbert Talbot (d.1346) that he should be granted Iscennen on the grounds that he was a descendant of Llywelyn ap Rhys Fychan ap Rhys Gryg. Talbot argued that Llywelyn was in the king's peace in the time of Edward I and therefore his family should not have been dispossessed and the lordship not granted to Giffard. The case wasn't particularly strong, but it played out in court for years. The grandson of Gilbert Talbot finally quitclaimed the lordship to John of Gaunt and Blanche in 1362, thus ending any claim the Talbots may have attempted.

Carreg Cennen played a role in the Glyn Dŵr uprising in the early fifteenth century. Given its prominent position, it became a military outpost to be garrisoned. Its commander at the start of the rebellion, Philip Scudamore, switched to the Welsh side, but he was eventually captured and beheaded (although his brother remained steward throughout). He was recorded as overseeing repairs to the castle following the damage done to it by Welsh rebels between 1403 and 1410. The castle then played a small role in the Wars of the Roses in the middle of the fifteenth century. However, when that war was over, it was decided to slight the castle to make it indefensible, as it had become a haven for robbers.

The Laws in Wales Acts of 1536 and 1542 incorporated Iscennen into the new county of Carmarthenshire.

Castles

Carreg Cennen Castle: situated on a limestone crag some 300 feet above the River Cennen, this stunning castle strikes an imposing image for miles around. It was probably built by John Giffard (d.1299), lord of Iscennen, at the end of the thirteenth century. The castle is privately owned and open to the public (see pp. 192, 195 & 196).

~

Kidwelly Castle
by J.M.W. Turner
(© image courtesy
Lytham St Annes
Art Collection,
Fylde Council)

THE LORDSHIP OF KIDWELLY

The Marcher lordship of Kidwelly was created during the reign of Henry I in the early twelfth century from the two existing Welsh *commotes* of Cydweli and Carnwylion. The boundary lies a short distance south of the royal castle of Carmarthen, meaning that their fortunes during the near-constant warring were often intertwined. It is bordered to the north by Cantref Mawr, to the east is the Gower peninsula, with the Bristol channel to the south. Given the proximity to the predominantly Welsh region of Cantref Mawr it was often one of the first Marcher lordships to suffer attacks during uprisings. The castle is situated on a cliff top above the tidal stretch of the Gwendraeth river. Thus, Kidwelly Castle, like the other castles along the coast, was able to be resupplied from the sea.

The lords of Kidwelly

Bishop Roger of Salisbury (d.1139); **Maurice de Londres** (d.1166); **William de Londres** (d.1211); **Thomas de Londres** (d.1216); **Hawise de Londres** (d.1274); **Patrick de Chaworth** (d.1258); **Payn de Chaworth** (d.1279); **Patrick de Chaworth** (d.1283); **William de Valence** (d.1296); **Henry of Grosmont** 4th earl and 1st duke of Lancaster, earl of Leicester, earl of Lincoln, earl of Moray (d.1361); **John of Gaunt** 2nd duke of Lancaster, duke of Aquitaine, earl of Richmond, earl of Leicester, earl of Derby (d.1399); **Henry Bolingbroke** 3rd duke of Lancaster, 3rd earl of Derby, 4th earl of Leicester, earl of Northampton and Hereford, became Henry IV of England (d.1413); **subsequent monarchs through the Duchy of Lancaster**.

It is unlikely that there was an early castle built during the first Norman invasion into south-west Wales in 1093, as the *Brut* records that, in 1095, the French laid waste to Gower and Kidwelly following the Welsh counter-attacks of 1094: '*The following year the French ravaged Gower and Cydweli* [Kidwelly] *and Ystrad Tywi, and the lands remained waste.*'

When Henry I came to the throne in 1100, he was directly involved in the budding Norman colonisation of south-west Wales. While putting down the rebellion of the Montgomery brothers, Henry persuaded their ally, Iorwerth ap Bleddyn of Powys, to defect, with promises of lands in south Wales. After the Montgomery brothers were defeated, however, the king failed to deliver on all the land that had been promised. When Iorwerth complained, he was tried on spurious charges and imprisoned. Henry then put Hywel ap Goronwy, a Welsh leader, in charge of Kidwelly and the rest of eastern Dyfed. This did not last long as Hywel was betrayed and treacherously killed in 1106; thus, Norman control over Kidwelly was secured.

As part of the strategy to colonise the region, Henry I had appointed several leading Normans to key lordships, with Roger, bishop of Salisbury granted Kidwelly in around 1106. Roger was a senior member of Henry's court, holding several key posts. He was also an avid castle-builder. Apart from Kidwelly, he had built his home castle of Sherbourne. He was responsible for the construction of Devises Castle (said to be the most beautiful castle in the world in that time), as well as Old Sarum Castle near Salisbury. Like many Norman barons he founded an abbey, in the case of Kidwelly, establishing a daughter house of Sherbourne Abbey. The founding charter of the abbey in *c.*1110 is in fact the earliest record we have of Kidwelly Castle, as the charter was signed in the great hall. The castle, like most others at the time, would initially have been a wooden structure surrounded by a large ditch. Some evidence has been discovered suggesting that Bishop Roger may have built part of the castle with stone, although that is still only conjecture.[5] Around the castle there developed a growing population of settlers comprised of Normans, Flemish and English.

Bishop Roger was most likely rarely present in Kidwelly as he spent most of his time at court or at his other manors. He was, therefore, an early example of the absentee Marcher lord. When Henry I died, Bishop Roger was immediately a royal favourite at the court of the new king, Stephen, who even said of him, 'I would give him half of England until the end of time if asked for it ...'.[6] Despite this, jealousies from other factions at court, and perhaps the king's own envy, led to Roger falling from grace and his circle being driven from court in 1139.

When Henry I died in 1135, the Welsh rebellion that followed had immediate consequences for Kidwelly. English settlers in the Gower peninsula had been overrun – a shock to the Norman community of the south-west. The success of this attack mobilised the family of Gruffudd ap Rhys ap Tewdwr, the head of the house of Deheubarth, and spurred them into action. Gruffudd went straight to Gwynedd to try to enlist their help to further the uprising. Whilst he was away in 1136, his wife Gwenllian led an army into the field, with her two sons, to confront a Norman army as it left Kidwelly. The Normans were led by Maurice de Londres (d.1166) from Ogmore in Glamorgan. The battle ended in disaster for Gwenllian and her sons. She was captured and beheaded, with both of her sons either falling in battle or being captured. The field where the battle took place is near the castle and is still referred to as Maes Gwenllian. A stone memorial to her memory has been erected near the castle's main gate to mark her bravery.

Tomb of Maurice de Londres (d.1166) at Ewenny Priory

It is unclear whether Maurice de Londres became lord of Kidwelly around this time, though it would certainly have been by 1139 at the latest, when Bishop Roger fell out of favour with King Stephen. Maurice's father William de Londres (d.b.1126) had been closely associated with Kidwelly in the time of Bishop Roger, and therefore it is likely that he was present at the initial conquest of Kidwelly and Gower in the early twelfth century. He was also a witness in 1115 of Bishop Roger's grant of Kidwelly Priory to Sherbourne Abbey. In the turbulent times of the Welsh uprisings, Maurice would have been able to claim lordship over Kidwelly by the simple fact that he was present and was strong enough to defend it. In any case, the de Londres family became established there as well as at their home castle at Ogmore.

Throughout Stephen's reign and the civil war that raged in England, the castle of Kidwelly would have been under pressure from the sons of Gruffudd ap Rhys.

Carmarthen Castle was destroyed in 1137 and again in 1146, the year after Earl Gilbert had rebuilt it to try to shore up Marcher defences. We also know that Llanstephan was in Welsh hands that same year. The Welsh controlled large areas around Carmarthen in 1150 and had occupied the castle. However, Kidwelly appears to have remained under Norman control. The *Brut* records that

> *The following year* [1150] *Cadell ap Gruffudd repaired the castle of Carmarthen, for the splendour and strength of the kingdom; and he ravaged Cydweli* [Kidwelly].

The civil war ended with the accession of Henry II to the throne. Following the submission of Rhys ap Gruffudd in 1158, the people of Kidwelly might have hoped for a period of stability. However, the peace was not to last, and in the early 1160s Rhys attacked Carmarthen, sacking many of the castles in Ystrad Tywi, one of which may have been Kidwelly. Henry II came to south-west Wales to subdue Rhys in 1163, but an unsuccessful campaign in 1165 in north Wales allowed Rhys to gain the upper hand in Deheubarth in the late 1160s. Maurice de Londres died in 1166 with his son William (d.1211) becoming lord of Ogmore and Kidwelly. He was able to enjoy a period of relative stability following the appointment of Rhys as Justiciar of south Wales in 1172.

After Henry II's death in 1189, the agreement that had kept the area comparatively at peace for the previous 17 years, collapsed. The Lord Rhys campaigned in south-west Wales, sacking and burning castles, with Kidwelly, Llanstephan, Laugharne and St Clears all falling to him in 1189. There is a curious entry in the *Brut* for 1190 which states, '*In that year the Lord Rhys built the castle of Cydweli.*' Given that we know that there was already a castle there, it seems more likely that he carried out repairs, but it is possible that he also made some significant additions to the structure. Rhys's inability to take Carmarthen, though, meant that his gains were not secure. Indeed, royal records indicate that Kidwelly Castle was back in the hands of William de Londres by around 1192. He received grants for the defence and upkeep of the castle in 1194 at the latest.[7] After the Lord Rhys died in 1197 the pressure on the Marcher lords abated somewhat, as Rhys's many sons were busy feuding amongst themselves. Despite this, it is clear that the situation was far from peaceful, for in 1201 the *Brut* records that '*Maredudd ap Rhys, a fine, accomplished young man, was slain in Carnwyllion.*' Maredudd was a younger son of the Lord Rhys, who was based in Cantref Bychan. He was ambushed by the men of Kidwelly while out marauding with his retinue – another example of the near-constant state of conflict in the region.

When William de Londres, the son of Maurice, died in 1211, the heir was his brother Thomas, who became the lord of Kidwelly and Ogmore, though not for long. The Welsh campaign in 1215, led by Llywelyn ab Iorwerth (d.1240), resulted in the sacking and capturing of Kidwelly Castle as part of the larger assault on southern Wales. The strategic castles at Carmarthen and Cardigan were also taken, which gave the Welsh military superiority. Thomas de Londres died in 1216. It is not known whether this was a result of the Welsh attacks or otherwise. He left a daughter, Hawise, who was only about five years old at the time of his death. The gains of Llywelyn and his allies were secured by the Treaty of Worcester in 1218, including Llywelyn's possession of Carmarthen Castle, which was granted to him until the young King Henry III was to come of age in 1227 at the earliest. Llywelyn granted Kidwelly to Rhys Gryg (d.1234) as part of the larger partition of Ystrad Tywi that he received.

The treaty also tried to compel the Welsh to return those lands taken from the Marcher lords as soon as possible; however, without strong military backing, they were not able to secure this immediately. During the early reign of the young King Henry III, Llywelyn was ordered to return the castle of Kidwelly to the rightful heir, Hawise de Londres, which was being held in wardship while she was underage. However, when Llywelyn went south, allegedly to fulfil that order, he went on another offensive. He burned many of the castles in Dyfed, restoring none to the Marcher lords. Rather than Kidwelly Castle being returned to Hawise, Rhys Gryg maintained control. His father having ceded lands to the Welsh by the Treaty of Worcester, William Marshal the younger (d.1231)

Kidwelly Castle, in possession of Rhys Gryg from 1216–23 (© Philip Hume)

decided to take matters into his own hands in 1223. He launched an invasion into south-west Wales with an army that he had raised from his Irish estates, retaking large swathes of territory including the key castles of Carmarthen and Cardigan, and also dislodging Rhys Gryg from Kidwelly, thus taking the lordship into his own control. In 1231 fortunes were reversed when, taking advantage of the death of William Marshal, Llywelyn campaigned again, with Kidwelly sacked and Rhys Gryg taking possession once more.

After the death of Llywelyn in 1240, his heir Dafydd was not strong enough to hold the gains his father had won. In 1243, Henry III compelled Maredudd ap Rhys Gryg to return the castle to Hawise de Londres who was now of age. Hawise married three times and it was her third husband, Patrick de Chaworth (d.1258), who became the lord of Kidwelly. Patrick was active in royal service when Llywelyn ap Gruffudd took up arms in 1256. Kidwelly survived the general sacking of the area by Llywelyn in 1257 following the heavy defeat of an English army in the Tywi valley. In 1258, Patrick was in royal service with Maredudd ap Rhys Gryg, who had now allied with the king. They were sent to negotiate a peace treaty or truce with the Welsh near Cemais. However, Patrick and Maredudd decided that they would attack them outright rather than negotiate. The *Brut* states

> *When Maredudd and Patrick saw the other men, they broke truce and rushed upon them. And then Patrick was slain and many knights and foot-soldiers along with him.*

With the lord of Kidwelly dead, the castle was besieged by Welsh forces. The town was burned up to the castle gates but the castle itself was strong enough to resist the siege.

Patrick and Hawise had two sons, Payn (d.1279) and Patrick (d.1283). Payn was a central figure in the early reign of Edward I, having gone on Crusade with Edward to the Holy Land between 1270 and 1274, returning when Edward was crowned at Westminster Abbey. In 1276, Payn was made captain of west Wales, becoming commander of the southern army in Edward I's campaign of 1277. Payn died without an heir in 1279, with his brother Patrick becoming lord of Kidwelly. Patrick was also active in the region for Edward and was involved in Edward's Welsh campaign of 1282. It was during the tenure of the two de Chaworth brothers that many of the stone features of the castle that are present today were built.

Many of Kidwelly Castle's stone features date from the late thirteenth century (© Philip Hume)

When Patrick de Chaworth died in 1283 his heir was his one-year-old daughter Maud. Edward I granted the lordship on a life term to his uncle William de Valence, the lord of Pembroke, who had served him well in the war of 1282. There was also the matter of £1,000 which Edward owed him, so this grant was used to offset the debt. William de Valence would have enjoyed the revenues of Kidwelly rather than being an active lord. It is also highly probable that de Valence was involved in the further upgrade of the castle that the de Chaworth brothers had begun.

When de Valence died in 1296 the lordship reverted to Maud de Chaworth who was now of age. She had been granted in marriage in 1298 to Henry of Lancaster (d.1345), the second son of the king's brother Edmund Crouchback and grandson of Henry III. Henry's elder brother, Thomas, the 2nd earl of Lancaster was a prominent opponent of Edward II and the Despenser family during the Despenser wars of the early fourteenth century. Thomas led the baronial faction that was defeated at the battle of Boroughbridge, which resulted in him being beheaded in 1322 (the king had kindly commuted the sentence from hanging, drawing and quartering). On his brother's death, Henry did not immediately inherit his titles and lands, as he would have been seen as still too close to the rebels. When Edward II was forced to abdicate in 1326, Henry made a successful petition to be granted the earldom of Lancaster in 1327.

Around 1310, Henry and Maud de Chaworth had a son whom they also named Henry. Born at Grosmont Castle, he was often referred to as Henry of Grosmont. Perhaps because of his failing eyesight, his father granted all his Welsh holdings to his son in 1333, Henry of Grosmont, who took great pleasure in styling himself 'Lord of Kidwelly' until he took his father's main titles.[8] Henry was very close to Edward III, campaigning with him regularly in France in the early part of the Hundred Years' War, and excelling as a commander in Gascony in 1345. When his father died that same year, Henry became the 4th earl of Lancaster and the wealthiest magnate in the realm. He was made an original knight of the Order of the Garter in 1348, and was made duke of Lancaster in 1350. Thus, Kidwelly became a part of the Duchy of Lancaster, which had Palatinate powers. This meant that all the business within the Duchy was the business of the duke without royal intervention. Kidwelly had been a Marcher lordship attached to Carmarthen, but was now removed entirely from any royal control. Henry was in almost continuous service to the king before he died of illness in 1361. The lordship of Kidwelly passed to his daughter Blanche who was married to John of Gaunt (d.1399), the third son of Edward III. Their son was Henry Bolingbroke who supplanted Richard II as king of England to become Henry IV. As related at the end of the section on Iscennen, Henry IV specified that the Duchy of Lancaster should be held separately from all other Crown possessions and should descend through the monarchy as a private estate. Thus, Kidwelly was held personally by the monarchs through the Duchy of Lancaster rather than the Crown.

Kidwelly was clearly rarely visited by these important men. However, as it was a key administrative centre, they continued to spend money on improving it. Most notably the Lancastrians (John of Gaunt) were responsible for building the great gatehouse that we see today. Kidwelly became part of the southern Duchy of Lancaster along with Ogmore and several other Welsh lordships. It would have been visited annually by an 'accountant' of the Duchy in order to make sure that the money was flowing correctly.

The defensive nature of the castle was put to use during the rebellion of Owain Glyn Dŵr. He rose against English rule in 1400 and slowly gathered momentum until he was a force to concern the king. Glyn Dŵr campaigned in the south in 1403, burning Kidwelly town and besieging the castle, but he was unable to take it. The siege was led by a local named Henry Don, who had been a steward of the Duchy of Lancaster and was a local man of influence. The rebellion had run its course by 1409 and Don was imprisoned. Interestingly his grandson, Gruffudd Don, who had been at the siege of Kidwelly with him, eventually became a steward of the castle and an important figure in the local administration. Following the rebellion, the castle was in a constant state of repair and renovation. It remained an administrative centre for the Duchy of Lancaster in the region.

The Laws in Wales Acts of 1536 and 1542 incorporated Kidwelly into the county of Carmarthenshire.

Castles and churches

Kidwelly Castle: an imposing presence above the River Gwendraeth, Kidwelly Castle is testament to the wealth of its later owners, the dukes of Lancaster. The first castle was built on the site in the early twelfth century. In the fourteenth century, as part of the Duchy of Lancaster, some of the most striking additions to the castle were built, including the impressive gatehouse (see pp. 3, 94, 199, 203 & 204).

St Mary's Church: the remains of Kidwelly Priory are embodied in St Mary's Church, with most of the surviving building dating from around 1320.

~

The Lordship of Llanstephan

The Marcher lordship of Llanstephan was dominated by its castle. It is situated prominently on a headland between the Tywi and Taf rivers. The strategic value of the site was underlined by the fact that the Normans chose to build the castle on the remains of an Iron Age fort. It is situated along the key Norman route through south Wales, lying between the ferries across the two aforementioned rivers. Like many Marcher lordships in the area, its fortunes rose and fell with the overall political situation in Wales and England. Llanstephan of course benefitted from the fact that it could be relieved from the sea, and therefore its Norman lords held a reasonably firm grip on it, with a few short periods of Welsh occupation. Llanstephan had a remarkably stable history, with two families holding the lordship for over 200 years between them.

The lords of Llanstephan

Robert d'Abetot (d.1097); Robert Marmion (d.1102–06); Roger Marmion (d.1129); Robert Marmion (d.1144); Maurice fitz Gerald (d.1176); Robert Marmion (d.1181); Geoffrey Marmion (d.1166); Geoffrey Marmion (d.c.1179); William de Camville (d.1207–08); Geoffrey de Camville (d.1219); William de Camville (d.1260); Geoffrey de Camville (d.1308); William de Camville (d.1338); Richard of Penrice (d.1356); Robert of Penrice (d.1377); Crown property granted to Simon Burley (d.1388); Crown property 1388–91; Robert of Penrice (d.1410); John of Penrice (d.1411); property of the Crown until granted to Humphrey, duke of Gloucester, then granted with earldom of Pembroke.

Brief History

As with all the lordships in south-west Wales, the history of Norman Llanstephan starts with the death of Rhys ap Tewdwr in 1093 and the subsequent Norman seaborne invasion led by William fitz Baldwin. By the end of 1093, Llanstephan Castle had probably been built as a satellite of the main castle in the region at Rhyd-y-gors. This clustering of castles around a central base provided mutual defence in the event of a Welsh attack. The castles were all built on rivers and estuaries, which allowed them to be supplied and relieved by sea. Llanstephan Castle was built in a strategic position guarding the mouth of the rivers Taf and Tywi. Records are scarce but the Norman lord that most likely built the castle was Robert d'Abetot (d.1097).[9] His early occupation of the site did not last long as there was a major Welsh uprising in 1094, which destroyed all the castles that the Normans had built

Llanstephan Castle dominates the tidal estuary of the Tywi river (© Crown Copyright 2022 Cadw)

except for Rhyd-y-gors and Pembroke. Upon the death of William fitz Baldwin in 1096, Rhyd-y-gors Castle was abandoned. We can therefore be somewhat certain that Llanstephan would not have been occupied at that time either.

In 1097 Robert d'Abetot died without an heir. D'Abetot's lands were granted to Robert Marmion (d.c.1106) by William (Rufus) II, although Marmion would not have been able to occupy Llanstephan, as the Welsh still held the upper hand. When Henry I came to the throne in 1100, he strengthened the Norman hold over south-west Wales by constructing a new castle at Carmarthen by 1109. This royal castle became the administrative centre for the region, and the lordship of Llanstephan would have been tied to it by feudal service as it had been to Rhyd-y-gors. The heir to Robert Marmion was his son Roger Marmion (d.1129), and it is highly probable that Roger would have come to Llanstephan at around the same time as Henry I was stabilising south-west Wales for foreign settlement. Even though there was a Welsh revolt in 1116 and Carmarthen was attacked, there is no record that Llanstephan suffered the same fate.

When Roger died in 1129 he left two sons: Robert (d.1144) and Geoffrey (d.1166), both minors, with Robert being confirmed in his inheritance by 1133. Following the death of Henry I in 1135, Robert supported King Stephen and was mainly at his manor of Tamworth in Staffordshire. Geoffrey, however, became a supporter of Henry I's daughter, Matilda, and during the Anarchy in England he seized the family lands in Lincolnshire.

At this time of unrest in England, and with the Welsh reclaiming territory, a prominent local person took control of Llanstephan – Maurice fitz Gerald, the son of Gerald of Windsor and his wife Nest. His lordship is indicated in an interesting letter in 1141 from David fitz Gerald, his brother, who was the bishop of St Davids. In the letter the bishop warned Maurice to stop interfering with land in Llanstephan that had been granted to Carmarthen Priory in the time of Henry I.[10] Circumstances were highly unstable for the Norman and Flemish occupiers at the time, with the princes of Gwynedd campaigning south in 1137 and burning down the castles of Llanstephan and Carmarthen amongst others, but they don't appear to have occupied them. Maurice would have repaired Llanstephan, but the threat of attack was always present. In 1146 the three Welsh princes of Deheubarth, Cadell, Maredudd and Rhys ap Gruffudd again sacked the castle in a ferocious battle which resulted in them taking possession of it. A few days after it fell, the local Normans and Flemish came to Llanstephan to take it back. Only the young Maredudd was present to defend it with a light garrison. His heroic defence is vividly recorded in the *Brut*:

> *A few days after that, there came unexpectedly a great multitude of the French and Flemings to lay siege to the castle, with the sons of Gerald the Steward and William fitz Hai as leaders at their head. And when Maredudd ap Gruffudd, the man to whom the custody of the castle and its defence had been entrusted, saw his enemies coming so unexpectedly as that, he encouraged his men and urged them to fight, letting his spirit have the better of his age: for though he was as yet but young of age, nevertheless his was the action of a knight and an unperturbed leader in urging his men to fight and in cutting his enemies with arms himself. And when his enemies saw how very small was the force defending within the castle, they raised ladders against the walls on every side. And with vigour he and his men overturned the ladders, so that their enemies fell into the ditch, driving the others to flight and leaving many of them dead ... For while yet a youth he defeated many men proven in battles, although he had with him but a small force.*

Llanstephan then remained in Welsh possession until Henry II came to the throne in 1154. Robert Marmion (d.1144), having lost his lands in Lincolnshire, did not survive the Anarchy. Based at his manor at Tamworth, he antagonised the earl of Chester by fortifying a church near Coventry Castle in 1144. When the earl came to deal with Robert, he rode out ahead of his men to engage the coming attackers. In an act of great irony, Robert forgot that he had entrenched the church and his horse fell into the ditch resulting in a broken leg. Unable to move, a lowly fighter from the other side jumped into the trench and cut off his head. Apparently, Robert was known as a 'warlike man, almost unequalled in his time for his ferocity, adroitness and daring, renowned for his successes far and wide'; however, this did not stop him from coming to an inglorious end.[11]

After the civil war, King Henry II moved to restore the status quo as it had been in 1135 at the time of his grandfather's death. The heir to Robert Marmion was his son, another Robert (d.1181). Sometime early in Henry's reign, Robert exchanged his father's lands in Wales and Warwickshire for the lands his uncle Geoffrey (d.1166) had taken during the civil war in Lincolnshire. This resulted in Geoffrey becoming the new Marcher lord of Llanstephan. However, it remained in Welsh hands until 1158 when Henry II invaded southern Wales and forced Rhys ap Gruffydd, then ruler of Deheubarth, to submit and return all that he had taken during the reign of Stephen. Geoffrey Marmion thus held Llanstephan until his death in 1166. He had two sons. His eldest, Geoffrey, was the lord of Llanstephan until he died in around 1179. Geoffrey's heir was his daughter Albreda, who married twice: first to William de Berkeley of Cobberley and then to William de Camville in 1175; thus William de Camville (d.1207–08) became lord of Llanstephan by right of his wife in 1179.

The death of Henry II in 1189 led to the end of the peace agreement with the Lord Rhys, who pushed up through much of south-west Wales, taking the castles of Llanstephan, Laugharne, Kidwelly and St Clears with little resistance. Although some historians state that the Welsh held Llanstephan for years, William de Camville seems to have retaken it by 1192.[12] This is supported by royal records showing that William received grants for the keeping of Llanstephan Castle as the Welsh threat continued through the 1190s. With the death of the Lord Rhys in 1197, the imminent threat to the castle subsided for a time.

Following this period of unrest, William made over the castle to his eldest son Geoffrey (d.1219). William and his wife Albreda travelled to Woodstock to confirm this with King John directly. The king recognised the grant and allowed Geoffrey to 'hold of his parents by the service of one knight's fee to be performed in south Wales for all services, as the charters of his parents testified'.[13]

Trouble arose again when Llywelyn ab Iorwerth took advantage of the weakness of the English Crown in 1215 to invade southern Wales with the assistance of all the rulers of Deheubarth. Carmarthen was sacked quickly by the Welsh army. Llanstephan, left exposed, fell a week later and was destroyed. Geoffrey would have been powerless to win it back, despite King John giving financial support and other assistance. Geoffrey died in 1219 without possession of Llanstephan. The lordship remained in the hands of the Welsh for the next few years.

Geoffrey's heir was his son William (d.1260), who was a minor at the time of his father's death, and his wardship was given to William Longespée, earl of Salisbury. During the minority, William Longespée aided William Marshal (d.1231) in his campaign of 1223 to recapture those areas lost to the Welsh. The campaign was successful and Llanstephan was restored to the de Camvilles to be held by the earl of Salisbury until William came of age. The earl died in 1226 and William de Camville came into his inheritance in 1228.

Seal of William de Camville, from an early thirteenth century charter (© The National Archives/ PRO E 210/8314)

There followed a period of relative stability in the south, which abruptly changed with the arrival on campaign of Llywelyn ap Gruffudd. In 1257, having failed to take Carmarthen Castle, the Welsh army moved against several Marcher castles, with Llanstephan, Laugharne and Narberth sacked and burned. However, the Welsh hold was not secure; indeed, William was back in possession of Llanstephan at the time of his death in 1260.

William de Camville's heir was his son Geoffrey (d.1308). Geoffrey de Camville married Maud, who was the granddaughter and heir to Henry de Tracy of Barnstaple, Devon, the barony descending to Geoffrey on Henry's death in 1274. Maud died around 1279 and Geoffrey then married a certain Joan of an unknown parentage. It was Geoffrey who rebuilt the outer ward of the castle in stone, replacing the timber structure that had existed. In 1275, King Edward I ordered a survey of the lordship of Carmarthen. The survey confirmed that Geoffrey held the barony of Llanstephan and *commote* of Penrlyn Deuddwr from Lord Edmund, first earl of Lancaster, the king's brother and royal agent.

Geoffrey de Camville served in both of Edward I's campaigns in 1277 and 1282. When he died in 1308, his heir was his eldest son William de Camville (d.1338), who came into his inheritance early in 1309 after paying a relief of £5. He had married Matilda, the youngest daughter of John Giffard of Brimpsfield, who was lord of Cantref Bychan and Iscennen, and a close friend of the king. William died around July 1338 leaving five daughters, with Eleanor gaining the Llanstephan inheritance. She took the lordship and castle to Richard of Penrice, her husband, who died in 1356. Their son Robert (d.1377) was ordered to repair and strengthen the castle having let it fall into disrepair; he lost the lordship, though, when he was convicted of murdering a woman in Llanstephan in 1377. The lordship was then granted to Simon de Burley, who was the tutor to the future King Richard II. Burley was executed in 1388, with the lordship passing to the Crown. Llanstephan returned to the Penrice family when Robert's son, another Robert (d.1410), bought back the family estates in 1391 for 500 marks. The picture becomes quite confused after this. The castle was sacked by forces loyal to Owain Glyn Dŵr and seems to have been lost to the Penrice family again. In 1403, Henry IV re-granted it to Sir John of Penrice after he recaptured it from the rebels. When John died in 1411, the castle became a Crown property and was granted to the earls of Pembroke, including the duke of Gloucester and Henry Tudor. The castle eventually fell into disrepair.

The Laws in Wales Act of 1536 incorporated Llanstephan into the new county of Pembrokeshire for judicial and administrative purposes. However, the Act of 1542 recognised the historic ties with Carmarthen and moved Llanstephan into the county of Carmarthenshire.

Llanstephan Castle, showing the walled-up gatehouse

~

THE LORDSHIP OF LAUGHARNE

The Marcher lordship of Laugharne (sometimes Talacharn) lies to the south-west
of Carmarthen at the confluence of the rivers Taf and Coran. It is situated on
the strategic route through south Wales at the point of the ferry crossing with
Llanstephan on the River Taf. The early history of the lordship is obscure, but
we know that the de Brian family was established in the lordship from the early
thirteenth century, and most likely from the twelfth century. Their lineage can
be confusing to follow, as the family named every first-born son Guy from the
thirteenth century onwards. They were one of the rare families who maintained
an uninterrupted male line throughout the thirteenth and fourteenth centuries.
The de Brians were also in possession of the barony of Walwyn's Castle, which
was attached to Pembroke and Haverford.

The lords of Laugharne

William de Brian (d.1244); **Guy de Brian** (d.1268); **Guy de Brian** (d.1307); **Sir Guy
de Brian** (d.1349); **Sir Guy de Brian** (d.1390); **William de Brian** (d.1395); **Henry Lord
Scrope** (d.c.1403); **Alice de Brian** (d.1435): **James Butler** 5th earl of Ormond, earl of
Wiltshire (d.1461); **Henry Percy**, 4th earl of Northumberland (d.1489); **Henry Percy**, 5th
earl of Northumberland (d.1527); **Henry Percy**, 6th earl of Northumberland (d.1537).

The early history of Laugharne is obscure. There are very few references in the sources, and therefore one must surmise some information based on other events in the region. It seems certain that there would have been a basic ringwork earth and timber castle built there as part of the Norman invasion of 1093. It seems also highly likely that the castle would have been destroyed before 1100. That it was rebuilt and refortified during the reign of Henry I is also highly probable. The castle site lay on the key ferry crossing over the Taf river between Laugharne and Llanstephan. Historians have generally considered the first reference to the castle to be in the *Brut* for 1116; however, this reference is more likely to refer to the castle of Abercywyn in the lordship of Ystlwyf (see below Ystlwyf lordship). So, in all probability, the first direct reference we have of the castle at Laugharne is actually from 1172, when the *Brut* recorded: *'And on Easter Monday he had parley with Rhys at Laugharne on the way. And thence he went to England.'*

Henry II was returning to England from his expedition to Ireland when he met the Lord Rhys at Laugharne. Henry was looking to secure peace, so in a change of strategy, he appointed Rhys as the Justiciar of south Wales. There is no record of who the lord of Laugharne may have been at the time, although it is tempting to think it may have been a de Brian. There was a 'Wido de Brian' who held lands in Pembroke near Haverford around this time. He is also recorded as owning land once held in Devon by the fitz Baldwins, who built Rhyd-y-gors Castle.[14] When Henry II died in 1189, the Lord Rhys immediately considered the agreement he had to be void, with Laugharne recorded as one of the castles that was occupied. The castle came back into Anglo-Norman control by the end of the twelfth century, but its security remained fragile.

Laugharne was among the many castles destroyed in Llywelyn ab Iorwerth's campaign of 1215, being granted by Llywelyn to Maelgwn ap Rhys, a son of the Lord Rhys. The Marcher lords were unable to recover any lost lands until they mounted a counter-attack in 1223 under the command of William Marshal the younger (d.1231). The two key castles of Carmarthen and Cardigan were taken back into English hands, and Laugharne too was recovered for its lord.

The de Brian family held extensive lands in south Devon, though it is difficult to date precisely when they came into their Welsh possessions (they also held the barony of Walwyn's Castle). The first documentary evidence is in a charter granted to the town of Haverford by William Marshal (d.1219) in around 1215, of which William de Brian (d.1244) was a witness.[15] He was succeeded by his son Guy de Brian (d.1268), who we know received a grant from the king in 1247 to hold an annual fair in Laugharne, so the family must have been granted the lordship before

Laugharne Castle: seat of the de Brian family in Wales (© Philip Hume)

then.[16] Guy de Brian was responsible for the start of the construction of the castle that we see today, modernising the castle to upgrade its defences. Guy was also active in royal service during the Welsh resurgence led by Llywelyn ap Gruffudd (d.1282). In 1257, he was part of the English army that was comprehensively defeated in the Tywi valley. The victory over the English army gave the Welsh superiority in the region, which they used to destroy several castles in Deheubarth, including Laugharne. Either during the battle or whilst trying to defend his castle, Guy de Brian was captured and held for ransom. To secure his release, the tenants of Laugharne were asked to raise the fine, which they did (along with a contribution from the king), and he was freed the following year. When Guy de Brian died in 1268, his heir was another Guy (d.1307), who was also an active lord, continuing his father's renovations of the castle. It is also probable that he granted the borough charter to the town of Laugharne, which it still operates under today. He was active in the Welsh wars of Edward I in 1277 and 1282.

When Guy died in 1307, he was succeeded by yet another Guy (d.1349), who was 23 years old when he came into the lordship. Unfortunately, he was not as dynamic as his father and grandfather, as there is no evidence that he undertook any work on the castle, with it falling into a state of disrepair during his tenure. As a result of his ill-health, he transferred the management of Laugharne to his son, Guy (d.1390), in 1330, even though he was still well underage, with Guy not formally entering into his inheritance until he was 30, on the death of his father in 1349. This Guy de Brian was an energetic lord who enjoyed a long and successful career in royal service, as well as modernising and improving the castle at Laugharne.

Charter and seal of Guy de Brian, 1382 (© The National Archives/PRO, DL27/141)

Guy became close to Edward III, serving him in various capacities throughout his career, with appointments that included Keeper of the Great Seal, Admiral of the West, ambassador to the Pope, and in 1370 he became a Knight of the Garter. He also received an annuity of 200 marks per annum because he carried the king's standard at the battle of Calais. He was married twice, first to Joan Carew, the daughter of a Pembrokeshire magnate. His second marriage was to Elizabeth Montagu, which brought him estates throughout England, including Tewkesbury where there is a tomb effigy in the church at the abbey (although he is buried at the church in Slapton in Devon).

The descent of the lordship of Laugharne became extremely complicated thereafter. Guy (d.1390) had five children with Elizabeth, but only two of them produced offspring. As the eldest son, Guy, died before his father in 1386, the inheritance at first passed to a younger son, William. When he passed away without issue in 1395, the inheritance went to the daughters of Guy (d.1386), Phillipa and Elizabeth. Phillipa was married to Henry, Lord Scrope, who was instructed in 1403 by the king to ensure that the defences of Laugharne Castle were up to date to defend against the Welsh forces during the Glyn Dŵr rebellion.[17] The marriage between Phillipa and Lord Scrope ended without children, so the lordship passed to her sister Elizabeth, who had a daughter, Maud. She was married to, firstly, John

Fitzalan, the 7th earl of Arundel, whose only son died a minor. She then married Sir Richard Stafford, with their daughter, Avice, becoming their heiress. Avice was married to James Butler, the earl of Ormond, and when she died childless in 1457 the lordship stayed with her husband during his lifetime. However, James appears to have been an unscrupulous character, who used legal chicanery to hold on to the de Brian estates, to which he had no rights as he was not a direct descendant of the de Brians. Furthermore, he was attainted in 1461 after the battle of Mortimers Cross for fighting on the losing Lancastrian side, with the result that he lost all his lands and titles. He was captured later that year after the battle of Towton and beheaded, apparently after fleeing the battle.

Following James's death, the inheritance was disputed because of the legal tricks he had used in an attempt to retain as much of the estate as possible, despite having no legitimate claim to it. There were others who continued to dispute the inheritance as well, until the matter was finally settled in 1488 by the court of Henry VII. In the end, the Welsh estates reverted to a direct descendant of Guy de Brian (d.1390). Guy and Elizabeth had a daughter, another Elizabeth, who had married Sir Robert Fitzpaine. Their line descended unbroken until it passed to Henry Percy, the 4th earl of Northumberland. Henry Percy had been on the side of Richard III, which would normally have put him into the political wilderness. However, he did not commit his troops in battle at Bosworth, preferring to see how the events unfolded. In the end, Henry VII was victorious, which may explain why the earl was soon reconciled with the king. The lordship remained part of the Northumberland estate until 1537.

The Laws in Wales Act of 1536 incorporated Laugharne into the new county of Pembrokeshire for judicial and administrative purposes; however, the Act of 1542, recognising the historic ties with Carmarthen, removed Laugharne into the county of Carmarthenshire.

Castles

Laugharne Castle: there was a castle at the mouth of the Taf river from the beginning of the twelfth century. The de Brian family updated the castle defences to stone starting in the middle to late thirteenth century. The castle was rebuilt by John Perrot in the late sixteenth century, to be the impressive Tudor manor, the remains of which we see today. The castle is open to the public and managed by Cadw (see pp. 76, 215 & 218).

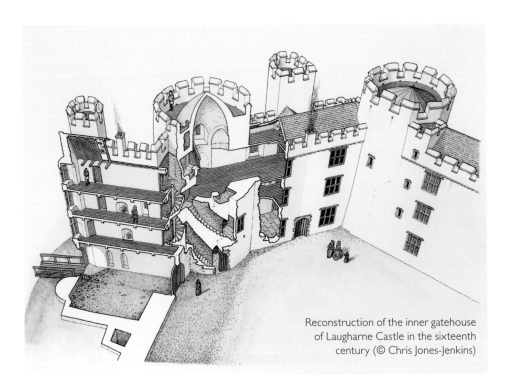

Reconstruction of the inner gatehouse of Laugharne Castle in the sixteenth century (© Chris Jones-Jenkins)

The Lordship of Ystlwyf

Ystlwyf, also known as Oysterlow, was a small lordship situated on the River Taf at the confluence of the River Cywyn. There are only slight remains of a motte and bailey castle on the southern point of the lordship overlooking the Taf. The ruins of a church are also near the castle. Otherwise, there is very little to alert a visitor that there was ever anything resembling a lordship here. The early history of this lordship is also obscure, with only a few references to it in the primary sources.

The lords of Ystlwyf

Robert Tortmains (d.a.1119); unknown; **the Crown** for a period to 1171; **Lord Rhys** (d.1197); **Hywel Sais** (d.1204); 1200–15, **William Marshal** 1st earl of Pembroke, 2nd creation (d.1219); 1215–23, **Maelgwn ap Rhys** (d.1231); 1223–41, **William Marshal** 2nd earl of Pembroke (d.1231); **Richard Marshal** 3rd earl of Pembroke (d.1234); **Gilbert Marshal** 4th earl of Pembroke (d.1241); 1241, Gilbert Marshal granted it to **Maredudd ap Rhys Gryg** (d.1271); **Rhys ap Maredudd** (d.1292), forfeited in 1287 for rebellion; **William de Valence** (d.1296); the lordship was held by the **earls of Pembroke** holding suit at Carmarthen until it passed to **the Crown** on the extinction of the Hastings line.

The lordship of Ystlwyf was a satellite of the castle of Rhyd-y-gors, which was established in 1093 by William fitz Baldwin under the auspices of William (Rufus) II during the initial Norman invasion after the death of the prince of Deheubarth, Rhys ap Tewdwr. It was one of several which were conquered by various Norman barons who joined fitz Baldwin in his establishment of castles near the mouth of the Tywi river. The occupied lands used the boundaries of the existing Welsh *commote* system. Whilst these early castles did not survive the eleventh century, their existence would have been a cause for future conquest and settlement. By inserting themselves into the existing *commote*, they were able to establish the early Norman structure of administration more readily.

The early descent of the lords of Ystlwyf is obscure. However, historical detective work indicates that the first lord of Ystlwyf was most likely Robert Tortmains (d.a.1119) or 'crooked hands'. His father (or brother) Ralph held lands in Somerset from the bishop of Wells and the abbot of Glastonbury. When Ralph died, his successor in England was a certain Geoffrey, so the fact that it was Robert who succeeded him in Wales probably indicates a cadet branch of the Tortmains. Following the initial success of the Norman conquest of south Wales, there was an immediate backlash from the local Welsh. The *Brut* records that all the castles of the French in the south-west were destroyed, apart from Rhyd-y-gors and Pembroke.

During the reign of Henry I the fortunes of the Normans were reversed. A new royal castle at Carmarthen was built by 1109 and the local lordships were once again established, holding from the king through Carmarthen. It was during Henry's reign that we get a glimpse of the workings of the lordship of Ystlwyf. During the uprising in 1116 (led by the heir to Deheubarth, Gruffudd ap Rhys), the records state that the Normans turned to a local Welsh ruler named Bleddri ap Cadifor to help defend the castle of Abercymwyn, which was most likely Ystlwyf. This is interesting because Bleddri was a descendant of the Welsh ruler of the *commote* who had died just before the Tortmains arrived. Indeed, Bleddri pops up in the scant records a few times. He is a good example of a local Welsh ruler who decided that accommodation was more fruitful than conflict. Apart from being called upon to defend the castle, he was in Norman service as an interpreter and even achieved the status of a knight with his own lands.[18]

It appears Robert Tortmains also acquired lands in Gower, indicating that he had been part of the earl of Warwick's conquest of that region in 1106. It is not certain where these lands were held, but evidence suggests that it was near Oxwich. In trying to establish who the descendants of Robert were, the information at hand is too patchy to say anything with certainty. Sometime before 1171, the lordship must have reverted to the Crown, as in that year Henry II granted it to the Lord Rhys. Henry confirmed him in the lands that he had conquered and granted him Ystlwyf as a separate lordship, holding of the king. While Rhys was the lord of Ystlwyf, he bestowed some lands there on the Cistercian abbey of Whitland in neighbouring St Clears. When Rhys died in 1197 the lordship went to his son Hywel Sais (d.1204), who at one time had been a hostage of King Henry II to guarantee the Lord Rhys's good behaviour. Hywel Sais was unable to hold the lordship for long without the power of his father to support him. In 1200, King John granted the lordship to William Marshal (d.1219), the newly appointed earl of Pembroke, in lieu of lands that had been lost to the Welsh in Emlyn. William Marshal remained the lord of Ystlwyf until the invasion of south-west Wales by the ruler of Gwynedd, Llywelyn ab Iorwerth, in 1215. Llywelyn was able to unite the sons and grandsons of the Lord Rhys to advance through the entire region, sacking most of the Marcher castles as they went. At the conference in Ceredigion to divide the conquered lands, Ystlwyf was granted to the eldest surviving son, Maelgwn ap Rhys (d.1231).

With the political situation too fragile in the early years of the minority of Henry III, and fully occupied as regent, William Marshal was unable to reverse his losses. His heir, another William Marshal (d.1231), however, took matters into his own hands in 1223, raising an army from his Irish lordships before sailing to Pembroke to launch a campaign of re-conquest. He was able to bring Ystlwyf (amongst others) back into the Marshal holdings. William Marshal had Welsh assistance from the son of Hywel Sais, Cynan, whom he rewarded with Ystlwyf and Emlyn (see Cilgerran/ Emlyn in the Pembrokeshire lordships section). This brought Ystlwyf into the orbit of Pembroke and away from Carmarthen, where it had been established.

Cynan lost the lordship when Gilbert Marshal (d.1241) moved against him following the death of Llywelyn ab Iorwerth in 1240. Gilbert granted Ystlwyf and Emlyn to his local favourite (and a cousin of Cynan), Maredudd ap Rhys Gryg, ostensibly because Cynan was in a state of war with King Henry III. Upon the death of Maredudd in 1270, it passed to his son, Rhys ap Maredudd; but when Rhys rose in revolt in 1287, he forfeited all his lands including Ystlwyf. William de Valence, who had become lord of Pembroke following the extinction of the Marshal line, claimed that the lordship belonged to him by right of the Marshals. Edward I took exception and filed suit against de Valence in 1292, to reclaim the rights to the lordship, which he won. Ystlwyf was taken back into royal hands and made part of the Principality of Wales at Carmarthen for a time. Edward I then granted it back to de Valence later that year, but on the condition that the lord of Pembroke held it on the same terms as the other lordships pertaining to Carmarthen.[19] From this point forward, Ystlwyf was held by the earls of Pembroke until the Hastings line died out in 1389 and it came into royal hands. It was given to subsequent earls of Pembroke as part of their grant to the earldom.

The Laws in Wales Act of 1536 incorporated Ystlwyf into the new county of Pembrokeshire for judicial and administrative purposes. However, the Act of 1542 recognised the historic ties with Carmarthen, so removed Ystlwyf into Carmarthenshire.

~

The Lordship of St Clears

The Marcher lordship of St Clears was likely to have been founded as part of the initial Norman conquest of eastern Dyfed before 1100, by the fitz Baldwins and their affinity. The castle of St Clears was built at the confluence of the Taf and Cynin rivers where the Taf was still navigable for Norman ships. There are very few references to St Clears in the records, but what seems clear is that any Norman settlement was concentrated around the castle in the early period. The remains of the castle reveal that it only had a stone keep that was built on top of the mound that we see today. That the castle was never built entirely of stone would indicate that it was not an important holding for its lords, given the trend for building stone castles in the late thirteenth century.

The lords of St Clears

Possibly **Bretel de Saint Clair** (d.b.1150); **William Fitz Hait/ Hay** (d.a.1182); **Simon Hay** (d.b.1195); **William de Braose** (d.1211); **Reginald de Braose** (d.1228); **William de Braose** (d.1230); the lordship was divided in the Braose inheritance and split into thirds between the families of **de Cantilupe, de Bohun and Mortimer**.

Brief History

The early history of the lordship of St Clears probably began when William fitz Baldwin built Rhyd-y-gors Castle in a royally-sponsored invasion in 1093. Like all the Norman castles that were built then, it was probably abandoned by 1100, as

Aerial view of the remains of St Clears Castle (© Paul Davis)

such structures did not have the strength to withstand the Welsh counter-attack. It was likely, therefore, that St Clears only became firmly established after Henry I built the castle at Carmarthen by 1109, which brought a strong royal presence to the region. This was also after the introduction of the Flemish immigrants into western Dyfed, which stabilised the region further for Norman expansion. There is only strong circumstantial evidence as to the early founders of St Clears, but it points at the Saint Clair family from Stoke Trister in Devon. As seen already, many of the early Norman adventurers that settled in eastern Dyfed were from Devon. Whilst there is no concrete proof that the Saint Clairs came with William fitz Baldwin in the initial conquest, it seems highly probable given their Devonshire connection.[20] The name of the castle also lends itself to this theory as to its origins.

The male line of the Saint Clair family became extinct sometime before the 1150s. In another example of a prominent local figure taking control of a lordship (see Kidwelly, Llanstephan and Cilgerran), William fitz Hay or fitz Hait acquired St Clears sometime before 1150. We know this from Gerald of Wales, who was writing some years later, which is also the first time that the lordship is referred to as St Clears. Fitz Hay was the son of Princess Nest and Hait, the sheriff of Pembroke, an early Flemish immigrant who rose to a position of authority. He is easily identifiable as the sheriff in the Pipe Roll of 1130, in which capacity he had the responsibility of appearing at the Exchequer to present the accounts for the region. William fitz Hay was a half-brother to the sons of Gerald of Windsor and Nest, and he was present when they unsuccessfully tried to retake Llanstephan Castle from the Welsh in 1146 (an example of how the local settlers worked together to defend their interests – although in this case they were not successful). The last reference to William fitz Hay was in the Pipe Roll of 1182. He was succeeded at St Clears by his son Simon Hay, sometime before 1189.[21]

As an interesting aside, Gerald of Wales mentions St Clears specifically in his recounting of his *Journey through Wales* with the Archbishop of Canterbury in 1188 to recruit for the upcoming Crusade. There was a young Welshman rushing to sign up for the Crusade who was murdered by 12 archers from St Clears. As punishment for their crime, all 12 were made to take the sign of the Cross and join the Crusade.

The castle of St Clears was taken by the Lord Rhys (d.1197) in 1189 when he campaigned through all of Dyfed following the death of Henry II. Rhys granted the castle to his son Hywel Sais (d.1204) along with several other conquered lordships in Dyfed. A campaign in 1195 by William de Braose (d.1211) brought St Clears back under Anglo-Norman control. De Braose was confirmed in possession, which indicates two things. Firstly, that the male line of the Hay family had become extinct. Secondly, that de Braose had a legitimate claim to the lordship of St Clears. This came through his great-grandfather, William de Braose of Bramber (d.c.1093), who was married to Agnes de Saint Clair from the family of Devon. St Clears stayed in the de Braose family throughout the turbulent years that followed. With the death in 1211 of William de Braose, who was persecuted by King John, the lordship was taken into royal hands.

The Welsh campaign of 1215 brought it back into the Welsh fold again, with St Clears granted to Maelgwn ap Rhys, which he had to relinquish after William Marshal's (d.1231) re-conquest of Dyfed in 1223. The lordship then belonged to Reginald de Braose, the son of William (d.1211), who had been reconciled with the Crown in 1217. Upon his death in 1228, his son William de Braose (d.1230) inherited the family's estates. However, his career came to a spectacular end when he was found in the bed chamber of the wife of Llywelyn ab Iorwerth (d.1240). Llywelyn showed no mercy and had him publicly hanged. His daughters were all too young to inherit his vast estates and St Clears would have been held in wardship, usually by the earl of Pembroke.

Following the death of Llywelyn in 1240, Gilbert Marshal made a speculative grab for St Clears, but was reminded by the king that he had no right to it and that it belonged to the de Braose patrimony.[22] The inheritance was settled at the same time as the Marshal inheritance in 1246, with St Clears split between the three daughters of William, thus adding to the estates of the families of their husbands – Mortimer, de Bohun, and de Cantilupe (Haverford was split in the same way). When the de Cantilupe line subsequently died out, their portion went to the Hastings family; thus, when Laurence Hastings (d.1348) became the earl of Pembroke, that third of St Clears passed into the holdings of the earl of Pembroke. The lordship remained divided with the third passing through the descendants of the Mortimers and the earls of Pembroke. The de Bohun third passed to the Crown in 1288, along with the two-thirds of Haverford.

The Laws in Wales Act of 1536 incorporated St Clears into the new county of Pembrokeshire for judicial and administrative purposes. However, the Act of 1542 recognised the historic ties with Carmarthen and so incorporated St Clears into Carmarthenshire.

Castles and other sites of interest

St Clears Castle: the earthen remains of a castle are now a park at the south end of the town. All that is visible is the large earthen motte that stands at the northern end of what was a large bailey (see p. 222).

Hywel Dda Centre: a garden and heritage centre in Whitland which is dedicated to the contemplation of and furthering of knowledge of Hywel Dda and his laws (see p. 31).

~

ENDNOTES

PRELIMS AND ONE

1 Sir John E. Lloyd, *The History of Carmarthenshire*, Vol. 1 (London Carmarthen Society, 1935), 231.

2 R.R. Davies, *Lordship and Society in the March of Wales 1282–1400* (Oxford University Press, 1978) 68.

3 J. Wyn Evans, 'The Bishops of St Davids from Bernard to Bec', in *Pembrokeshire County History*, Vol. II, R.F. Walker (ed.) (Pembrokeshire Historical Society, 2002), 294.

4 R.F. Walker, 'The Lordships of Pembrokeshire in the Thirteenth and Fourteenth Centuries', in *Pembrokeshire County History*, Vol. II (Pembrokeshire Historical Society, 2002), 146.

5 Davies, *Lordship and Society*, 180.

6 Neil Ludlow, *Carmarthen Castle, The Archaeology of Government* (University of Wales Press, 2014), 18.

7 Dillwyn Miles, *The Lords of Cemais* (Cemais Publications, 1997), 22–4.

8 D.D. Jenkins, *The Law of Hywel Dda: Law Texts from Medieval Wales* (Llandysul, 2000). See also J. Goronwy Edwards, 'Hywel Dda and the Welsh Law-Books', The Hywel Dda Millennary Lecture (Bangor, 1929); reprinted as 'Hywel Dda and the Welsh Law-books', in D. Jenkins (ed.), *Celtic Law Papers* (Brussels, 1973), 135–60.

9 T.M. Charles-Edwards, 'The Seven Bishop-Houses of Dyfed' in *Bulletin of the Board of Celtic Studies 24* (1970–72), 247–62.

10 On the Surexit, see D. Jenkins and M.E. Owen, 'The Welsh Marginalia in the Lichfield Gospels Part I' in *Cambridge Medieval Celtic Studies 5* (1983), 37–66; and 'The Welsh Marginalia in the Lichfield Gospels Part II: The 'Surexit' Memorandum' in *Cambridge Medieval Celtic Studies 7* (1984), 91–120. Breint Teilo is examined by P. Russell, 'Priuilegium sancti Teliaui and Breint Teilo' in *Studia Celtica 50* (2016), 41–68.

11 On the Law of the March, see R.R. Davies, 'The Law of the March' in *Welsh History Review 5*, (1970), 1–30; and also Sara Elin Roberts, 'What's Yours is Mine: Cyfraith Hywel and the Law of the March' (Mortimer History Society Essay Prize Winner, 2018/19). *Journal of the Mortimer History Society 3* (2019), 1–15.

12 Sara Elin Roberts, 'Plaints in Welsh Mediaeval Law' in *Journal of Celtic Studies 4* (2004), 219–61.

13 Morfydd E. Owen, 'A Fifteenth-Century Lawbook from Cefnllys' in *Transactions of the Radnorshire Society 81* (2011), 77–93.

14 Sara Elin Roberts, 'Legal Practice in Fifteenth-Century Brycheiniog' in *Studia Celtica 35* (2001), 307–23.

15 There is a wealth of material published on the castles of south-west Wales, both Anglo-
Norman and native Welsh, and the following is a selection, excluding the guide books
to the numerous sites that are in the care of Cadw, such as Kidwelly and Laugharne.
Mention should also be made of two works in progress, namely Neil Ludlow on Pembroke
Castle and David Austin on Carew Castle. Reference may also be made to the relevant
sections of John R. Kenyon, *Castles, Town Defences and Artillery Fortifications in the United
Kingdom and Ireland: a Bibliography 1945–2006* (Shaun Tyas, 2008); and also to the annual
bibliographies available on the Castle Studies Group's website.

Paul R. Davis, *Towers of Defiance: The Castles & Fortifications of the Princes of Wales*
(Y Lolfa, 2021);

Paul R. Davis, *Forgotten Castles of Wales and the Marches* (Logaston Press, 2021);

John Goodall, *The English Castle 1066–1650* (Yale University Press, 2011);

John R. Kenyon, *The Medieval Castles of Wales* (University of Wales Press, 2015);

John R. Kenyon, 'Recent castle studies and Carmarthenshire' in *Carmarthenshire
Antiquary 36* (2000), 45–57;

John R. Kenyon and D.J.C. King, 'The castles of Pembrokeshire' in R.F. Walker (ed.),
Pembrokeshire County History: Medieval Pembrokeshire, 522–47, (Pembrokeshire Historical
Society, 2002);

D.J.C. King, 'Haverfordwest Castle c.1110–1577' in D. Miles (ed.), *A History of the Town and
County of Haverfordwest*, 34–51 (Gomer, 1999);

Neil Ludlow, *Carmarthen Castle: The Archaeology of Government* (University of Wales
Press, 2014);

Neil Ludlow, 'The castle and lordship of Narberth' in *Journal of the Pembrokeshire Historical
Society 12*, (2003), 5–43.

TWO

1 Kari Maund, 'Dark Age Wales' in *History of Wales 25,000 BC to AD 2000*, Prys Morgan
(ed.) (Tempus Publishing Ltd, 2001), 49–53.

2 William Rees, *An Historical Atlas of Wales, from Early to Modern Times*, 3rd edition (Faber
and Faber, 1967).

3 There is an excellent discussion of the legal and practical issues concerning entitlement
to inheritance of Welsh kingdoms in T.M. Charles-Edwards, *Wales and the Britons, 350–
1064* (Oxford University Press, 2014), 329–37. Also see J. Beverley Smith, 'Dynastic
Succession in Medieval Wales', in *Bulletin of the Board of Celtic Studies 33*, (1986), 199–232;
and, J. Beverley Smith, 'The Succession to Welsh princely inheritance: the evidence
reconsidered', in R.R. Davies (ed.), *The British Isles 1100– 1500: Comparisons, Contrasts and
Connections* (Edinburgh, 1988), 64–81.

4 For further reading on Wales before 1066 see: T.M. Charles-Edwards (as above); Sir John
Lloyd, *A History of Wales from the Earlies Times to the Edwardian Conquest, Vol. 1*
(Longmans, 1954); and W. Davies, *Wales in the Early Middle Ages* (Leicester University
Press, 1982).

A good summary is provided by: Glynn Roberts, 'Wales on the Eve of the Norman
Conquest' in *Aspects of Welsh History* [Selected papers of the late Glyn Roberts]
(University of Wales Press, 1969).

Two books that focus on the history of Welsh rulers from the period after the departure
of the Romans through to 1282 are: Kari Maund, *The Welsh Kings: Warriors, Warlords and
Princes* (The History Press, 2017); and David Moore, *The Welsh Wars of Independence*
(Tempus Publishing, 2005) – the latter runs through to 1415.

THREE

1. I.W. Rowlands, 'Conquest and Survival', in *Pembrokeshire County History Vol. II*, R.F. Walker (ed.) (Pembrokeshire Historical Society, 2002), 1–8; and I.W. Rowlands, 'The Making of the March: Aspects of the Norman Settlement of Dyfed' in *Proceedings of the Battle Conference on Anglo-Norman Studies III*, 1980, R. Allen Brown (ed.) (Boydell Press, 1981), 142–8.

2. I.W. Rowlands, 'Conquest and Survival', 11–13; I.W. Rowlands, 'The Making of the March', 146–8.

3. For Henry I's approach to Wales see, R.R. Davies, 'Henry I and Wales', in *Studies in Medieval History* [presented to R.H.C. Davis], H. Mayr-Harting and R.I. Moore (eds) (London, 1985), 133–47.

4. J.E. Lloyd, *A History of Wales from the Earliest Times to the Edwardian Conquest Vol. 2*, 3rd Edition (Longmans, 1954), 452.

5. J. Beverley Smith, 'Princes, Lords and English Monarchy: Ceredigion 1081–1197', in *Cardiganshire County History Vol. 2*, Geraint H. Jenkins, Richard Suggett & Eryn M. White (eds) (University of Wales Press, 2019), 254–61.

6. *The Great Roll of the Pipe for the Thirty-First Year of the Reign of Henry I Michaelmas 1130*, Judith Green (ed.) (Pipe Roll Society, 2012).

FOUR

1. J.E. Lloyd, *A History of Wales*, 462.

2. David Crouch, 'The March and the Welsh Kings', in *The Anarchy of King Stephen's Reign*, Edmund King (ed.), (Oxford University Press, 1994), 261–2.

3. J.E. Lloyd, *A History of Wales*, 511.

4. Two good sources for the Norman conquest of Ireland are: David Carpenter, *The Struggle for Mastery, Britain 1066–1284*, (Penguin, 2004), 215–23; and *The Geraldines and Medieval Ireland, The Making of a Myth*, Peter Crooks and Sean Duffery (eds) (Four Court Press, 2017).

FIVE

1. John Gillingham, *The English in the Twelfth Century: Imperialism, National Identity and Political Values* (Boydell & Brewer Ltd, 2008), 66.

2. Bruce Coplestone-Crow, 'Llansteffan Castle and the Abetot, Marmion and Camville Families 1093–1338' in *The Carmarthenshire Antiquary 54* (2018), 14–15.

3. Huw Pryce, 'The Dynasty of Deheubarth and the Church of St Davids', in *St David of Wales: Cult, Church and Nation*, J.W. Evans and Jonathan M. Wooding (eds.) (The Boydell Press, 2007), 306–7.

4. David Crouch, *William Marshal*, 3rd edition (Routledge, 2016), 101.

5. J.E. Lloyd, *History of Wales*, 645.

6. David Carpenter, *The Struggle for Mastery*, 300.

7. *The History of William Marshal*, Nigel Bryant (trans.) (The Boydell Press, 2018), 391.

8. For a good account of events leading up to Marshal's campaign and the campaign itself see: David Carpenter, *The Minority of Henry III* (Methuen, 1990), 192, 279, 306–14.

9. David Carpenter, *Henry III* (Yale University Press, 2020), 242–3.

10. Dillwyn Miles, *The Lords of Cemais* (Cemais Publications, 1997), 22–3.

11. John Kenyon, *Kidwelly Castle Guide* (Cadw, 2017), 9.

12. Sir John E. Lloyd, *History of Carmarthenshire*, 183.

SIX

1   Sir John E. Lloyd, *History of Carmarthenshire*, 188–90.
2   Richard Cassidy, 'Rolls and Ransoms in the March of Wales', Henry III Fine Rolls Project, April 2010.
3   Lloyd, *History of Carmarthenshire*, 194.
4   Ibid, 195.
5   Paul Martin Remfry and Nigel Ruckley, *Castell Carreg Cennen and the families of Deheubarth, Giffard and Lancaster* (Castle Studies Research and Publishing, 2010), 21–24.
6   Carpenter, *The Struggle for Mastery*, 256.

SEVEN

1   R.F. Walker, 'The Lordships of Pembrokeshire in the Thirteenth and Fourteenth Centuries', *in Pembrokeshire County History Vol. II* (Pembrokeshire Hist. Soc., 2002), 156.
2   Davies, *Lordship and Society*, 137–8.
3   Ibid, 114.
4   Ibid, 214–5.
5   Ibid, 188–98.
6   R.A. Griffiths, 'The Extension of Royal Power, 1415–1536', in *Pembrokeshire County History Vol. II*, (Pembrokeshire Historical Society, 2002), 237–43.
7   Ibid, 261.

EIGHT

1   Gerald of Wales, *The Journey through Wales* and *The Description of Wales*, Lewis Thorpe (trans.) (Penguin, 2004), 148–9.
2   *The Great Roll of the Pipe for the Thirty First Year of the Reign of Henry I Michaelmas 1130*, Judith Green (ed.) (Pipe Roll Society, 2012), 107–8.
3   Crouch, *The March and the Welsh Kings*, 274–5.
4   Crouch, *William Marshal*, 101.
5   Carpenter, *Henry III*, 240–3.
6   Ibid, 467–74.
7   Roger Turvey, 'The Jurisdiction and Comital Authority of the Earls Palatine in Medieval Pembrokeshire' in *The Journal of the Pembrokeshire Historical Society 4* (1991), 97.
8   R.F. Walker, 'The Earls of Pembroke, 1138 to 1389', in *Pembrokeshire County History Vol. II* (Pembrokeshire Historical Society, 2002), 73–117.
9   R.A. Griffiths, 'The Extension of Royal Power, 1415–1536' in *Pembrokeshire County History Vol. II* (Pembrokeshire Historical Society, 2002), 231–62.
10 Gerald of Wales, *A Journey through Wales*, 151.
11 Terence James, 'The Origins and Topography of Medieval Haverford' in *Journal of the Pembrokeshire History Society 4*, (1991), 53.
12 Ibid, 57.
13 *The Acts and Letters of the Marshal Family, Marshals of England and Earls of Pembroke, 1145–1248*, David Crouch (ed.) (Cambridge University Press, 2015), 108–11.
14 James, *Origins and Topography of Medieval Haverford*, 62.
15 Miles, *Cemais*, 14.
16 R.F. Walker, 'The Lordships of Pembrokeshire in the Thirteenth and Fourteenth Centuries' in *Pembrokeshire County History Vol. II* (Pembrokeshire Historical Society, 2002), 152.
17 Miles, *Cemais*, 21–2.
18 Cassidy, *Rolls and Ransoms in the March of Wales*.
19 Walker, 'Lordships of Pembrokeshire', 157.

20 Neil Ludlow, 'The Castle and Lordship of Narberth', in *Journal of the Pembrokeshire Historical Society 12*, (2003), 9.

21 Ibid, 12.

22 R.F. Walker, 'Lordships of Pembrokeshire', 170.

23 I.W. Rowlands, 'Conquest and Survival', 9.

24 J. Wyn Evans, 'Bishops of St Davids', 278.

25 Ibid, 292–3.

NINE

1 R.R. Davies, *Lordship and Society*, 28–30.

2 J.E. Lloyd, *A History of Wales*, 511, using *Pipe Rolls Henry II* 6–8.

3 R.A. Griffiths, *The Principality of Wales in the Later Middle Ages* (University of Wales Press, 2018), 117.

4 Paul Martin Remfry and Nigel Ruckley, *Castell Carreg Cennen*, 28.

5 John Kenyon, *Kidwelly Castle*, 5–6.

6 David Crouch, *The Reign of King Stephen 1135–1154* (Pearson Education Ltd., 2000), 51.

7 Bruce Coplestone-Crow, 'Llansteffan', 14–15, using *Pipe Rolls 3–4 Richard I*.

8 John Kenyon, *Kidwelly Castle*, 12.

9 Bruce Coplestone-Crow, 'Llansteffan', 8.

10 Ibid, 10–11.

11 Peter Coss, *Oxford Dictionary of the National Biography* online, Reference https://doi.org/10.1093/ref:odnb/18081

12 See EN 7.

13 See EN 7, 15.

14 I.W. Rowlands, 'The Making of the March', 149.

15 *The Acts and Letters of the Marshal Family*, David Crouch (ed.) (Cambridge University Press, 2015), 110.

16 Richard Avent, *Laugharne Castle Guide* (Cadw, 1995), 9.

17 Ibid, 15.

18 Bruce Coplestone-Crow, 'Ystlwyf/ Oysterlow: Welsh Commote and Norman Lordship' in *The Carmarthenshire Antiquary 46*, (2010), 5–9.

19 Davies, *Lordship and Society*, 261.

20 Rowlands, *The Making of the March*, 149.

21 I am grateful to Neil Ludlow who has kindly shared his notes on St Clears.

22 Sir John E. Lloyd, *A History of Carmarthenshire*, 182.

A SELECT BIBLIOGRAPHY FOR THE WELSH
MARCHER LORDSHIPS 1066–1284

SELECTED PRINTED PRIMARY SOURCES

The Acts and Letters of the Marshal Family: Marshals of England and Earls of Pembroke, 1145–1248, Crouch, D. (ed.) (Cambridge University Press, 2015)

The Acts of Welsh Rulers, 1120–1283, Pryce, H. (ed.), with the assistance of Insley, C. (University of Wales Press, 2005)

The Anglo-Saxon Chronicle, Swanton, M. (ed. & trans.) (Phoenix Press, 2000)

Annales Cambriae, Ithel, Gough-Cooper, Henry (transcribed), Welsh Chronicles Research Group website http://croniclau.bangor.ac.uk/editions.php.en

Annales Monastici, Luard, H.R. (ed.), 5 vols (London, 1864–9)

The Annals of Dunstable Priory, D. Preest (trans.) & H. Webster (ed.) (Woodbridge, 2018)

Bowen, I., *The Statutes of Wales*, Gwasg y Gors (Taliesin, 1908, reprinted 2014)

Brenhinedd Y Saesson, or *The Kings of the Saxons*: Jones, T. (ed. & trans.) (University of Wales Press, 1971)

Brut Y Tywysogyon, or *The Chronicle of the Princes: Peniarth MS. 20 Version*, Jones, T. (ed. and trans.) (University of Wales Press, 1952)

Brut Y Tywysogyon, or *The Chronicle of the Princes: Red Book of Hergest Version*, Jones, T. (ed. and trans.) (University of Wales Press, 1955)

Calendar of Ancient Correspondence concerning Wales, Edwards, J.G. (ed. & trans.) (Cardiff University Press, 1935)

Calendar of Ancient Petitions relating to Wales: Thirteenth to Sixteenth Century, Rees, W. (ed.) (University of Wales Press, 1975)

Cartae et alia Munimenta quae ad Dominium de Glamorgancia Pertinent, Clark, G.T. (ed.), 6 vols (Cardiff, 1910)

The Chronicles of Medieval Wales and the March, Guy, B., Henley, G., Wyn Jones, O., Thomas, R. (eds) (Turnhout, 2020)

Domesday Book, A Complete Translation, Williams, A. & Martin, G.H. (eds) (Penguin, 2003); also, a free copy of Domesday Book is now available on the internet that can be searched by lord and place, making it very easy to see all the Domesday lands of a particular lord, or who owned which location: https://opendomesday.org/

Earldom of Gloucester Charters: The Charters and Scribes of the Earls and Countesses of Gloucester to A.D. 1217, Patterson, R.B. (ed.) (Oxford, 1973)

Geoffrey of Monmouth, *The History of the Kings of Britain*, Thorpe, L. (trans.) (London, 1966)

Gerald of Wales, *The Journey Through Wales*; and *The Description of Wales*, Thorpe, L. (trans.) (Penguin, 1978)

Gesta Stephani: The Deeds of Stephen, Potter, K.R. (ed. & trans.) (London, 1955)

Historia Gruffudd vab Kenan in *A Medieval Prince of Wales: The Life of Gruffudd ap Cynan*, Simon Evans, D. (trans.) (Llanerch Enterprises, 1990)

History of the Dukes of Normandy and the Kings of England by the Anonymous of Béthune, Shirley, J. (ed. & trans.) (Oxford, 2021)

History of William Marshal, Bryant, N. (trans & ed.) (The Boydell Press, 2018)

Littere Wallie Preserved in Liber A in the Public Record Office, Edwards, J.G. (ed.) (Cardiff University Press, 1940)

Llwyd, H., *Cronica Walliae*, Williams, I.M. (ed.) (University of Wales Press, 2002)

Magna Carta, Carpenter, D.A. (ed. & trans.) (Penguin, 2015)

Roderick, A.J. and Rees, W. (trans.), 'The Lordships of Abergavenny, Grosmont, Skenfrith and White Castle: Accounts of the Ministers for the year A.D. 1256–1257,' *Miscellany*, South Wales and Monmouth Record Society, 3 vols (1950–1957)

Roger of Wendover, *Flowers of History*, Giles, J.A. (trans.), 2 vols (London, 1849)

The Welsh Assize Roll 1277–1284, Conway Davies, J. (ed.) (Cardiff, 1940)

Walker, D. (ed.), 'Charters of the Earldom of Hereford 1095–1200', *Camden Miscellany*, vol. 22 (1964), 1–75

Ward, J., *Women of the English Nobility and Gentry 1066-1500* (Manchester, 1995)

SECONDARY SOURCES: PRE-1066

Charles-Edwards, T.M., *Wales and the Britons, 350–1064* (Oxford University Press, 2014)

Davies, M. & Davies, S., *The Last King of Wales: Gruffudd ap Llywelyn, c.1013–1063* (The History Press, 2012)

Davies, W., *Wales in the Early Middle Ages* (Leicester University Press, 1882)

Maund, Kari, *The Welsh Kings: Warriors, Warlords and Princes* (The History Press, 2017)

Moore, David, *The Welsh Wars of Independence* (Tempus Publishing, 2005) – runs through to 1415

Ray, K. & Bapty, I., *Offa's Dyke: Landscape and Hegemony in Eighth Century Britain* (Oxbow, 2019)

Roberts, G., 'Wales on the Eve of the Norman Conquest', in *Aspects of Welsh History* [Selected papers of the late Glyn Roberts] (University of Wales Press, 1969), 275f

GENERAL AND OVERVIEW 1066–1300 (OR SUBSTANTIAL PART)

Carpenter, D.A., *The Struggle for Mastery, Britain 1066–1284* (Penguin, 2003)

Carr, A.D., *Medieval Wales*, (Macmillan, 1995)

— 'Anglo-Welsh Relations, 1066–1282' in *England and her Neighbours 1066–1453, Essays in Honour of Pierre Chaplais*, Jones, M. & Vale, M. (eds) (The Hambledon Press, 1989)

Crouch, D., *The Image of Aristocracy in Britain, 1000–1300* (Routledge, 1992)

— *Medieval Britain, c.1000–1500* (Cambridge University Press, 2017)

Davies, J., *A History of Wales* (Penguin, 2007)

Davies, R.R., *The Age of Conquest: Wales, 1063–1415* (Oxford University Press, 1992; reprinted 2007)

— *The British Isles, 1100–1500: Comparisons, Contrasts and Connections* (John Donald, 1988)

— 'Colonial Wales' in *Past and Present* 65 (1974), 3–23

— *Domination and Conquest: The Experience of Ireland, Scotland and Wales, 1100–1300* (Cambridge University Press, 1990)

— *The First English Empire: Power and Identities in the British Isles, 1093–1343* (Oxford University Press, 2000)

— 'Frontier Arrangements in Fragmented Societies: Ireland and Wales' in Bartlett, R. & MacKay, A. (eds) in *Medieval Frontier Societies* (Clarendon Press, 1989)

— 'Kings, Lords and Liberties in the March of Wales, 1066–1272' in *Transactions of the Royal Historical Society* 29 (1979), 41–61

— 'The Law of the March' in *Welsh History Review* 5 (1970), 1–30

— *Lords and Lordship in the British Isles in the Late Middle Ages*, Smith, B. (ed.) (Oxford University Press, 2009)

— *Lordship and Society in the March of Wales, 1282–1400* (Oxford University Press, 1978)

— 'The Peoples of Britain and Ireland, 1100–1400. I. Identities; II. Names, Boundaries and Regnal Solidarities; III. Laws and Customs' in *Transactions of the Royal Historical Society* 4–6 (1994–1996), 1–20; 1–20; 1–23

Davies., R.R. and Jenkins, G.H. (eds), *From Medieval to Modern Wales: Historical essays in honour of Kenneth O. Morgan and Ralph A. Griffiths* (University of Wales Press, 2004)

Davis, Paul R., *Towers of Defiance, The Castles & Fortifications of the Princes of Wales* (Y Lolfa, 2021)

— *Forgotten Castles of Wales and the Marches* (Logaston Press, 2011; revised and extended edn 2021)

Edwards, J.G., 'The Normans and the Welsh March' in *The Proceedings of the British Society*, 42 (1956), 155–177

Frame, R., 'Conquest and Settlement', in Harvey, B. (ed.), *The Twelfth and Thirteenth Centuries: 1066–c.1280* (Oxford University Press, 2001)

— 'Lordship and Liberties in Ireland and Wales, c.1170–c.1360', in Pryce, H. and Watts, J. (eds), in *Power and Identity in the Middle Age: Essays in Memory of Rees Davies* (Oxford University Press, 2007)

— *The Political Development of the British Isles: 1100–1400*, 2nd edition (Clarendon Press, 1995)

Gillingham, J., *The Angevin Empire* (Edward Arnold, 2001)

Griffiths, R.A., *Conquerors and Conquered in Medieval Wales* (St Martin's Press, 1994)

Griffiths, R.A. and Schofield, P.A. (eds), *Wales and the Welsh in the Middle Ages: Essays presented to J Beverley Smith* (University of Wales Press, 2011)

Guy, B., *Medieval Welsh Genealogy: An Introduction and Textual Study* (Boydell Press, 2020)

Huws, D., *Medieval Welsh Manuscripts* (University of Wales Press, 2000)

Kenyon, John R., *The Medieval Castles of Wales* (University of Wales Press, 2015)

Le Patourel, J., *Feudal Empires: Norman and Plantagenet* (Hambledon, 1984)

Liebermann, M., *The March of Wales, 1067–1300: A Borderland of Medieval Britain* (University of Wales Press, 2008)

— 'The Medieval "Marches" of Normandy and Wales' in *English Historical Review* 125 (2010), 1357–1381.

— *The Medieval March of Wales: The Creation and Perception of a Frontier, 1066–1283* (CUP, 2010)

Lloyd, J.E., *A History of Wales from the Earliest Times to the Edwardian Conquest*, 3rd edn., 2 vols (Longman, 1911–1939; reprinted 1988)

Mann, K., 'The March of Wales: A Question of Terminology' in *Welsh History Review* 18 (1996), 1–13

Morris, J.E., *The Welsh Wars of Edward I* (Clarendon Press, 1901; reprinted 1968)

Power, D., *The Norman Frontier in the Twelfth and Early Thirteenth Centuries* (Cambridge University Press, 2004)

Prestwich, M.C. (ed.), *Liberties and Identities in the Medieval British Isles* (Boydell and Brewer Press, 2008)

Pryce, H. & Watts. J., *Power and Identity in the Middle Ages: Essays in memory of Rees Davies* (Oxford University Press, 2007)

Rees, W., *A Historic Atlas of Wales from Early to Modern Times*, 2nd edition (Faber, 1959)

Reeves, A.C., *The Marcher Lords* (Llandybïe, 1983)

Roberts, S.E., 'What's Yours is Mine: Cyfraith Hywel and the Law of the March', in *Journal of the Mortimer History Society* 3 (2019), 1–15

Sanders, I.J., *English Baronies: A Study of their Origin and Descent, 1086–1327* (Clarendon Press, 1960)

Smith, B., *Colonisation and Conquest in Medieval Ireland: the English in Louth, 1170–1330* (CUP, 1999)

Smith, J.B., 'Dynastic Succession in Medieval Wales' in *Bulletin of the Board of Celtic Studies 33* (1986), 199–232

Stephenson, D., *Medieval Wales, c.1050–1332: Centuries of Ambiguity* (University of Wales Press, 2019)

— 'Empires in Wales: from Gruffudd ap Llywelyn to Llywelyn ap Gruffudd' in *Welsh History Review*, 28 (2016), 26–54

Stevens, M.F., *The Economy of Medieval Wales 1067–1536* (University of Wales Press, 2019)

Stringer, K.J. & Jotischky, A. (eds), *Norman Expansion: Connections, Continuities and Contrasts* (Ashgate, 2013)

Turvey, R., *The Welsh Princes, the Native Rulers of Wales 1063–1283* (Longman/ Pearson Education, 2002)

Walker, D., *Medieval Wales* (Cambridge University Press, 1990)

1066–1200

Barlow, F., *William Rufus* (Yale University Press, 2000)

Bartlett R., *England under the Norman and Angevin Kings: 1075–1225* (Clarendon Press, 2000)

Bates, D., *William the Conqueror* (Yale University Press, 2018)

Crouch, D., *The Reign of King Stephen, 1135–1154* (Pearson, 2000)

— 'The March and the Welsh Kings' in King, Edmund (ed.), *The Anarchy of King Stephen's Reign*, (Clarendon Press, 1994)

Davies, R.R., 'Henry I and Wales' in *Studies in Medieval History Presented to R.H.C. Davis*, Mayr-Harting, H. & Moore, R.I. (eds) (London, 1985), 133–47

Evans, D. Simon, *A Medieval Prince of Wales: The Life of Gruffudd ap Cynan* (Llanerch Enterprises, 1990) contains a translation of the '*Historia Gruffudd vab Kenan*'

Gillingham, J., *The English in the Twelfth Century, Imperialism, National Identity and Political Values* (The Boydell Press, 2000)

— 'Henry II, Richard I and the Lord Rhys' in Gillingham, John, *Imperialism, National Identity and Political Values* (The Boydell Press, 2008)

— *Richard I* (Yale University Press, 2002)

— *Richard Coeur de Lion: Kingship, Chivalry and War in the Twelfth Century* (Hambledon Press, 1994)

King, E., *King Stephen* (Yale University Press, 2012)

Morris, M., *The Norman Conquest* (Windmill, 2013)

Warren Hollister, C., *Henry I* (Yale University Press, 2003)

Warren, W.L., *Henry II* (Yale University Press, 2000)

1200–1300

Ayton, A.I., 'Politics, Policy and Power: the Marcher Lords and the English Crown in the March of Wales, 1254–1272' (University of St Andrews, unpublished PhD thesis, 2020)

Billaud, R., 'The Lord Edward and the Administration of Justice across his Apanage, 1254–1272', in King, A. & Spencer, A.M. (eds), *Edward I: New Interpretations* (York Medieval Press, 2020)

Carpenter, D.A., 'Dafydd ap Llywelyn's submission to King Henry III in October 1241: A New Perspective' in *Welsh History Review* 23 (2007), 1–12

— *Henry III: The Rise to Power and Personal Rule, 1207–1258* (Yale University Press, 2020)

— *The Minority of Henry III* (University of California Press, 1990)

Cavell, E., 'Widows, Native Law and the long shadow of England in thirteenth-century Wales' in *English Historical Review 133* (2018), 1387–1419

Crook, D. & Wilkinson, L.J. (eds), *The Growth of Royal Government under Henry III* (Boydell and Brewer Press, 2015)

Davies, S., *Edward I's Conquest of Wales* (Pen & Sword, 2017)

Holden, B.W., 'King John, the Braoses and the Celtic Fringe, 1207–1216' in *Albion 33* (2001), 1–23

— '"Feudal Frontiers?" Colonial Societies in Wales and Ireland, 1170–1330' in *Studia Hibernica 33* (2004/ 2005), 61–79

King, A. & Spencer, A.M. (eds), *Edward I: New Interpretations* (York Medieval Press, 2020)

Morris, M., *A Great and Terrible King: Edward I and the Forging of Britain* (Hutchinson Press, 2008)

Neal, K.B., 'Words as Weapons in the Correspondence of Edward I with Llywelyn ap Gruffydd' in *Parergon* 30 (2013), 51–71

Prestwich, M.C., *Edward I*, 2nd edition (Yale University Press, 1997)

— *Plantagenet England, 1225–1360* (Oxford University Press, 2005)

— *The Three Edwards: War and State in England, 1272–1377*, 2nd edition (Methuen Press, 2003)

— *War, Politics and Finance under Edward I* (Rowman and Littlefield Press, 1972)

Pryce, H., 'Anglo-Welsh agreements, 1201–77' in Griffiths, R.A. & Schofield, P.R. (eds), *Wales and the Welsh in the Middle Ages* (University of Wales Press, 2012)

Smith, J.B., 'Llywelyn ap Gruffudd and the March of Wales' in *Brycheiniog* 20 (1982–1983), 9–22

Stephenson, D., 'Llywelyn ap Gruffudd and the Struggle for the Principality of Wales' in *THSC* (1983), 36–47

— 'A Treaty too far? The Impact of the Treaty of Montgomery' in *The Montgomery Collections*, vol 106, 2018

Williams, Diane M. & Kenyon John R. (eds), *The Impact of the Edwardian Castles in Wales* (Oxbow Books, 2010)

CENTRAL AND NORTH REGION

Barraclough, G., *The Earldom and County Palatine of Chester* (Blackwell, 1953)

Brown, A.E., 'The Castle, Borough and Park of Cefnllys' in *The Transactions of the Radnorshire Society* 42 (1972), 11–22

Butler, L., *Denbigh Castle* (Cadw, 2007)

Butler, L., Knight, J., *Dolforwyn Castle, Montgomery Castle* (Cadw, 2004)

Cavell, E., 'Aristocratic Widows and the Medieval Welsh Frontier: The Shropshire Evidence: The Rees Davies Prize Essay' in *Transactions of the Royal Historical Society* 17 (2007), 57–82

— 'Emma d'Audley and the clash of laws in thirteenth-century Northern Powys' in Skinner, P. (ed.) in *The Welsh and the Medieval World: Travel, Migration and Exile* (University of Wales Press, 2018)

— 'Periphery to Core: Mortimer women and the negotiation of the king's justice in the thirteenth-century March of Wales' in *Journal of the Mortimer History Society* 2 (2018), 1–19

Charles, B.G., 'An early charter of the Abbey of Cwmhir' in *TRHS* 40 (1970), 68–74

Crump, J.J., 'The Mortimer Family and the Making of the March' in *Thirteenth Century England* 6 (1997), 117–126

Davies, J., 'Montgomery – 1224–1332: A New Town in the central March of Wales' in *Montgomery Collections 2013*

Eyton, R.W., *The Antiquities of Shropshire, vols 1–12* (London, 1854–60)

Given-Wilson, C.J., 'Chronicles of the Mortimer Family, *c*.1250–1450' in Eales, R. & Tyas, S. (eds), *Family and Dynasty in Late Medieval England: Proceedings of the 1997 Harlaxton Symposium* (Donnington: Shaun Tyas, 2003; reprinted in the *Mortimer History Society Journal* vol 3, 2019)

Gruffydd, K. Lloyd, 'The Manor & Marcher Lordship of Mold during the Early Middle Ages, 1039–1247' in *Ystrad Alun, the Journal of the Mold & District Civic Society*, vol 3, 2003

Holden, B.W., *Lords of the Central Marches: English Aristocracy and Frontier Society, 1087–1265* (Oxford University Press, 2008)

— 'The Making of the Middle March of Wales, 1066–1250' in *Welsh Historical Review* 20 (2000), 208–26

Hume, P., 'The Mortimers and Radnorshire (part 1): the Conquest of Maelienydd' in *Journal of the Mortimer History Society* vol 3, 2019

— 'The Mortimers and Radnorshire (part 2): Marriage and Inheritance – Radnor and Elfael' in *Journal of the Mortimer History Society* vol 4, 2020

Jones, A., 'Legal Culture in a Medieval Marcher Lordship: a Comparative Analysis of the Dyffryn Clwyd Court Rolls' in *Journal of the Mortimer History Society*, vol 1, 2017

Lieberman, M., 'Striving for Marcher liberties: The Corbets of Caus in the thirteenth century' in Prestwich, M. (ed.), *Liberties and Identities in the Medieval British Isles* (Boydell Press, 2008)

Morgan, R., 'The barony of Powys, 1275–1360' in *Welsh History Review* 10 (1980) 1–42

Pratt, D., 'Anatomy of conquest: Bromfield and Yale 1277–84' in *Denbighshire Historical Society Transactions* Vol 56 (2008)

— 'The de Warenne lords of Bromfield and Yale' in *Denbighshire Historical Society Transactions*, Vol 62 (2014)

— 'The medieval borough of Chirk', in *Denbighshire Historical Society Transactions*, Vol 46 (1997) Preshous, D., Baugh, G., Leonard, J., Watson, G. & Wigley, A., *The Story of Bishop's Castle* (Logaston Press, 2016)

Pritchard, T.W., *Mold Town and Country, an historical account* (Bridge Books, 2012)

Remfry, P.M., *The Castles and History of Radnorshire* (Castle Studies Research & Publishing, 2008)

— *Clifford Castle 1066 to 1299* (SCS Publishing, 1994)

— *Clun Castle, 1066 to 1282* (SCS Publishing, 1994)

— *Kington and Huntington Castles, 1066 to 1416* (SCS Publishing, 1997)

— *Montgomery Castle, a Royal Fortress of King Henry III* (Castle Studies Research and Publishing, 2005)

— *Painscastle 1066 to 1405* (SCS Publishing, 1999)

— *Radnor Castle 1066 to 1282: A Short Guide* (SCS Publishing, 1995)

— *Richards Castle, 1048 to 1219* (SCS Publishing, 1997)

— *Whittington Castle, and the families of Montgomery, Peveril, Maminot and Fitzwarin* (Castle Studies Research and Publishing, 2007)

Roderick, A.J., 'The Four Cantrefs: A Study in Administration' in *Bulletin of the Board of Celtic Studies* 10 (1939–1941), 246–56

Rogers, M., 'The Welsh Marcher Lordship of Bromfield and Yale, 1282–1485' (unpublished PhD thesis, University of Wales, 1992)

Smith, J.B., 'The Middle March in the Thirteenth Century' in *Bulletin of the Board of Celtic Studies*, 24 (1970), 77–93

Smith, L., 'The Lordships of Chirk and Oswestry, 1282–1415' (unpublished DPhil thesis, University of London, 1970)

Stephenson, D., 'Cedewain in the thirteenth century: from Maredudd ap Rhobert to the end of native rule' in *The Montgomeryshire Collections*, vol 109, 2021

— 'Crisis and continuity in a fourteenth-century lordship: the struggle for Powys, 1312–32' in *Cambrian Medieval Celtic Studies*, 66 (2013), 56–78.

— 'Fouke le Fitz Waryn and Llywelyn ap Gruffudd's claim to Whittington' in *Shropshire History and Archaeology*, 77 (2002), 26–31

— 'Llywelyn Fawr, the Mortimers and Cwmhir Abbey: the politics of monastic building' in *TRHS* 80 (2010), 29–41; reprinted in the *Journal of the Mortimer History Society*, vol 3, 2019

— 'The Lordship of Ceri in the Thirteenth Century' in *The Montgomeryshire Collections* 95 (2007)

— 'The Making of a Welsh lordship: the mysterious case of Cedewain' in *The Montgomeryshire Collections*, vol 108, 2020

— *Medieval Powys: Kingdom, Principality and Lordships, 1132–1293* (Boydell and Brewer Press, 2016)

— *Political Power in Medieval Gwynedd: Governance and the Welsh Princes* (University of Wales Press, 2014)

— 'The Politics of Powys Wenwynwyn in the Thirteenth Century' in *Cambridge Medieval Celtic Series* 7 (1984), 39–61

Stevens, M.F., *Urban Assimilation in Post-Conquest Wales: Ethnicity, Gender and Economy in Ruthin 1282–1348* (Studies in Welsh History) (University of Wales Press, 2010)

Suppe, F., *Military Institutions on the Welsh Marches, Shropshire 1066–1300* (The Boydell Press, 1994)

Turner, R. & Jones-Jenkins, C., 'The history and digital reconstruction of Holt Castle, Denbighshire' in *Archaeologia Cambrensis 165* (2016), 241–82

SOUTH-WEST REGION

Copplestone-Crow, Bruce, 'Llansteffan Castle and the Abetot, Marmion and Camville Families 1093–1338' in *CAS*, vol 54, 2018

— 'Ystlwyf/ Oysterlow: Welsh Commote and Norman Lordship' in *CAS*, vol. 46, 2010

Crook P. & Duffey S. (eds), *The Geraldines of Medieval Ireland, The Making of a Myth* (Four Courts Press, 2017)

Dillwyn, M. (ed.), *The Description of Pembrokeshire* (Gomer Press, 1994)

— *The Lords of Cemais* (Cemais Publications, 1997)

Griffiths, R.A., *The Principality of Wales in the Later Middle Ages* (University of Wales Press, 1972, republished 2018)

Howells, B. (ed.), *Pembrokeshire County History, volume II* (Pembrokeshire Historical Society, 2002)

James, Terence, 'The Origins and Topography of Medieval Haverford' in *The Journal of the Pembrokeshire Historical Society*, vol. 4, 1991

Jenkins, G.H., Suggett, Richard & White, Eryn M. (eds), *Cardigan County History Volume 2* (University of Wales Press, 2019)

Lloyd, J.E., *A History of Carmarthenshire*, 2 vols (University of Wales Press, 1935–1939)

Lloyd, T., Orbach, J. & Scourfield, R. (eds), *Carmarthenshire and Ceredigion* (Yale University Press, 2006)

Ludlow, Neil, *Carmarthen Castle, The Archaeology of Government* (University of Wales Press, 2014)

— 'The Castle and Lordship of Narberth' in *The Journal of the Pembrokeshire Historical Society*, vol. 12, 2003

Remfry, Paul Martin & Ruckley, Nigel, *Castell Carreg Cennen and the families of Deheubarth, Giffard and Lancaster* (Castle Studies Research and Publishing, 2010)

Rowlands, I.W., 'The Making of the March: Aspects of the Norman Settlement of Dyfed' in *ANS* 3 (1981), 142–57

Thomas, Dr Spencer, 'The Descent of the Lordships of Laugharne and Eglwyscummin: Norman Marcher Lordships in South-west Carmarthenshire' in *CAS*, vol. 6, 1970

Turvey, R., 'The Jurisdiction and Comital Authority of the Earls Palatine in Medieval Pembrokeshire' in *The Journal of the Pembrokeshire Historical Society*, vol. 4, 1991

— 'Nevern Castle: A New Interpretation' in *The Journal of the Pembrokeshire Historical Society*, vol. 3, 1989

SOUTH-EAST REGION

Bartlett, R., *The Hanged Man* (Princeton University Press, 2004)

Bradney, J., *A History of Monmouthshire*, 5 vols in 10 (London, Cardiff, Aberyswyth, 1907–1993)

Clarke, C.A.M. (ed.), *Power, Identity and Miracles on a Medieval Frontier* (Routledge, 2017)

Cook, M. & Kidd, N., *The March of Ewyas: The Story of Longtown Castle and the de Lacy Dynasty* (Logaston Press, 2020)

Courtney, P., *Medieval and Later Usk* (University of Wales Press, 1994)

— 'The Norman Invasion of Gwent: a Reassessment' in *Journal of Medieval History*, vol. 12, issue 4 (1986), 297–313

Crouch, D., 'The Slow Death of Kingship in Glamorgan, 1067–1158', in *Morgannwg*, vol. 29, 20–41

Draisey, D., *A History of Gower*, (Logaston Press, 2002)

Griffiths, R.A. (ed.), *Boroughs of Medieval Wales* (University of Wales Press, 1978)

— *The Gwent County History: Volume 2: The Age of the Marcher Lords, c.1070–1536*, Griffiths, R.A. (general ed.), T. Hopkins, R. Howell (University of Wales Press, 2008)

Howell, R., 'The Demolition of the Roman Tetrapylon in Caerleon: An Erasure of Memory?' in *Oxford Journal of Archaeology*, vol. 19, issue 4 (2000), 387–95

Kissack, K.E., *The Lordship, Parish and Borough of Monmouth* (Lapridge Publications, 1996)

Knight, J.K. & Johnson, A. (eds), *Usk Castle, Priory and Town* (Logaston Press, 2008)

Lewis, C., 'The Norman Settlement of Herefordshire under William I' in *Anglo-Norman Studies*, vol. VII (1984), 195–213

Mein, A.G., *Norman Usk: The Birth of a Town* (privately published, Usk, 1986)

Mitchell, L.E., *Portraits of Medieval Women: Family, Marriage and Politics in England 1225–1350* (Palgrave Macmillan, 2003)

Nelson, L.H., *The Normans in South Wales 1070–1171* (University of Texas Press, 1966)

Priestley, S.G. & Turner, R.C., 'Three Castles of the Clare family in Monmouthshire during the Thirteenth and Fourteenth Centuries' in *Archaeologia Cambrensis*, vol.153 (2004), 9–52

Pugh, T.B. (ed.), *Glamorgan County History: Volume 3: The Middle Ages* (Glamorgan County History Committee, 1971)

Rees, W. 'The Medieval Lordship of Brecon' in *The Transactions of the Honourable Society of Cymmrodorion* (1915–16), 165–224

Rowlands, I.W., 'William de Braose and the Lordship of Brecon' in *Bulletin of the Board of Celtic Studies*, vol. 30 (1982–1983), 123–33

Shoesmith, R. & Johnson, A. (eds), *Ludlow Castle: Its History & Buildings* (Logaston Press, 2000)

Somerville, R., *History of the Duchy of Lancaster* (Chancellor and Council of the Duchy of Lancaster, 1953)

Spurgeon, C.J., 'Builth Castle' in *Brycheiniog* vol. 18 (1978–1979), 47–59

Stephenson, D., 'Conquerors, Courtiers and Careerists: The Struggle for Supremacy in Brycheiniog 1093–1282' in *Brycheiniog,* vol. 44 (2013), 27–49

Taylor, A.J., 'Usk Castle and the Pipe Roll of 1185: With a Note on an Expenses Account of 1289' in *Archaeologia Cambrensis*, vol. 99 (1946–7), 249–55

Turner, R. & Johnson, A. (eds), *Chepstow Castle: Its History & Buildings* (Logaston Press, 2006)

Walker, R.F. & Spurgeon, C.J., 'The Custody of the De Clare Castle in Glamorgan and Gwent, 1262–1263' in *Studia Celtica*, vol. 37 (2003), 43–73

Williams, A.G., 'Norman Lordship in South-East Wales during the Reign of William I' in *Welsh History Review*, vol. 16, issue 4 (1993), 445–66

PEOPLE

Altschul, M., *A Baronial Family in Medieval England: The Clares, 1217–1314* (John Hopkins University Press, 1965)

Balfour, D., 'The Origins of the Longchamp Family' in *Medieval Prosopography* 18 (1997), 73–92

Burtscher, M., *The FitzAlans, Earls of Arundel and Surrey, Lords of the Welsh Marches, 1267–1415* (Logaston Press, 2008)

Cole, M., 'Llywelyn ab Iorwerth: The Making of a Welsh Prince' (unpublished PhD thesis, University of St Andrews, 2012)

Crouch, D., *William Marshal*, 3rd edition (Routledge, 2016)

Crump, J.J., 'Repercussions of the Execution of William de Braose: a Letter from Llywelyn ab Iorwerth to Stephen de Segrave' in *Historical Research*, vol. 73, issue 181 (2000), 197–212

Davies, S., *The First Prince of Wales? Bleddyn ap Cynfyn, 1063–75* (Cardiff, University of Wales Press, 2016)

Davis, Paul R., *Three Chevrons Red* (Logaston Press, 2013)

Dryburgh, P.R., 'The career of Roger Mortimer, first Earl of March (*c.*1287–1330)' (unpublished PhD thesis, University of Bristol, 2002)

Evans, B.P., 'The Family Mortimer' (unpublished PhD thesis, University College of Wales, 1934)

Hopkinson, C. & Speight, M., *The Mortimers, Lords of the March* (Logaston Press, 2002)

Jack, I.R., 'The Lords Grey of Ruthin, 1325 to 1490: a study in the lesser baronage' (unpublished PhD thesis, Royal Holloway, University of London, 1961)

Jones, C.O., *Llywelyn Bren* (Llygad Gwalch Cyf, 2006)

Julian-Jones, M., 'The Land of the Raven and the Wolf: family power and strategy in the Welsh March, 1199–*c*.1300, Corbets and the Cantilupes' (unpublished PhD thesis, Cardiff University, 2015)

Lewis, F.R., 'William de Valence *c*.1230–1296, Part 1' in *Aberystwyth Studies* 13 (1934), 11–35

— 'William de Valence *c*.1230–1296, Part 2' in *Aberystwyth Studies* 14 (1936), 69–94

Meisel, J., *Barons of the Welsh Frontier: The Corbet, Pantulf, and Fitz Warin Families, 1066–1272* (University of Nebraska Press, 1980)

Morris, M., *The Bigod Earls of Norfolk in the Thirteenth Century* (Boydell and Brewer Press, 2005)

Mortimer, I., *The Greatest Traitor: The Life of Sir Roger Mortimer, Ruler of England 1327–1330* (Jonathan Cape, 2003; reprinted by Vintage Books, 2010)

Pascual, L.D., 'The de Bohun dynasty: power, identity and piety, 1066–1399' (unpublished PhD thesis, Royal Holloway University of London, 2017)

Patterson, R.B., *The Earl, The Kings & the Chronicler: Robert, Earl of Gloucester and the Reigns of Henry I and Stephen* (Oxford University Press, 2019)

Phillips, J.R.S., *Aymer de Valence, Earl of Pembroke, 1307–1324: Baronial Politics in the Reign of Edward II* (Oxford University Press, 1972)

Power, D., 'The Briouze Family in the Thirteenth and early Fourteenth Centuries: Inheritance Strategies, Lordship and Identity' in *Journal of Medieval History* 41 (2015), 341–61.

Ridgeway, H., 'The Ecclesiastical Career of Aymer de Lusignan, Bishop Elect of Winchester, 1250–1260' in Blair, J. & Golding, B. (eds), *The Cloister and the World: Essays in Medieval History in Honour of Barbara Harvey* (Clarendon Press and Oxford University Press, 1996)

— 'William de Valence and His *Familiares*, 1247–1272' in *Historical Research* 65 (1992), 239–57

Smith, J.B., *Llywelyn ap Gruffudd: Prince of Wales* (University of Wales Press, 1998; reprinted 2014)

Stephenson, D., 'Madog ap Maredudd, *Rex Powissensium*' in *Welsh History Review* 24 (2008), 1–28

— *Patronage and Power in the Medieval Welsh March: One Family's Story* (University of Wales Press, 2021)

— '*Potens et Prudens*: Gruffudd ap Madog, lord of Bromfield, 1236–1269' in *Welsh History Review* 22 (2004), 409–31

Turvey, R. *The Lord Rhys, Prince of Deheubarth* (Gomer Press, 1997)

— *Llywelyn the Great* (Gomer Press, 2007)

— *Owain Gwynedd, Prince of the Welsh* (Y Lolfa, 2013)

Underhill, F.A., *For Her Good Estate: The Life of Elizabeth de Burgh, Lady of Clare* (Moonwort Press, 1999; new edition 2020)

Veach, C., *Lordship in Four Realms: The Lacy Family, 1166–1241* (Manchester University Press, 2014)

Walker, D., 'Miles of Gloucester, Earl of Hereford' in *Transactions of the Bristol and Gloucestershire Archaeological Society*, vol. 77 (1958), 66–84

Walker, R.F., 'Hubert de Burgh and Wales, 1218–1232' in *English Historical Review* 87 (1972), 465–94

Ward, J.C., *The Estates of the Clare Family, 1066–1317* (unpublished PhD thesis, University of London, 1962)

Warner, K., *The Rise and Fall of a Medieval Family: The Despensers* (Pen & Sword, 2020)

Wightman, W.E., *The Lacy Family in England & Normandy 1066–1194*, (Oxford University Press, 1966)

INDEX OF PEOPLE

239

Breteuil, Roger of (d.a.1087) 38
de Brian family (*Laugharne*) 21, 103, 106, 109, 153,
 168, 213–7, *215*, *216*
 Alice (d.1435) 213
 Elizabeth 216
 Elizabeth (m. Sir Robert Fitzpaine) 217
 Guy (d.1268) 103–4, 109, 168, 213–5
 Guy (d.1307) 213, 215
 Guy, Sir (d.1349) 213, 215
 Guy (d.1386) 216
 Guy, Sir (m. Joan Carew, Elizabeth Montagu)
  (d.1390) 213, 215–7, *216*
 Maud (m. John Fitzalan, Richard Stafford) 216
 Phillipa (m. Henry, Lord Scrope) 216
 Wido 214
 William (d.1244) 153, 213–4
 William (d.1395) 213, 216
Brugge, Walter 126
de Burgh, Hubert, Justiciar of England (d.1243) 97–9
de Burley family (*Emlyn*) 165, 168, 207, 212
 Simon (d.1388) 165, 168, 207, 212
Butler, James, earl of Ormond, lord of Laugharne
 (m. Avice de Stafford) (d.1461) 213, 217

Cadell ap Gruffudd (*Deheubarth*) (d.1175) 63–6, 77,
 202, 209
Cadell ap Rhodri (*Seisyllwg*) (d.910) 33–5, 134
Cadwaladr ap Gruffudd (*Gwynedd*) (d.1172) 60–1,
 63–4, 67, 71
Cadwgan ap Bleddyn (*Powys*) (d.1111) 46–8, 52–3
de Camville family (*Llanstephan*) 22, 84, 106, 207,
 210–2, *211*
 Eleanor (m. Richard of Penrice) 212
 Geoffrey (d.1219) 207, 210
 Geoffrey (m. Maud de Tracy) (d.1308) 22, 207, 211–2
 William (m. Albreda Marmion) (d.1207–8)
  207, 210
 William (d.1260) 22, 207, 211, *211*
 William (d.1338) 207, 212
de Cantilupe family 97, 101, 154, 164, 168, 221, 224
 George (d.1273) 164, 168
 William (m. Eva Marshal) (d.1254) 101, 168
Caradog ap Gruffudd ap Rhydderch (*Gwynllwg*)
 (d.1081) 37–9
Carew, Joan (m. Guy de Brian) 216
Carew, Thomas of 127
Catherine of Valois *see Valois*
de Chaworth family (*Kidwelly*) 21, 103–4, 106, 109,
 115, 144, 199, 204–5
 Maud (m. Henry, 3rd earl of Lancaster) 205

Patrick (m. Hawise de Londres) (d.1258) 103–4,
 109, 199, 204
Patrick (d.1283) 21, 199, 204–5
Payn fitz Patrick (d.1279) 21, 115, 144, 199, 204
de Clare family (*Ceredigion, Pembroke*) 9, 22, 53–4,
 56, *57*, 61–2, *61*, 63–4, 68–9, 71, 73–5, 79, 87–8, 101,
 137, 139–40, 155, 157, 165, 172
 Baldwin fitz Gilbert (d.1095) 69
 Gilbert, earl of Gloucester & Hertford, lord of
  Glamorgan (d.1230) 69, 101
 Gilbert, earl of Gloucester (d.1295) 155
 Gilbert fitz Gilbert 'Strongbow' (d.c.1149) 63–4,
  68–9, 137, 139–40, 172
 Gilbert fitz Richard (d.1117) 53, 56, 69, 139
 Gilbert fitz Richard, 'of Striguil' (d.1185) 69, 140
 Gilbert 'the Red', 6th earl of Hereford, 7th earl of
  Gloucester, lord of Glamorgan (d.1295) 22, 69
 Isabel (m. William Marshal) (d.1220) 69, 87–8, 101
 Richard, earl of Gloucester & Hertford, lord of
  Glamorgan (d.1262) 69, 101
 Richard fitz Gilbert, lord of Clare & Ceredigion
  (d.1136) 56, 61–2, *61*, 69
 Richard fitz Gilbert 'Strongbow', 2nd earl of
  Pembroke, lord of Striguil (d.1176) 68–9, 74–5,
  101, 137, 140, 172
 Walter, lord of Striguil (d.1138) 64, 69
Clifford family (*Cantref Bychan, Cantref Selyf*) 55,
 57, 71, 115, 118, 186–91, 193, 196
 Matilda (m. John Giffard of Brimpsfield, d.1299)
  (d.1284) 115, 189–91, 196
 Walter (the younger) (d.1268) 190
 Walter fitz Richard fitz Pons (later styled Walter
  Clifford) (d.c.1190) 71, 186–8, 193
Clydog ap Cadell (d.920) 34–5, 134
Cromwell, Thomas (d.1540) 131
Cynan ap Hywel (*Cilgerran/ Emlyn*) (d.a.1241) 83,
 95, 102, 143, 167, 220

Dafydd ab Owain Gruffudd (*Gwynedd*) (d.1203) 77
Dafydd ap Gruffudd (*Gwynedd*) (d.1283) xxi, 107,
 111, 113–6, 120, 122, 194–5
Dafydd ap Llywelyn (m. Isabella de Braose)
 (*Gwynedd*) (d.1246) 97, 100–4, 107, 119, 167, 204
Despenser, Hugh, the Younger (d.1326) xii, 145, 155,
 168, 175, 193, 197, 205
Devereux, Walter, Lord Ferrers 130, 165
Don, Gruffudd 206
Don, Henry 206

INDEX OF PLACES AND GENERAL INDEX